BONDAGE
of the MIND

BONDAGE
of the MIND

**How Old Testament Fundamentalism
Shackles the Mind and Enslaves the Spirit**

*Toward a Better Understanding
of the Religious Experience*

R. D. GOLD

ALDUS BOOKS

Menlo Park, California

Aldus Books, Inc.
325 Sharon Park Drive, Suite 111
Menlo Park, CA 94025-6805

For details of copyright permissions, see pages 254-256

Distributed to the trade by Midpoint Trade Books, NY

Publisher's Cataloging-In-Publication Data
(Prepared by The Donohue Group, Inc.)

Gold, R. D.
    Bondage of the mind : how Old Testament fundamentalism shackles the mind and enslaves the spirit / R.D. Gold.

    p. ; cm.

    "Toward a better understanding of the religious experience."
    Includes bibliographical references and index.
    ISBN: 978-0-9796406-0-5

1. Religious fundamentalism. 2. Jewish fundamentalism. 3. Faith and reason.
4. Religion and science. I. Title.

BL238 .G65 2008
200/.9

ISBN 978-0-9796406-0-5

10 9 8 7 6 5 4 3 2 1

To My Wife

People are smart enough so that truth will prevail over falsity.

—Benjamin Franklin

CONTENTS

PREFACE

THIS IS A BOOK about truth.

In the sixth century BCE,[1] well before Socrates—even before the word *philosopher* (lover of wisdom) was coined—the Greeks were already debating what is truth. One hundred years later Parmenides took the position that what is, is, and what is not, is not. All is one, he declared, a single, eternal reality. Socrates, more circumspect, is reputed to have said, "Truth is difficult to find out. That is why I ask questions." Plato held that truth could be reached through abstract reason, while Aristotle, the first person to develop the concept of evidence, argued that truth could be understood through observation. But whatever the starting point, the path to truth for the ancient Greek philosophers was built on reason.

At roughly the same time, a little farther to the east, the Hebrew prophets were explaining the world in terms of divine revelation. In the year 458 BCE, Ezra came back to Judah from exile in Babylonia with written authorization from the Persian emperor to teach and enforce "the law of your God which is in your hand." What he had in his hand was the Torah, and teach it and enforce it he did, zealously. Echoing Parmenides, Ezra preached that there was indeed a single, eternal reality, and that single eternal reality was the Torah that God revealed to his chosen people, Israel.

For the past twenty-five hundred years, these have been the two major strands of thought running through Western civilization. In one camp are those who believe that truth about the world can be found through scholarly inquiry, evidence, and reason, that truth emerges through the use of the human mind. In the other camp are those who believe that truth about the world can be found only in God's word and God's will, handed down from on high in divine revelation, and that this revealed truth trumps reason—indeed, *is* reason.

Five hundred years after Ezra, Christianity took revealed truth on a different tack, building on the Torah and the rest of the Old Testament, adding its own gospel, dogma, and doctrines, demanding unquestioning faith and threatening harsh consequences for those who dared to question. The result, notwithstanding Thomas Aquinas's efforts in the thirteenth century to reconcile Aristotelian reason with orthodox Christian doctrine, was that public debate about truth was effectively shut down for well over a thousand years. There were some stirrings in the seventeenth century, as a few philosophers of note began to question the belief that God gave the Pentateuch to Moses. But the ecclesiastical authorities moved quickly to contain these doubts, and they dealt severely with the doubters.[2] The rabbinate of the day was just as closed minded and took just as hard a line. When the philosopher Baruch Spinoza, a Dutch Jew, wrote that "it is clearer than the sun at noon that the Pentateuch was not written by Moses, but by someone who lived long after Moses," he was excommunicated.

Religious truth also trumped scientific fact. A notorious case involved Galileo, probably the greatest scientist of his time. The Church denounced Galileo for supporting Copernicus's heretical theory that Earth was not at the center of the universe but rather, along with all the other planets, revolved around the sun. Given the choice of recanting or going to prison (and probably to his death), Galileo readily recanted—although legend has it that when he did he added under his breath, "Eppur si muove" (and yet it moves).

Eventually cracks in the wall of religious orthodoxy began to appear. The world was changing and it was impossible for the clergy to stem the tide of biblical criticism that came with the Enlightenment and took hold firmly in the middle of the nineteenth century. With this scholarly criticism the public debate about truth began to open up.

We hear a lot today about religious fundamentalism, the literal reading of sacred texts and their infallibility as the word of God, the ultimate moral authority that determines what man should and should not do. Here in the United States the fundamentalist movement started back in the 1920s, as a reaction by some in the Protestant Church to this new biblical criticism and the "liberals" who espoused it. The fundamentalists claimed that the liberals were abandoning the gospel and, by so doing, they were betraying the true Christianity. The liberals, for their part, warned that the Church was doomed unless it adapted its anachronistic theology to the changing times. These same battle lines remain drawn to this day (although shortly after World War II the fundamentalists began calling themselves by a softer name, evangelicals).

The debate about truth has not been limited to liberal and fundamentalist Christians. Exactly the same struggle has been taking place between liberal and Orthodox Jews. The biblical criticism that began in the nineteenth century was undertaken by a number of young Jewish scholars as well, and they gave birth to the liberal Jewish movements that took hold and flourished, especially in the United States. And just as the Christian fundamentalists are still fighting liberal Christianity tooth and nail, so are the Orthodox Jews—*the Jewish fundamentalists*—fighting liberal Judaism and just as hard. Taking the same hard line as their Christian brethren, Orthodox Jews—who, like fundamentalists everywhere, maintain the unshakable conviction that it is they, and they alone, who are in sole and certain possession of The Truth and, therefore, the exemplars of a divinely ordained moral behavior—claim that liberal Jews (whom they disdainfully call "secular") are abandoning the Torah and, by so doing, they are betraying the true Judaism.

But are they really? Are the doctrines of Orthodox Judaism really true?

The relevance of these questions goes far beyond the confines of the Jewish community. Christian fundamentalism is firmly anchored in the same literal reading of the Old Testament that is at the core of

Orthodox doctrine, and indeed would be incomprehensible without it.[3] The concept of the Messiah, one of Christianity's most fundamental tenets—without which, one could reasonably argue, Christianity could not exist—comes from the Old Testament. Indeed, the whole idea of a divinely revealed truth, essential to the evangelical belief system, comes from a literal reading of the Torah. Pull up the anchor that is the literal truth of the Torah and you set adrift the whole foundation of Christian fundamentalism. Thirty years ago the French Dominican priest and biblical archeologist Roland de Vaux summed it up succinctly with this candid observation: "If the faith of Israel is not founded in history, such faith is erroneous, and, therefore, our faith is also."[4]

De Vaux's conundrum is a big deal. In 2005 the *Wall Street Journal* ran a front-page feature on how evangelical and secular organizations are slugging it out for the hearts and minds of our children. The *Journal* quoted one teenage girl, who attended a ten-thousand-member evangelical megachurch in Florida, as saying she was glad her church taught creationism because "that helps me defend my belief that evolution is false."[5]

In 2006, Kathleen Harris, at the time a congresswoman and formerly the secretary of state of Florida who came to national prominence in the disputed presidential election in 2000, was running for the Republican nomination to the Senate. In an interview with the weekly newspaper of the Florida Baptist State Convention, Harris called the separation of church and state a "lie" and warned that if we don't elect Christians, we'll end up as "a nation of secular laws [where we] are going to legislate sin."[6]

It would be a serious error to dismiss this kind of thinking as confined to the Bible Belt. Efforts to undermine the teaching of evolution are afoot in no fewer than forty states. In some public school districts even geology is under attack because its time line for Earth collides with what scripture tells us. Stem-cell research, a promising new technology that may lead to major breakthroughs in medical science, is opposed by many people (including the current administration) on the grounds that it runs counter to their religious beliefs. In the run-up to the presidential election in 2004, some conservative bishops made national headlines when they told parishioners that a vote for John Kerry or even for candidates with Senator Kerry's policies would lead to eternal damnation.

However you come down on these issues, there is no denying that religious fundamentalism has become an increasingly potent social and political force in America today. The *Economist* of London, always a keen observer of America's political trends, ran an article in 2005 on precisely this convergence of religion and politics, concluding that "the new battleground of American politics is about religious attitudes as much as [party] affiliation."[7] The *New York Times* writer Thomas Friedman calls attention to a "terrible trend in the world today . . . drifting toward a widespread religious and sectarian cleavage the likes of which we have not seen for a long, long time."[8]

I consider religious fundamentalism to be one of the most noxious forces in the history of mankind, and, lamentably, it is on the rise again. Not a day passes that we don't witness Islamic fundamentalists wreaking havoc somewhere in the world. Here at home, we see Christian fundamentalists (now estimated at about a quarter of the electorate) elbowing their way into a powerful position on the American political landscape, with potentially far-reaching, deleterious consequences. Orthodox Jews, the Jewish fundamentalists, are also becoming more aggressive—more subtly here, more openly in Israel—but perhaps for fear of being labeled an anti-Semite there is little serious discussion of it.[9] I am a Jewish American myself, but I don't like the Orthodox trying to turn Israel into a Jewish Iran any more than I like evangelicals such as Kathleen Harris trying to turn the United States into a Christian Iran.

Now you can analyze to death the impact of religious fundamentalism and bemoan the creeping loss of people's inherent freedoms. But the *real* debate—the one I attempt to provoke in this book— should be about the truth of the whole belief system that impels the fundamentalists to think and act the way they do. And to get to the truth, you have to drill down deep, through the layers of fundamentalist rhetoric, into the bedrock of their dogma. Only then will you be in a position to make an informed, reasoned judgment as to whether or not their arguments are honest and logical and whether or not their doctrines are true. If you conclude that their doctrines are *not* true, then no matter what they say, no matter how they frame their arguments, no matter how much they invoke God's name and God's will, it would make no sense for you to believe them. And if you don't believe them, it would make even less sense for you to exchange much of your personal freedom for the straightjacket of enforced obedience to strict religious law.

I wrote this book to provoke readers, Jew and non-Jew alike, to step back and ask themselves a very simple question: *Does all this religious fervor really make any sense?* And if it doesn't, what is it doing—and what does it have the potential to do—to my life? My own answer to this question is what this book is all about. In the pages that follow I build an argument to demonstrate that the doctrines of Orthodox Judaism, like the doctrines of religious fundamentalism of all stripes, are false and make no sense at all.

You might think that most people already know that Orthodox Jews and evangelical Christians (let alone Islamic fundamentalists) are misguided zealots, and you don't need a book to prove it. This might have been true twenty-five years ago, but it is not true today. Yes, many people do recoil instinctively from religious fundamentalism. But it is a fact that increasing numbers of Americans do not. Just look at the spectacular growth of the evangelical megachurches.[10] There has even been a surprising backsliding in Reform Judaism, away from the emphasis on personal choice that has always been one of its salient characteristics.

An unstable world in which individuals seem to have less and less control over their lives has led more and more people to seek refuge in the security blanket of a fundamentalist belief system that explains that what is happening is God's will. Liberal Christians and Jews may dismiss the fundamentalists as religious nuts, but that is a mistake.

The irreverent iconoclast Christopher Hitchens has declared that "what can be asserted without evidence can also be dismissed without evidence."[11] Not anymore. Today we need to be able to counter the fundamentalists' arguments not with what we feel instinctively, but with hard facts.

If we cavalierly dismiss religious fundamentalism without taking a closer look at the phenomenon and where it all comes from, we do so at our peril. And where it all comes from, the acknowledged common pillar on which the belief system of evangelical Christianity as well as Orthodox Judaism is based, is the purported truth of the Old Testament and, more specifically, of its first five books, the Torah. Hence, any sincere quest for the truth must begin by submitting the fundamentalists' literal reading of the Torah to the twin tests of empirical evidence and legitimate principles of reasoning.

Nicholas Kristof, another writer for the *New York Times*, makes this insightful observation: "One of the biggest mistakes liberals have made has been to forfeit battles in which faith plays a crucial role. Religion has always been a central current of American life, and it is becoming more important in politics because of the new Great Awakening unfolding across the United States.... When liberals take on conservative Christians, it tends to be with insults—by deriding them as jihadists and fleeing the field. That's a mistake."[12]

Commenting on Kathleen Harris's impolitic declarations, Leonard Pitts, a columnist for the *Miami Herald*, issues a similar warning: "Maybe your instinct is to laugh at [Harris] and move on. That would be a mistake. Because here's the thing about what she told the newspaper: She meant it. . . . And I doubt she's the only one. The forces of Christian fundamentalism have made terrific inroads in the Republican mainstream over the past quarter-century. Some would argue that [now] they *are* the Republican mainstream."[13] A few days after Pitts wrote this column, Kathleen Harris handily won Florida's Republican nomination for senator.

The forces of Jewish fundamentalism are no longer benign, either. Possibly as a reaction to their fears that assimilation and intermarriage pose a serious threat to Jewish survival, the Orthodox have stepped up their efforts to convert non-Orthodox Jews, to recruit them to become "returnees"—without regard for the trauma such a conversion often brings to the liberal Jewish families involved.

Perhaps on a visit to Israel the prospective convert is approached by a friendly fellow who (taking a leaf out of the Moonies' playbook) invites him to dinner with "a nice group of people you'll really like." Or he may be here in America, possibly feeling low or alienated for one reason or another, and is approached by what the Orthodox euphemistically call an "outreach" organization. But whatever the venue and whatever the technique, it is a siren song that lures the unsuspecting into a sticky web of claims about God's word and God's will, designed to convince them that Orthodoxy is the only viable path to Jewish fulfillment and salvation. In the 1960s there was a popular Broadway musical called *Stop the World I Want To Get Off*. In a very real sense, this is what the Orthodox are offering the convert. But before he stops the world and gets off, wouldn't you think he would first want to have as clear an idea as possible of what he would be getting off into and, more important, whether or not it made any sense to do so?

There is a minor industry out there turning out books, monographs, lectures, tapes, Internet support groups, you name it, all aimed at convincing the secular that the Torah is the true word of God. I have taken three publications as representative of the genre: *On Judaism* by Rabbi Emanuel Feldman, *Choose Life* by Rabbi Ezriel Tauber, and *Living Up . . . to the Truth* by Rabbi Dovid Gottlieb. Orthodox proselytizers often give these three tracts to those they are trying to convert. I shall assess what each of these men is saying—and pay particular attention to Gottlieb, because he claims that the literal truth of the Torah can be proven by reason and logic. When I present their views, however, it is important for the reader to keep in mind that I do not do so simply to offer for debate the opinions of a few individuals. I present the views of these three Orthodox writers as concrete points of reference that define the doctrine and rationale of

Jewish fundamentalism. What these men claim is true is what mainstream Orthodoxy claims is true. And when I offer evidence to counter what these men are telling us, I am not merely disputing the views held by three rabbis. I am disputing the dogma of Old Testament fundamentalism.

When assessing the validity of Orthodox dogma, I have sought the most reliable empirical evidence from the most credible sources. I will present, at times extensively, the findings and conclusions of the most authoritative scientists and scholars in their respective fields of inquiry. Throughout the book I also refer to contemporary articles published in major newspapers. This introduces pertinent current commentary on the basic themes I develop, grounding them in the real world in which the reader lives today.

One final observation. At first blush it might appear that by dismantling the core doctrines of Orthodox Judaism—and, by extension, of religious fundamentalism writ large—my purpose is to discredit all religious belief. The reader will soon discover that this is not so. Orthodox Judaism is not authentic Judaism, as the Orthodox claim, any more than Christian fundamentalism is authentic Christianity, as the evangelicals claim. The reader does not face a choice that is limited to fundamentalism (I believe all of it) or atheism (I believe none of it). Piety is not a license to run other people's lives,[14] but if one so chooses, religion can play a positive role in one's life—sociologically, philosophically, and psychologically. It's all in how you look at it, and what I am proposing is that you look at it from a new and different perspective. I bring all this together in the book's last chapter, "Understanding the Religious Experience." Athens and Jerusalem need not be at loggerheads.

January 2008

INTRODUCTION

THE TORAH (together with the book of Joshua)[1] is a sweeping saga, an odyssey that starts when Abraham enters into a covenant with God and, at God's direction, travels from Ur to Canaan, where he settles down. His grandson, Jacob, later renamed Israel, has twelve sons—the children of Israel—the progenitors of the twelve tribes. Jacob's favorite son, Joseph, sold into bondage by his jealous brothers, is taken to Egypt, and when a famine forces his brothers and their families to go down from Canaan to Egypt, the children of Israel end up spending over four centuries there in cruel servitude. Then a deliverer appears in the person of Moses, who leads the children of Israel (now more than two million strong) out of Egypt and—after forty years wandering in the desert, where God spectacularly reveals himself at Mount Sinai—back to the Promised Land. Following God's instructions, Moses's handpicked successor, Joshua, conquers Canaan with a series of bold attacks (often aided by divine miracles), purifies the country by either killing the idolatrous Canaanites or driving them out, and then distributes the land among the twelve tribes of Israel as their eternal, God-given inheritance.

It's a gripping epic. But is it true? Did it really happen?

Orthodox Jews claim it did, unquestionably. And this belief, together with the belief (also unquestioned) that God wrote the Torah* and gave it—word by word, indeed letter by letter—to Moses

---

*Throughout the book I shall refer to the Orthodox claim that God "wrote" the Torah. This does not mean the physical act of writing something down. It is merely a convenient shorthand for saying that the Orthodox—indeed all religious fundamentalists—believe that God is the author of the Torah, that the Torah is God's creation.

1

during the miraculous revelation at Mount Sinai, is the cornerstone of Orthodox doctrine.

The unshakable Orthodox conviction that in the covenant God gave all of what they call the "Land of Israel" (today, Israel proper together with most of Gaza and the West Bank) to the people of Israel has always been, and continues to be, a major obstacle to peace between Israelis and Palestinians. Not that the equally entrenched stance of Hamas, Islamic Jihad, al Aqsa, and the other radical Palestinian factions who deny Israel's right to exist and are committed to driving the Jews into the sea, is any better. It isn't, and indeed, given their commitment to indiscriminate terror, one could argue that it is infinitely worse. But whenever the thorny issue of the settlements is raised, the Orthodox faithful invariably insist that in the covenant God bequeathed the Land of Israel to his chosen people, Israel, so that today all of the land is the Jewish people's rightful inheritance for all time.

This fundamentalist mantra was set forth explicitly five years ago by Benyamin Elon, an Orthodox rabbi who at the time was Israel's Minister of Tourism. Elon wanted Israel to annex the West Bank and Gaza because, he said, God promised it to the Jews. "You can't understand the Middle East," he declared, "if you don't understand the Prophets." Referring to the Palestinians, Elon added, "They will [have to] understand that we are the children of Israel that came back to the land of Israel."[2] This remains the Orthodox position. In early 2006 the Council of West Bank and Gaza Rabbis publicly called for Israeli soldiers to refuse to obey the government's orders to dismantle the Gaza settlements, saying they "go against the laws of the Torah."[3]

If you accept the Orthodox proposition that God wrote the Torah, then it follows that all the Torah's commands and prohibitions are the direct and true word of God, that they accurately reflect his divine will, and that, therefore, they must be scrupulously obeyed. The problem is that there is a large and growing body of credible evidence—textual, archeological, and historical evidence—that points sharply in the other direction. Here are a few examples:

- Richard Elliott Friedman is one of the country's most highly regarded biblical scholars. In 1987 Friedman published *Who Wrote the Bible?*, a landmark book that methodically lays out why all nonfundamentalist biblical scholars today agree that the Torah had multiple, human authors. Friedman explains who they were, when and where they wrote the Torah, and *why* they wrote it.

- Israel Finkelstein is one of the world's leading biblical archeologists. In 2001 Finkelstein and the historian Neil Asher Silberman published *The Bible Unearthed*, a fact-filled book that zeros in on the widening chasm between the Bible's stories and the findings of modern archeology over the past thirty years.

- William W. Hallo, a professor emeritus at Yale University, is a widely recognized authority on the ancient Near East. His studies place the texts of the Torah in the context of the contemporary Near East, and he offers abundant, documented evidence that the texts were not unique, but rather reflected the general customs and practices of the region and the times.

Approaching the Torah from different angles, all three eminent scholars arrive at the same two basic conclusions. First, that man, not God, wrote the Torah. And second, that the stories in the Torah are not an accurate account—not even close—of the real history of the ancient Jewish people.

Now one may wish to believe in the supernatural events reported in the Torah and in the doctrines of Orthodoxy for all sorts of reasons—unquestioning faith, for example, or family tradition, personal inspiration, emotional satisfaction, a desire to belong to an all-embracing community that offers structure and direction, fear, superstition, or simply because one wants to believe. But none of these reasons provides a rational justification for accepting the doctrines of Orthodoxy—or, for that matter, of any fundamentalist belief system.

There is an old Jewish line that goes: Before I talk, let me say a few words. It is very, very difficult to be rational and logical about deep-seated human emotions. Do you remember the original *Star*

Trek television series? One of the leading characters, Spock, was half-human and half-Vulcan, endowed with a computerlike brain and devoid of any emotion. Every now and then, after someone would act in an unexpected way that reflected his human emotions, Spock would look completely baffled, arch an eyebrow, and remark: "But that is not logical." And everyone would have a good laugh at Spock's expense, knowing that often you can't explain human behavior by logic and reason.

So it is with faith, one of the most deep-seated of all the human emotions. Five years ago the chief justice of the Alabama Supreme Court refused to heed a federal court ruling that a stone rendering of the Ten Commandments in a public area of the courthouse in Montgomery violated the constitutional separation of church and state and should be removed.[4] The eight associate justices overruled the chief justice and ordered the monument moved to a private area of the building. This decision didn't sit well with many in Alabama's deeply religious community, and several people gathered around the courthouse to express their displeasure vigorously. As workers were rolling the monument away, one particularly aggrieved man shouted out vehemently: "They ain't takin' away my Ten Commandments! They ain't takin' away my Bible! And they ain't takin' away my faith!"[5] So, yes, it is indeed difficult to be rational about deeply ingrained religious beliefs. But that is precisely what you must do if you want to reach the truth. You have to put your emotions to one side and submit the religious doctrines in question to critical analysis, to see if they can stand up to the twin tests of empirical evidence and legitimate principles of reasoning.

The Orthodox try to defuse any critical assessment of their doctrines by claiming that such an assessment applies too high a standard, the standard of irrefutable proof. If you set aside this impossible standard, they tell us, then the preponderance of evidence weighs heavily in their favor (and, they add, if you have an open mind, it will convince you that their doctrines are true). But this is a straw man.[6] By trying to convince us that high standards are somehow unreasonable or unfair when evaluating their claims, the Orthodox are hoping we will abandon the principles of rational belief that we rely on in our everyday life. They are hoping we will not react to Joshua's claim to have stopped the sun with the same skepticism with which we would react to an analogous contemporary claim (for example, that Eisenhower stopped the sun at Normandy). They are hoping we will not apply to the familiar stories of Abraham and Moses the same standards of credibility we would apply to the unfamiliar—but equally amazing—stories of Vishnu and Shiva described in Hindu texts.

No serious scholar would disagree with the proposition that irrefutable proof is far too demanding a standard by which to assess *any* argument. The standard I apply in this book is not of irrefutable proof but of proof beyond reasonable doubt. This is not only the familiar standard used in the law courts of Western society, but it is also the inherent standard we all use repeatedly every day when we make such mundane decisions as whether or not to believe an article we read in the newspaper, an ad we see on television, or a story we hear at a party.

Preponderance of evidence is an excellent way to prove something beyond a reasonable doubt—if the evidence is reliable. But what if it isn't? What if the evidence is based on a series of assumptions, which, if examined critically, are found wanting for independent, objective substantiation? What if the evidence is presented in a series of arguments that, eloquent though they may be, are riddled with inconsistencies, fallacies of logic, and blatant errors of historical fact? If this is the case, then no matter how preponderant the evidence, it proves absolutely nothing at all. A ton of bad evidence is just as worthless as an ounce of bad evidence. There's just more of it.

In reality, the danger we face in judging the claims of Orthodoxy is not that we apply unusually high standards, but that we completely suspend the ordinary standards of rational belief we depend on every day. We forget to sit back and ask the simple question: All things considered, *does what they are telling me make any sense?*

The Orthodox also claim that because the Torah contains its own complete, internally consistent set of values, it is impossible to approach its truth from a Western perspective. You can approach it, they insist, only from a "Jewish perspective." There are two serious defects with this line of reasoning. First, it could just as easily be applied to the most extreme value systems. Nazi Germany, for example, had its own set of values that certainly were consistent with what was written in *Mein Kampf*, but does that make *Mein Kampf* true? An internally consistent set of values (a favorite Orthodox mantra, by the way) is, by itself, no evidence for the truth of anything. Second, there is no credible reason to believe that questions about the truth of the Torah should be, or even could be, answered by culture-specific standards of evidence. Should we approach Nazism from a Nazi perspective? Should we approach Stalin's Russia from a Soviet perspective? No. Standards of evidence are general-purpose tools available to anyone from any culture to use freely and without restriction.

Now as you can imagine, every Orthodox rabbi past and present would readily testify to the truth of the doctrines of Orthodoxy, and they would all point to the sheer volume of rabbinical scholarship as proof that their arguments are true. Ten thousand rabbis, like the proverbial ten thousand Frenchmen, can't be wrong. But, of course, they *can* be wrong. What is important is not how much evidence there is, but how good it is. And when all is said and done, the fact remains that the entire testimony of these thousands of Orthodox rabbis—all of it—is based on a single collection of ancient texts, the Torah. This means that all the claims of Orthodox Judaism are based on a single source of evidence.

This fact, and it is a fact, is extremely important. It is also easy to overlook. Think for a moment. If you read a claim in a newspaper—say that it rained yesterday in Chicago—and then later hear five different people make the same claim, should your confidence in that claim increase? Well, it depends. If it turns out that all five based their assertions on exactly the same newspaper article that you yourself read, then obviously not. The apparently corroborating evidence is no more reliable than the original article was. The subsequent assertions do not constitute additional, independent lines of evidence.

This example is not hypothetical. As we saw following the 9/11 terrorist attack on the World Trade Center, someone made the sinister claim on the Internet that it was Israel and the Jews (aided and abetted by the CIA) who were behind the attack and, as proof, offered the "fact" that four thousand Jews were warned beforehand to stay away from the Twin Towers on September 11. This bizarre explanation spread like wildfire throughout the Muslim world. It was repeated over and over and over again as more and more people picked up and then sent the same message on the Internet and spread it by word of mouth, citing as "authoritative sources" all the different "news reports published" on the Internet. Getting this story thrown at them from so many different places, most Muslims came to regard it as verified truth—and, sadly, many still believe it to this day. But of course it was not true at all. It was a canard, started by one person, that multiplied exponentially in the Muslim world like a computer virus.

The people who believed this blatant lie did so because the evidence to support it had, in their minds, been substantiated "in print" and had come from what appeared to be many different authoritative sources (and because it was a story they wanted to believe). This is a dramatic demonstration that subsequent claims all based on the same source add no weight at all to the truth of the original claim. Evidence of this type is only as reliable as the original source.

So it is with the Torah, the original—and sole—source for the Orthodox claims that their doctrines are true. Because the Torah is the single evidentiary source for every Orthodox claim, the fact that every Orthodox rabbi in the world for the past two thousand years has argued that the Torah is true adds no weight to their arguments. The question you must ask yourself is: *How reliable is this original source as a true historical account of the ancient Jewish people?* In Part 1 of this book I shall attempt to answer this question.

So how strong must the evidence be for us to believe that the doctrines of Orthodox Judaism are true? If we are to apply the everyday standard of proof beyond reasonable doubt, we should judge the document on which Orthodox Judaism is based—the Torah—just as we would judge any document of similarly uncertain origin and making similarly remarkable claims. As a starting point we can ascribe no certainty of origin to the Torah, because if we assume at the outset (as the Orthodox do) that God wrote the Torah, its truth is established a priori, and there is, therefore, no further need to prove anything.

Any number of documents make remarkable claims comparable to those in the Torah, ranging from ancient Hindu and Buddhist texts through the writings of Nostradamus to modern reports of encounters with aliens. True, these are all testimony that we in the West are strongly inclined to reject, due to their antecedent implausibility. But the inherent implausibility of these texts is, in reality, no greater than that of the Torah, despite our deeply ingrained cultural bias. What is important here is not what we were raised to believe, or what we want to believe, or even what we do in fact believe. The Orthodox evidence must be sufficiently convincing that, were it presented in favor of the Hindu sacred texts, we would judge that they are true. Were it presented in favor of Nostradamus's texts, we would judge them to be true. And so on down the line. Applying a lesser standard to the Torah would be to abandon the very principles of rational belief that we use in every other sphere of our lives.

PART I

THE
EVIDENCE

CHAPTER ONE

THE ILLUSION
OF THE REVELATION
AT MOUNT SINAI

A physicist, a chemist, and an economist are marooned on a desert island. They were able to salvage from the shipwreck a large supply of canned food, but they have no way to open the cans. After a series of complex calculations, the physicist proudly announces that he can open the cans by dropping a coconut from a tree on each can from a particular height at a particular angle. The chemist, in turn, offers a solution based on the principles of chemistry. But it is the economist who comes up with by far the easiest solution of all. He says: "Assume a can opener."

FOR ORTHODOX JEWS, the watershed event in the history of the Jewish people was the revelation at Mount Sinai. In his book *On Judaism*, Rabbi Emanuel Feldman goes so far as to say that "this Divine Revelation at Sinai is the most significant event in the history of mankind."[1] As described so dramatically in Exodus 19, while the "nation of Israel" stood awestruck and transfixed by the blaring of the horns and the flames and smoke rising out of the trembling mountain, God revealed himself and (through Moses) gave his chosen people, Israel, the Torah and his commandments. God then made a covenant with the Jewish people, promising them both the Land of Israel (the Promised Land) and a happy, bountiful life in it if they obeyed his law faithfully—and an accursed, hellish life if they didn't. All this is described with graphic precision in the Torah itself. And, although Orthodox rabbis, both ancient and modern, argue endlessly over the details,[2] they all believe the essential elements of the story to be true. Maimonides's Eighth Article of Faith sums up this belief succinctly: "I believe with perfect faith that the whole Torah, now in our possession, is the same that was given to Moses our teacher."[3]

But how do we know this miracle really took place the way the Torah says it did? Because, the Orthodox reply, it was witnessed by an entire nation of two million people. And how do they know this? Because the Torah says so.[4]

Begging the Question

The circular argument I have just described is a good example of the common fallacy of begging the question, whereby one argues from the assumption that something is true to the conclusion that it is true. In this case, the Orthodox are arguing from the assumption that the Torah stories are true to the conclusion that the Torah stories are true. They assume the stories of the patriarchs are true. They assume the story of Joseph is true. They assume the Israelites' 430-year sojourn in Egypt is true. They assume the story of the exodus is true. They assume the census figures presented in the book of Numbers are true (especially because they are set down in such minute detail). From all these assumptions they proceed to the conclusion that the Torah's account of the revelation at Mount Sinai is true.

This is not a legitimate line of reasoning.

Begging the question—the fallacy of assuming the conclusion to be proven—is the single most common form of fallacious reasoning used in so-called proofs of fundamentalist religious doctrine. And as we saw with the old joke at the beginning of the chapter, with the right set of assumptions anything is possible. In its most blatant form, begging the question involves assuming a proposition in the course of arguing that the very same proposition is true. When college professors describe this fallacy to introductory logic students, the students' first reaction is to wonder how anyone could fall for such a flagrant error in reasoning. They imagine someone "proving" that 2+2=5 by assuming, as a premise, that 2+2=5. And of course no one would be fooled by that. But this is not how questions get begged in real life. More commonly, we fall victim to the fallacy by focusing on one specific part of some larger issue in question. Then, while trying to settle that specific point, we assume some other equally questionable part of the same larger issue as a premise of our reasoning.

This is exactly how the Orthodox prove that the miraculous revelation at Sinai really took place. They don't assume as a premise that the revelation occurred. Everyone would see through that in an instant. Instead, they assume that an entire nation—two million people strong if you accept the Orthodox estimates based on the counts given in the book of Numbers—was present in the Sinai desert and witnessed the miracle.[5] But of course, to accept this basic premise is to argue from the *assumption* that the Torah is true to the *conclusion* that the Torah is true. And that, friends, is, in a nutshell, the fundamental fallacy of Orthodox doctrine.

The question we must ask ourselves when assessing the value of this evidence is: *What is the source of the evidence?* Is it independent historical or archeological evidence? No, there is no independent evidence for any aspect of the exodus story, including the captivity in Egypt, the existence of Moses, or the presence of a whole nation wandering in the Sinai desert. To the contrary, most serious historians and archeologists today are convinced that at most only a handful of Israelite families were in and left Egypt, hardly an entire nation of two million people.

Do the numbers in Numbers make any sense? It's hard to see how.

The edition of the Torah edited by the liberal rabbi W. Gunther Plaut (commonly called the Plaut Torah) raises these objections to the counts in the book of Numbers:

> These numbers raise many difficulties both because of their size and because of other statistics recorded in the Bible (for instance, the notation in Num. 3:43 that there were only 22,273 first-born children among this multitude). . . . The most obvious problem is presented by the figure of some 600,000 arms-bearing men, which would suggest that about two million Israelites wandered in the desert. The logistics of so large a migration exceeds the bounds of likelihood.[6]

The Plaut Torah was published in 1981. Even then the number of people the Orthodox claim to have witnessed the revelation at Mount

Sinai was considered implausible by non-Orthodox rabbinical authorities. Over the course of the ensuing twenty-five years, archeology has demonstrated conclusively that Rabbi Plaut's skepticism was justified.

In his essay preceding the book of Numbers in the Plaut Torah,[7] William Hallo, then professor of Assyriology and Babylonian literature at Yale, makes a strong case that the figures given in the text are unreal in the extreme. They are incredibly high, he says, and lack any documented parallels from the biblical world in general. Furthermore, the way the Israelite tribes are organized in Numbers bears a striking similarity to a military organization in vogue in the fifth century BCE (when most modern scholars believe the final edition of the Torah was redacted).[8] And, as he does throughout his essays in the Plaut Torah, Hallo, referring to "the abundant testimony of the cuneiform archives," draws several other parallels between the text of Numbers and the texts of contemporary societies.[9]

As we shall soon see, the evidence is very persuasive that a constant process of elaboration and embellishment over an extended period of time is a much more plausible explanation of the story of the exodus and revelation—of both the remarkable events that supposedly happened and of the remarkable numbers of people that supposedly witnessed them. To accept the latter as true and then use it to argue that the former is true is clearly not a valid form of reasoning. Indeed, you would be hard pressed to find a more classic example of the fallacy of begging the question. Nonetheless, this illegitimate reasoning is the fundamental underpinning of the Orthodox assertion that their doctrines are true.

Secondhand Belief

Another argument the Orthodox offer to convince us that the miracles of the exodus and the revelation at Mount Sinai actually took place exactly as the Torah says they did is that just because we haven't seen something with our own eyes we should not necessarily disbelieve it. That statement is true enough. But when the Orthodox extend that logic to tell us that just because we did not see the miraculous revelation at Mount Sinai or all the other dubious events the Torah describes we should not disbelieve them, they are distorting the principle of secondhand belief.

It is clear that we rely on the reports of others for many of our beliefs, but it is also clear that we do not do so indiscriminately. We often require the convergence of multiple sources of evidence before adopting a belief, particularly if the claim is surprising or runs counter to ordinary experience. Most people believe, solely on the reports of others, that China exists. But we don't believe that Shangri-La exists. What is the difference? Well, we have many independent sources of evidence for the existence of China—newspapers, books, photographs, innumerable firsthand reports—but only a single source for the claim that Shangri-La exists. We firmly believe that Pompeii existed before it was destroyed by a volcanic eruption. But we do not believe the same thing of Atlantis, or at least we withhold judgment. The difference? The former is supported by historical reports as well as a host of archeological evidence uncovered by many different people. In contrast, the latter is supported by a single myth and nothing more.

Obviously, we don't always require such a convergence of evidence before believing a reported claim. If a trusted employee calls to tell us he has the flu, we take his word for it without giving it a second thought. But, if an unreliable employee reports that he has contracted a rare illness that requires him to take off every other Monday, we would justifiably be pretty skeptical. And even were our trusted employee to call to tell us that he was abducted by aliens last night and needs a day to recover, we would withhold belief—and probably look into getting him psychiatric help.

We give credence to a claim if it is more likely to be true than it is to be false. In its simplest terms, this is the principle of secondhand belief. Social scientists put it this way: It is legitimate to base our own beliefs on the reports of others when, and only when, our judgment of the antecedent probability of the event or state of affairs in question is higher than the probability that the report (or other evidence) is unreliable. Of course, there are certain events or states of affairs (the alien abduction story, for example), for which the antecedent probability is so low that it is almost impossible for a single source of evidence to be sufficiently credible to convince us.

What is the relevance of all this to the doctrines of Orthodox Judaism? The fact is, many of the Bible's historical claims have an antecedent probability that is infinitesimally small. Consider, for example, the claim in the book of Joshua that God aided Joshua in battle by making the sun stand still for a full day. What is the probability of the sun's standing still? Remember, we cannot assume a priori the existence of the Judaic God or the truth of the book of Joshua, because these two propositions are part and parcel of the larger claim to be proved (or disproved).

To appreciate the judgment you need to make here, imagine that you are assessing a contemporary report of such an event. Imagine that a trusted friend, or even a respected Nobel Prize-winning scientist, tells you that last week the sun over Israel stood still in the sky for a full day. What would your reaction be? Naturally, you would be supremely skeptical. You would wonder how Earth could have survived such a cataclysmic deceleration and acceleration. You would wonder why no one else in the world, in, say, Egypt or New York, noticed it (and recall, there were several developed civilizations at the time of Joshua, none of which recorded such an event). My guess is that no matter how sincere your interlocutor may seem, no matter how reliable he has been in the past, you would not believe that this really happened. Perhaps he is delusional. Perhaps he and others were the victims of a clever illusionist's trick. Perhaps he intends his report metaphorically, not literally at all. Perhaps he is pulling your leg.

Such a flagrant violation of the laws of physics is so unlikely, so contrary to the sum total of our experience, that it is hard to imagine a more improbable piece of evidence. In other words, it is hard to see how any application of the principle of secondhand belief would judge this report, this evidence, to be credible. And this is only one example of the kinds of events we must accept in order to endorse the truth of the doctrines of Orthodox Judaism.

One might argue that saying the sun stood still for a full day should not be taken literally; it may simply have been the way people of the time described the meteorological conditions prevalent that day. But this kind of explanation—that what appeared to be a miracle was, in reality, a natural occurrence described metaphorically—is emphatically rejected by the Orthodox, who rely on this and other equally implausible claims of miraculous events as evidence to support their fundamentalist doctrines.

The Orthodox will likely counter that violations of natural law are, in ordinary circumstances, extremely improbable, perhaps even impossible, but God is all-powerful and can easily perform such miracles if he so desires. There are two problems with this response. First, recall that the question at issue is the antecedent probability of the claims of Orthodox Judaism, not the probability of these claims *if* you make the question-begging assumption that God has all the motivations and characteristics ascribed to him in the Torah itself. Second, it is not even clear that the assumption of the existence of the Orthodox God would significantly change the situation. To see this, assume that your trusted friend had reported that last week *God* made the sun stand still. My guess is that even if you accept that God exists and could do this, you would remain just about as skeptical as before.

If you apply the ordinary standards of belief we use in everyday life, what would it take to convince you that your employee has the flu? Not much. What would it take to convince you that he has an unusual disease requiring a day off every other Monday? Somewhat more. That he was abducted by aliens? Quite a bit more. That he witnessed the sun standing still?

So, while the Orthodox are correct when they say that just because you haven't seen something with your own eyes you should not necessarily disbelieve it, the very simple and straightforward question you have to ask yourself is this: Which version of history has the greater antecedent probability: (1) the Orthodox version, based on a single source (the text of the Torah itself), that God wrote the Torah and miraculously gave it to Moses at Mount Sinai; or (2) the version to which all the leading academic biblical scholars and archeologists in the world subscribe, that the Torah was written over an extended period of time by several different individuals, codifying an oral tradition of legend and lore and reflecting the times and places in which they wrote it?

Myth Formation and the Spread of Beliefs

In *Living Up . . . to the Truth*, Rabbi Dovid Gottlieb presents a third argument in defense of a literal reading of the Torah's description of the exodus and the revelation at Mount Sinai. He calls this argument "The Kuzari Principle," which he defines thus: "Let E be a possible event which, if it really occurred, would have left behind enormous, easily available evidence of its occurrence. If the evidence does not exist, people will not believe that E occurred."[10]

Gottlieb uses this so-called principle, which is, in reality, an argument first formulated over eight hundred years ago by a medieval rabbi named Yehuda Halevi[11] to argue that the various events surrounding the exodus from Egypt (the parting of the waters, the wandering "nation of Israel" two million strong, the witnessed revelation at Sinai) must have actually happened, since otherwise no one would have been able to convince the Israelites that these events occurred. The missing evidence would have been so obvious that the Israelites would never have believed a person who tried to convince them that the events really happened.

At first, you might wonder what the missing evidence might be—that is, what evidence might the Israelites have noticed as missing if the exodus had not taken place? The examples that Gottlieb uses to make his principle seem plausible—for instance, a volcano erupting in Manhattan—involve a significant amount of missing physical evidence. But what the rabbi has in mind for the exodus story is not physical evidence—such as traces in the desert or distinctive marks on Mount Sinai (if we could find the mountain—which, by the way, no one has yet been able to locate). There *is* no such physical evidence, and none was available to the ancient Jews. The purported evidence is the collective memories of these events among the Israelites themselves.

If the events had not occurred, Gottlieb argues, no one would believe reports about them, since they could simply ask their parents, or grandparents, or great-grandparents whether they remembered (or had ever heard of) the events. Or they could simply ask themselves: If these amazing events actually took place, why have I never heard about them before? Thus, the Orthodox argument goes, if the stories were not true, the Israelites would never have come to believe them; because the Israelites did believe them, they are therefore true.

This line of reasoning is nonsense. The Kuzari Principle is no more applicable to the story of the exodus than it is to innumerable other national myths that have been widely believed among the descendents of those who could have witnessed the alleged events. If we are to be convinced by the rabbi's application of his principle to the exodus and the miraculous revelation at Sinai, we should be equally convinced that the ancient Egyptian god Ra existed, ruled Egypt for thousands of years as the first pharaoh, and performed many miracles, because it is an undeniable historical fact that the belief in Ra's exploits prevailed at some time or other among the descendents of those who would have witnessed them. From this historical fact, according to the rabbi's principle, it follows that the belief had to be true, for otherwise it could never have become widespread. But, if it was true *then* that Ra existed, it must be true *now* that Ra once existed. If the rabbi's principle is valid, the fact that no one believes in Ra anymore simply shows that we are all ignorant and mistaken.

You might think that this case is different because the Egyptians were an ancient, unsophisticated people, more susceptible to myth formation than we are today. But remember, we are talking about a culture that overlapped temporally with the ancient Jews and, by virtually every measure, was significantly more advanced than the Jewish culture of the time. There is no reason to think that the ancient

Egyptians were any more or less susceptible to the natural process of myth formation than were the ancient Jews. Whatever process led to the widespread belief in Ra's reign in Egypt could surely have led to the widespread belief in the exodus stories among the Israelites.

Or you might think this case is different—that the Ra story could be accepted at some point among the Egyptian populace—because the events described were said to have occurred in the distant past. But of course the same is true of the exodus events. According to the best historical estimates, the Torah was written sometime between the tenth and seventh centuries BCE—and recent archeological discoveries have led some scholars to conclude that the entire "first edition" of the Torah may have been written down toward the end of the seventh century BCE. Thus the exodus story describes events that, according to the Torah's internal chronology, occurred hundreds of years before (roughly in the thirteenth century BCE). That is a very long time and, if the archeologists are correct, just about as long as the entire duration of the Egyptian Old Kingdom. So even if the last inhabitants of the Old Kingdom came to believe that the first pharaoh was Ra, their mythical story was no more temporally distant from them than were the alleged events of the exodus from the Jews of 600 BCE. There is not the slightest difference in the timescales involved. Even great-great-grandpa would not have been an eyewitness to the events alleged in the two respective stories. Seven hundred years spans close to forty generations. Most of us, even today, know virtually nothing about our ancestors more than three or four generations back.

The Egyptian example is simply one of many obvious responses to the Kuzari argument. We could equally have discussed the belief in the mythical King Arthur among medieval inhabitants of England. (How could they have come to believe that their own country was once ruled by this remarkable king if it hadn't actually been the case? Couldn't people just ask their grandparents if they remembered or had heard about him?) Or how about Romulus, the mythical founder of Rome? ("Hey, Sextus, did you know that your great-grandfather was named Romulus and was raised by wolves?") Or the numerous and varied national myths that are central to Hinduism. Examples of populations that come to believe myths about their own histories, even spectacular and magical myths, are all too easy to come by.

As I am sure you have recognized by now, the rabbi's Kuzari Principle is completely bogus. It is not in any way an empirically verified principle. Rather, it is at root a nonsensical argument based on a naïve piece of armchair psychology[12] combined with an equally naïve view of the context and timescales involved in the process of myth formation. It was not a good argument in the twelfth century, but its naïvete in the medieval context was understandable. It is a tribute to the rabbi's skills of rhetoric that he can dredge up this old fallacious argument and make it seem plausible to modern readers.

Gottlieb's principle is an absurd caricature of the process of myth formation. To demonstrate how much it distorts what authentic social scientists really know about the cumulative nature of the spread of beliefs, let's examine a simple mathematical progression. Suppose that in the twelfth century BCE there was one person—just one person in the entire world—who believed (or wanted to convince people) that the revelation at Mount Sinai had occurred a hundred years before. Most people probably would not have listened to him. But suppose that he is able to convince just two people in the next generation— perhaps his own children—of the truth of his stories. Then suppose, conservatively, that each convert can convince two people in each subsequent generation of these beliefs. How many converts will there be after five hundred years—that is, after about twenty-five generations—by the seventh century BCE? The answer is 33.6 million people. This, of course, far exceeds the number of Jews around at the time, so eventually they all would have been convinced.

If you think I am exaggerating the mathematical progression for dramatic effect, you can easily work out the numbers for yourself. In reality, the numerical assumptions I used are fairly conservative. The Mormon religion was founded in 1830 by one man, Joseph Smith, who set out to convince others of an extensive and quite radical catalogue of doctrines and miraculous occurrences. Clearly, Smith's pool of potential converts was significantly more sophisticated than were the ancient Jews, and so we might have expected a more skeptical and resistant reception. Yet this religion now has 4.5 million believers after 180 years (about nine generations). This means that, on average, each believer over the course of the history of Mormonism has converted (or produced) five or six members of the following generation. If a religion can grow this quickly in the last 180 years of the second millennium CE, it could certainly grow as quickly during the first millennium BCE, a much more primitive age.

Among social scientists who study myth formation, it is well known that oral traditions evolve and are subject to a continual process of embellishment. What this means is that a spectacular event described in the Torah may not have been quite so spectacular in the early versions of the oral tradition. We can easily imagine that stories of Moses's exploits began, like those of King Arthur, as the stories of a great leader, perhaps even a person who led a small number of families out of Egypt. Over the course of the ensuing centuries, these accounts would gradually be elaborated and embellished, just as the myths of King Arthur were over a roughly comparable period of time. At no point would the elaboration meet with broad disbelief. Everyone would have heard of Moses and his great leadership. Perhaps initially he was said to have been inspired by God. Then he was said to have spoken directly to God, and to have transmitted God's message to the Israelites. Then stories of God's direct displays to the Israelites—smoke and thunder—were added. And so on.

Now I am not claiming that this chronology is correct. We don't even know if there *was* a historical Moses. But before we can accept the conclusion of the Kuzari argument as correct, we must be convinced that an alterative explanation is not possible. The problem the Orthodox face is that an alternative argument not only is possible, it is much more plausible than the Orthodox hypothesis. Indeed, the alternative argument is supported by all of the scientific and textual evidence available to us.

Another important feature of the spread of belief is what is sometimes called "the snowball effect." Initially, a proponent of a new religion is fighting against the predominant beliefs of his community and, to most of the people, his religion will seem to be more like a cult. But, as a new belief system becomes more common, it loses this cult-like quality. When half the community has accepted the amazing events that become the fundamental dogma of the new belief, then even the nonbeliever finds them no longer so strange—half of his friends will be believing them. The only question at this point is whether he will choose to give more credence to these beliefs than to competing religions. Many people will. This is, in fact, precisely how all religions spread.

CHAPTER TWO

THE FUNDAMENTALISTS VS. THE ARCHEOLOGISTS

A FEW YEARS AGO a young American archeologist friend sent me a copy of an article published in the Israeli newspaper *Ha'aretz* called "Deconstructing the Walls of Jericho," written by Tel Aviv University archeologist Ze'ev Herzog. Here's how it starts out:

> Following seventy years of intensive excavations in the Land of Israel . . . this is what archeologists have learned: The patriarchs' acts are legendary, the Israelites did not sojourn in Egypt or make an exodus, they did not wander in the desert, and they did not conquer the land in a military campaign. Perhaps even harder to swallow is the fact that the united monarchy of David and Solomon, which is described in the Bible as a regional power, was at most a small tribal kingdom. . . .
>
> Most of those who are engaged in scientific work in the interlocking spheres of the Bible, archeology and the history of the Jewish people—and who once went into the field looking for proof to corroborate the Bible story—now agree that the historic events' relation to the stages of the Jewish people's emergence are radically different from what that story tells us.[1]

I found Herzog's article so iconoclastic that I phoned my friend—himself a specialist in ancient Near Eastern archeology, who was shortly heading out to the region for another extended dig—and asked him if this was just so much sensationalistic polemic designed to sell newspapers or if there was anything to what Herzog was saying. He replied that not only was Herzog a serious archeologist who specializes in the Late Bronze Age (fifteenth to thirteenth centuries BCE), but also that the general thrust of the article was what had now become consensus among the leading archeologists in the field.

It turns out that all the archeological evidence—and there is a lot of it—points to the Torah being a fanciful account of Jewish history, not a historical record of what really happened. The Orthodox have no archeological evidence—none whatsoever—to offer in support of their doctrines, so they take the tack of dismissing modern archeology out of hand. What else can they do? But if we are serious in our quest for the truth we should not do that, as it would be intellectually irresponsible of us to ignore such a large body of serious scientific evidence that bears so directly on the question at hand.

The Orthodox also attack the findings of archeologists such as Ze'ev Herzog as the work of a group of Israelis who are pushing a secularist political agenda for Israel. They thereby try to suggest that the archeologists' motivation is political rather than scientific. This allegation is a classic red herring,[2] designed to divert our attention from the real issue—is the Orthodox reading of the Torah true?—to a totally different and, for our purposes here, totally irrelevant issue: current Israeli politics. The claim that the Israeli archeologists have a political agenda masks the fact that their position is exactly the same as that held by objective archeologists the world over, who have no religious or political axes to grind. The entire archeological community makes its judgments on the same evidence and using the same scientific methods.

It should not strike you as surprising that the increasing consensus among the world's leading academic archeologists and historians that the whole exodus story is just that, a story, with no foundation in fact, has met with tremendous resistance in nonacademic circles, because of the religious and political sensitivities of the subject. But if we are really interested in the truth, we should not mistake political and religious resistance to a scientific discovery for genuine scientific controversy. When it comes to archeological issues, the relevant question is not whether Orthodox rabbis or some Israeli politicians like what the scientists have discovered. The relevant question is what do those discoveries tell us about the world?

When the Orthodox have no alternative but to confront modern archeology, they build a defensive perimeter around their entrenched fundamentalist beliefs to try to protect them from the onslaught of more and more powerful evidence that calls these beliefs into question. Let's assess some of the principal Orthodox defenses against what modern archeology has found.

Argument 1

Negative evidence is not conclusive, so the jury is still out

The Orthodox are correct when they say that negative evidence is not irrefutable proof. Just because you can't find something doesn't mean it isn't there. However, they paint a picture of a few guys digging a few holes in the desert and coming up empty handed. Were this the case, they would be right. It would not prove anything. But this is not the case. This is not even remotely close to the case. Over the past few decades a huge amount of archeological evidence has been amassed about the events and cultures that occupied the areas described in the Bible. Much of it is powerful *positive* evidence that quite clearly demonstrates that the biblical account is false. It is not simply negative evidence—a failure to find anything at all—as the Orthodox would have us believe.

The fact is, the most authoritative biblical archeologists in the world have been searching for years for positive evidence to corroborate the Bible's stories. They have been digging and digging, using increasingly accurate scientific techniques. What they have found are enormous amounts of evidence of the existence of *other* cultures in the area, but in spite of all this effort, they have yet to find a single scrap of the kind of evidence they have been searching for, evidence that would support the biblical text as an accurate historical portrayal.

From 1991 to 1998 a young woman named Amy Dockser Marcus lived in Tel Aviv as the *Wall Street Journal*'s Middle East correspondent. Her book *The View from Nebo* is an easy-to-read account of how modern archeology has been deconstructing the biblical stories as a true history of the ancient Jewish people. She calls attention to the fact that just one archeologist, Eliezer Oren of Ben Gurion University, led an extensive ten-year search, probing "more than thirteen hundred different sites along the Mediterranean coastal strip of Sinai, the historic route that linked Egypt to Canaan and the lands beyond. They found everything from small ancient campsites, to cities complete with cemeteries, to granaries that the Egyptian army used to supply its troops as they marched toward Canaan."[3] But they found no evidence, none at all, of the Israelite exodus. We cannot say that the archeologists have irrefutable proof that the sojourn in Egypt and the exodus did not happen the way they are described in the Torah, but we must be clear eyed and face the fact that the solid evidence the archeologists have produced points us inexorably in this direction.

Furthermore, archeology is not always fated to what the Orthodox call "inconclusive negative evidence." Consider the stories of Jericho and Ai (the cities allegedly conquered by Joshua). We know where these cities are, and we know where to dig. And with modern dating techniques we know how deep to dig. The problem for the Orthodox version of ancient Jewish history is that repeated excavations of these cities have revealed that at the time of the exodus and Joshua's storied conquest, in about the thirteenth century BCE, there were no "great cities with walls sky high," as reported in Deuteronomy 9:1. In fact, at that time there were no cities at all at these locations, and no walls of *any* height. In this case, not only is there no evidence of the Israelites' conquest of Canaan, there is *positive* evidence that the cities described in the text were not around for the Israelites to conquer. They didn't emerge until much later. Moreover, the evidence from this period indicates that the demise of the Canaanite culture came about not through sudden conquest but as a gradual decline over the course of hundreds of years.

For an authoritative discussion of what modern archeology has to tell us about the events chronicled in the Torah and the book of Joshua, you can't beat *The Bible Unearthed*, written by the eminent Israeli archeologist Israel Finkelstein together with the historian Neil Asher Silberman.[4] *The Bible Unearthed* is required reading for anyone genuinely seeking the truth about the biblical stories. It is a beautifully written book, jam-packed with authoritative evidence of the true history of the ancient Jewish people. Finkelstein is relentless in disproving much of what the Orthodox dogma holds dear. But to the best of my knowledge, he has no religious or political agenda. He just happens to be a very dedicated and exceptionally good archeologist, whose work has produced, and continues to produce, powerful evidence that the Torah stories—as well as many of the stories in the books of the Former Prophets (Joshua, Judges, Samuel, and Kings)—are just that, *stories*, or, as William Hallo delicately puts it, how the Jewish people choose to remember their collective past.

Finkelstein and Silberman don't stop with the Torah, but continue to the return from exile in Babylonia in the fifth century BCE. It all makes for fascinating reading (for example, David and Solomon, far from being rulers of a vast and splendid kingdom, were little more than hill-country chieftains), but it would take us too far afield. We shall concentrate on what they have to say about the stories told in the Torah and the book of Joshua.

Here is how Finkelstein and Silberman respond—with *real* history, backed up by solid archeological findings—to the biblical account:

The sojourn in Egypt

Finkelstein and Silberman make a powerful case that the Israelite presence in Egypt in the thirteenth century BCE was very limited, perhaps no more than a handful of families:

> There is no recognizable evidence of Israelite presence in Egypt immediately before [the thirteenth century BCE, when the exodus was supposed to have taken place.] . . . The Merneptah stele [dated

1207 BCE] refers to Israel as a group of people already living in Canaan. But we have no clue, not even a single word, about the early Israelites *in* Egypt: neither in monumental inscriptions on walls of temples, nor in tomb inscriptions, nor in papyri. Israel is absent—as a possible foe of Egypt, as a friend, or as an enslaved nation. And there are simply no finds in Egypt that can be directly associated with the notion of a distinct foreign ethnic group (as opposed to a concentration of migrant workers from many places) living in a distinct area of the eastern delta, as implied by the biblical account of the children of Israel living together in the Land of Goshen (Genesis 47:27).[5]

The exodus

They make an equally powerful case that the exodus never happened:

> The escape of more than a tiny group from Egyptian control at the time of Ramses II seems highly unlikely, as is the crossing of the desert and entry into Canaan. In the thirteenth century, Egypt was at the peak of its authority—the dominant power in the world. The Egyptian grip over Canaan was firm; Egyptian strongholds were built in various parts of the country, and Egyptian officials administered the affairs of the region. . . . [Because] the main overland road that went from the delta into the heart of Canaan was of utmost importance to the pharaonic regime, the most potentially vulnerable stretch of road—which crossed the arid and dangerous desert of northern Sinai between the delta and Gaza—was the most protected. A sophisticated system of Egyptian forts, granaries, and wells was established at a day's march distance along the entire length of the road. . . .[6]
>
> Putting aside the possibility of divinely inspired miracles,* one can hardly accept the idea of a flight of a large group of slaves from Egypt through the heavily guarded border fortifications into the desert and then into Canaan in the time of such a formidable Egyptian presence . . . [and] the possibility of a large group of people wandering in the Sinai peninsula is also contradicted by archeology.[7]

---

* Of course, the Orthodox and other fundamentalists *never* put aside the possibility of miracles, because without the unquestioning acceptance of divine miracles their belief systems collapse.

Forty years wandering in the desert

Finkelstein and Silberman discuss the account of the forty years in the wilderness under the heading "Phantom Wanderers?"—a title that gives their readers a pretty clear indication of where they come down on this question: It didn't happen the way the Torah says it did. In fact, it didn't happen at all.

The conquest of Canaan

The conquest of Canaan didn't happen, either. It is another biblical myth. For much of the twentieth century archeology seemed to confirm the Bible's account, but as new evidence was uncovered archeologists were forced to abandon the conquest story. Almost all of the ancient cities that are listed in the Bible in the account of Joshua's conquest of Canaan—among them, Jericho, Ai, Gibeon, Hazor, and Lachish—have now been located and excavated, and what they tell us sharply contradicts the biblical story rather than corroborating it.

The Canaan of the Bible and the Canaan of history are diametric opposites. In the late thirteenth century BCE, according to the Bible, Canaan was a collection of great walled city-states ruled by powerful kings. According to the dramatic evidence modern archeology has uncovered—and Finkelstein and Silberman present a great deal of information about specific findings—Canaan was, at that time, an Egyptian province run by weak vassal princes firmly under Egyptian control, enforced by a vast Egyptian political and military presence.[8] The Bible makes no mention of Egyptians outside of Egypt. Yet "contemporary texts and archeological finds indicate that they managed and carefully watched over the affairs of the country."[9]

Not only were there no "great cities with walls sky high," as foretold in Deuteronomy, but also many of the cities (including Jericho) that are purported to have been conquered by Joshua's blitzkriegs weren't even occupied at the time he was supposed to have been there. Furthermore, Finkelstein and Silberman point out that

it is unlikely in the extreme that the Egyptian garrisons throughout the country would have remained on the sidelines as a group of refugees (from Egypt) wreaked havoc throughout the province of Canaan. And it is inconceivable that the destruction of so many loyal vassal cities by the invaders would have left absolutely no trace in the extensive records of the Egyptian empire. . . . Something clearly doesn't add up when the biblical account, the archeological evidence, and the Egyptian records are placed side by side.[10]

The origin of the Israelites

If the solid archeological evidence—*positive* evidence—demonstrates that the Israelites' four-hundred-year sojourn in Egypt, the exodus, and the conquest of Canaan did not take place, then where did the Israelites come from? The short answer is that they originated in Canaan, that they were there all the time. "How," asks Amy Dockser Marcus, "can you tell an Israelite from a Canaanite?" In the Bible, she says, the answer is easy.

> The Canaanites are idol worshippers. They hold religious ceremonies involving sex and drink, all part of their broader campaign to entice the Israelites from the true path of monotheism. They're morally inferior to the Israelites and culturally undistinguished. In the book of Joshua, entire Canaanite villages, men, women, and children are eradicated by a victorious army of tribes that have been freed from slavery in Egypt to march in and conquer the land. Except that's not how it happened.
>
> All the latest evidence indicates that there was no swift invasion around 1250–1225 BCE, the time generally attributed to the beginning of the Israelite settlement in Canaan. . . . After studying the remains of scores of villages of that period, the archeologists concluded that the people living there worshipped traditionally Canaanite gods, wrote in Canaanite alphabetic script, and used Canaanite-style pottery. It is difficult to tell an Israelite from a Canaanite because the Israelites and the Canaanites were one and the same people.[11]

What we have here, then, is exactly the opposite of what the Torah tells us. Extensive archeological excavations and surveys over the past thirty years have led Finkelstein and Silberman to conclude:

There was no sign of violent invasion or even the infiltration of a clearly defined ethnic group. Instead, it seemed to be a revolution in lifestyle. In the formerly sparsely populated highlands from the Judean hills in the south to the hills of Samaria in the north, far from the Canaanite cities that were in the process of collapse and disintegration, about two-hundred fifty hilltop communities suddenly sprang up. Here were the first Israelites. . . .[12]

The emergence of early Israel was an outcome of the collapse of Canaanite culture, not its cause. And most of the Israelites did not come from outside Canaan—they emerged from within it. There was no mass Exodus from Egypt. There was no violent conquest of Canaan. Most of the people who formed early Israel were local people—the same people whom we see in the highlands throughout the Bronze and Iron Ages. The early Israelites were—irony of ironies—themselves originally Canaanites![13]

I think we can confidently reject the Orthodox claim that biblical archeology is unreliable because it offers only negative evidence and, hence, is inconclusive. This allegation is simply not true. It does not match the facts.

Now let's take a look at some of the other defensive arguments the Orthodox present to counter what modern archeology is telling us.

Argument 2

All ancient histories were written as propaganda; there is no Egyptian record of the exodus because the Egyptians did not record their defeats

To a certain degree, the Orthodox are probably right when they say that all ancient histories were written as propaganda. But official histories are not the only sources that historians and archeologists look at when seeking evidence to determine historical truth. Among the most valuable sources are much more boring documents such as recordings of commercial transactions, manifests, and so on. To date, in all the vast array of Egyptian documents that have been uncovered, there is not one single mention of the Israelites' presence in Egypt, much less of their escape. There is no mention of the thousands—

millions if we are to believe the Torah's account of the exodus—of Israelites who allegedly spent centuries in Egypt. Nor has there been any discovery of Hebrew texts or artifacts that the Israelites themselves might have left behind that would attest to their presence there.

We are not dealing here with the simple omission from official Egyptian histories of an isolated defeat in battle. We are talking about a crucial episode in the alleged history of a nation of people who apparently left no enduring record of any sort whatsoever over the course of more than four hundred years. Along with other evidence, this has led most serious biblical archeologists and historians to conclude that the sojourn in Egypt and subsequent exodus, if they happened at all, probably involved only a handful of families and it is this family history that was later glorified and nationalized.

One is tempted here to repeat the Orthodox mantra with a slight twist: "All ancient histories were written as propaganda. All, that is, except ours."

Argument 3

The Sinai is a big, sandy area and one would not expect to find anything of a shepherding culture

Yes, the Sinai desert is a big, sandy area. And one might argue that it would be difficult for archeologists to find the material remains that a relatively small band of wandering Israelites might have left behind. Of course, if we are to believe the exodus story, the wandering Israelites were two million strong, hardly a small band. Furthermore, as Finkelstein and Silberman point out: "Modern archeological techniques are quite capable of tracing even the very meager remains of hunter-gatherers and pastoral nomads all over the world. Indeed, the archeological record from the Sinai peninsula discloses evidence for pastoral activity in such eras as the third millennium BCE and the Hellenistic and Byzantine periods. There simply is no such evidence at the supposed time of the exodus in the thirteenth century BCE."[14]

A particularly vexing problem for the Orthodox reading of ancient Jewish history is the failure of generations of researchers to locate Mount Sinai. No mountain has been located that matches the biblical account, despite nearly constant searching since the early 1900s. It is one thing to lose a burial site, quite another to lose a mountain. As one might expect, "discoveries" have been recorded all over the map. Some claim to have identified Mount Sinai as Mount Karkoum in the Negev; others claim to have found it in northern Hijaz. But none has been corroborated by any archeological findings. They are simply guesses. The most bizarre Orthodox theory that has surfaced lately is that nobody has found Mount Sinai because it is in Saudi Arabia.

Argument 4

The absence of anachronisms in the biblical stories proves that the Torah was not written later

The assertion that there are no anachronisms in the Torah (names, places, conditions, events, and so on that later authors projected back to the period described in the Torah) would be an argument in favor of the historical accuracy of the text—if it were true. For example, the Orthodox claim that, because the names of the patriarchs seem to be historically appropriate, the Torah could not be simply a myth made up hundreds of years later.

There are two problems with this argument. First, no non-Orthodox biblical scholar believes that the Torah was made up from whole cloth one day in the fifth century BCE. As we shall see, there is a great deal of evidence that the Torah was written over time by several different authors, compiling an ancient oral tradition into a single, rather inconsistent text. The inclusion of ancient names is not particularly surprising, any more than the inclusion of authentic names in *Beowulf*, even though that poem is likely the record of an older oral poem maintained by a troubadour tradition.

Second, the Bible is, in fact, rife with anachronisms of the very kind the Orthodox deny exist, exactly the kinds of anomalies one would expect to find when an author is writing about an ancient time with which he is unfamiliar. For instance, the Bible has Joshua conquering towering cities that modern archeology has demonstrated conclusively didn't exist until centuries later.

We are concentrating here on the Torah stories, but it is worth noting that the Bible would also have us believe that the "United Kingdom" of David and Solomon was a great empire, with its capital the walled city of Jerusalem, and that Solomon was a great builder. Modern archeology has demonstrated that the historical facts are quite different. Finkelstein and Silberman point out that Jerusalem became the great walled city described in the Bible only after the destruction of Samaria in 772 BCE. The authors of the biblical account were clearly familiar with the impressive city of the eighth century BCE and simply projected this picture back to the time of Solomon. Other great building projects the Bible attributes to Solomon, in cities such as Hazor, Megiddo, and Gezer, did not exist during Solomon's time; they came much later.[15] These, too, are examples of glaring anachronistic anomalies.

Argument 5

If you accept that God wrote the Torah and that miracles can happen, the absence of archeological evidence is irrelevant

I can't dispute that. It's an accurate statement. Here is how Rabbi Dovid Gottlieb works the argument:

> If the Exodus took place, what kind of archeological evidence would you expect to find? You are talking about a large number of people leaving Egypt. You would expect to find implements, clothing, vessels, weapons, and these sorts of things scattered all over the desert. What about bones? People die, especially if they were in the desert for forty years. The truth is though, we don't find anything. Nothing as of yet has been found as archeological evidence of the Exodus.
>
> Is this then evidence against the Torah's account? It depends on what you tested. Are you testing the Biblical story? If you are testing the Biblical story, you have to test it on its own terms. You have to accept all of it. It will do no good to take one element of the Biblical story, and then graft onto it other non-Biblical hypotheses

and then test the conglomerate, because that is a conglomerate that no one believes in.

Now in the case of the Exodus the Torah says explicitly that *during the forty year period their clothing and their vessels didn't wear out.* Now, if you are going to look through the desert for scattered clothing and vessels, then you are not testing the Bible. *The Bible would say that you won't find anything!* The Bible says that they are not there. If you are looking for clothes and implements, you are testing the assumption that there was an Exodus as the Bible says *together with your naturalistic account of the evidence which the Bible denies.* Nobody believes that! To test the Biblical story you have to take it in all its details.

Similarly with the bones. The *Midrash* asks, how did the people in the desert die?[16] Each year on the ninth of Av they dug a mass grave, everybody laid [*sic*] down in the grave, and in the morning those who survived got up, and the rest that were dead were covered up and that was their grave. They didn't die from time to time, everyday more or less scattered all over the desert.

Furthermore, the Sinai desert is a big place and sands shift over time. We are talking about sands shifting over a period of three thousand years. Where exactly would you dig? How deep would you dig? How many holes should you put down to have a chance of finding anything? It is not even thirty-nine burial places because in certain places they stayed for many years. There are maybe twenty burial places in the entire Sinai desert. How many holes do you need to put down to have a reasonable probability of finding twenty burial places, each burial place being the size of three square blocks? So, the fact that they haven't found the kind of evidence they are looking for is no proof whatsoever. It is not even evidence against the idea of an Exodus.[17]

What do you think of the rabbi's argument? *Does it make any sense to you?* Let's take a closer look at what the Orthodox are telling us.

First, according to Gottlieb, the Orthodox do recognize that there is no archeological evidence to corroborate the Torah's account of the exodus. But because there is really no way they can get around this incontrovertible fact, they take the classic rhetoric tack of claiming that, all right, what you are saying may be true, but it is irrelevant. Archeologists have been wasting their time. Had they read the Torah properly, they would have known that they would never find anything. This whole line of reasoning is transparently bogus, a crude attempt to keep us from submitting the Orthodox proposition that the Torah is true to the tests of empirical evidence and rational thought.

Second, Gottlieb notes that, according to the exodus story, the wandering Israelites remained in the same places for many years. As a matter of fact, the Torah has them camping in one place, Kadesh-barnea, for thirty-eight of the forty years. Wouldn't you think this would make it *easier* for archeologists to find some evidence of their presence there, rather than more difficult, almost impossible, as the rabbi would have us believe? Yet, as Finkelstein and Silberman point out, they found none whatsoever:

> The conclusion—that the Exodus did not happen at the time and in the manner described in the Bible—seems irrefutable when we examine the evidence at specific sites where the children of Israel were said to have camped for extended periods of time during their wanderings in the desert (Numbers 33) and where some archeological indication—if present—would almost certainly be found. Yet repeated excavations and surveys throughout the entire area have not provided even the slightest evidence for activity in the Late Bronze Age [the time the Exodus is supposed to have taken place], not even a single sherd left by a tiny fleeing band of frightened refugees. . . . From the long list of encampments in the wilderness, Kadesh-barnea and Ezion-geber [where no archeological evidence of Late Bronze Age occupation has ever been found, either] are the only ones that can be safely identified, yet they revealed no trace of the wandering Israelites.[18]

Argument 6

There is archeological evidence that does support, albeit indirectly, the Orthodox reading of the Bible

The modern tradition in biblical archeology started out as a concerted attempt to prove the accuracy of the Old Testament texts. The Orthodox often cite the biblical archeologist William Foxwell Albright, who began work in Palestine in the 1920s. Albright was a religious man, the son of a clergyman, and his explicit goal in bringing the techniques of scientific archeology to study biblical history was to refute critical claims against the historical truth of the Old Testament made by certain schools of biblical interpretation, especially those made by the Wellhausen school in Germany. The method he adopted was to assume that Old Testament texts contain an accurate historical narrative that could be verified and refined through the use of archeological techniques. By 1932, Albright was convinced: "Discovery after discovery has established the accuracy of innumerable details [in the Bible], and has brought increasing recognition to the value of the Bible as a source of history."[19]

In the close to fifty years since the most recent edition of Albright's *Archeology of Palestine*, biblical archeology has blossomed, uncovering more and more solid evidence about the period, and applying much more highly refined scientific techniques. The problem for Albright—and for the Orthodox and, indeed, for all fundamentalists—is that this evidence points in exactly the opposite direction, so much so that no serious academic archeologist today considers the Torah to be an accurate account of the ancient history of the Jews, and most would not even claim that it is even moderately accurate.

Philip Davies, a highly respected biblical archeologist and author of the book *In Search of "Ancient Israel,"*[20] gives the following succinct assessment of the current state of archeological evidence: "The gap between the Biblical Israel and the historical Israel as we derive it from archeology is huge. We have almost two entirely different societies. Beyond the name 'Israel' and the same geographical location, they have almost nothing in common."[21]

The Orthodox claim that the fact that archeologists have identified some of the places mentioned in the Torah is proof that the text is true. But rigorous logic does not permit us to infer the credibility of surprising or implausible claims from the truth of less surprising, more plausible claims. To illustrate this point, suppose we are judging the truth of an alibi. The defendant tells a long story about his actions and whereabouts on the night of the crime. Many of the claims, indeed perhaps all the directly verifiable claims, will be true. He says he left his second-floor apartment and went down the stairs. Do the facts that he really does live in an apartment, on the second floor, and that his building really has stairs, add credibility to the alibi? No. They merely show that he knows where he lives. This kind of veracity is completely irrelevant to the crucial claims of the alibi.

In viewing the Torah, we should make similar distinctions. It is unsurprising that the author or authors of the text got certain geographic facts right. This is roughly analogous to our defendant's being able to describe his apartment. Now, suppose that we are able to ascertain, through archeological investigation or because we know the geography of Israel, that certain of these geographic places existed at one time or another. How much credibility does this add to the miraculous occurrences reported in the Torah, such as the revelation at Mount Sinai? None at all. Legitimate reasoning simply doesn't work that way. Moreover, "they were unoccupied precisely at the time they reportedly played a role in the events of the wandering children of Israel in the wilderness."[22]

Apart from William Foxwell Albright, just about the only source the Orthodox point to for archeological substantiation that the Torah is accurate history is a book called *Israel in Egypt: The Evidence for the Authenticity of the Exodus Tradition*, by James K. Hoffmeier, Professor of Biblical Studies and Archeology at Wheaton College. With all due respect, one might question whether a midwestern Christian college whose web site features its "Billy Graham Center" is an intellectual environment conducive to open-minded intellectual inquiry about the Bible. Be that as it may, it is worth examining Professor Hoffmeier's views to see what they can tell us:

> Many historians and biblical scholars now maintain that a text's claims must be corroborated before they can be considered historical. This expectation is the opposite of the Western legal tradition of "innocent until proven guilty." . . . Unfortunately, [the] assertion that the burden of proof does not rest on the critical (minimalist) historian has become the prevailing attitude in biblical scholarship for the past several decades. In shifting the burden of proof to the ancient document and demanding that the maximalist historian

"prove" the historicity of a text's claim, the minimalist commits a
methodological fallacy . . . the "fallacy of presumptive proof,"
which consists in advancing a proposition and shifting the burden
of proof or disproof to others. . . . The minimalist approaches an
ancient text as "guilty until proven innocent," whereas the maximalist accepts what appears to be a historical statement unless
there is evidence to prove the contrary.[23]

I don't like the terms *minimalist* and *maximalist*, because they tend
to frame the discussion at the extremes on both ends.[24] It is perfectly
possible that some parts of an ancient text—any ancient text—can be
reasonably accurate history, other parts approximate history, other
parts hyperbole, other parts legend with some original kernel of fact,
and still others pure flights of fancy.

As for Hoffmeier's "fallacy of presumptive proof," reflect for a
moment on what he is telling us. He is proposing that we accept an
ancient text as an accurate historical statement—regardless, by the way,
of what it says—"unless there is evidence to prove the contrary." This
is exactly the approach the Orthodox take, except that they automatically reject out of hand the idea that there could possibly be any evidence to the contrary. But no rigorous scholar would ever accept at face
value what is written in an ancient text. He or she would submit it to
all sorts of tests, two of the most obvious being whether, on a prima
facie basis, the content appears to be accurate history or legend, myth,
or fable, and whether the content can be corroborated by independent
sources, such as other texts or archeological findings. In subjecting the
texts to these sorts of tests, the scholar is not making assumptions that
the information is necessarily wrong—or, as Hoffmeier puts it, "guilty
until proven innocent"—or right ("innocent until proven guilty"). It is
a non sequitur to equate the right of the accused to the presumption of
innocence with a "right" to the presumption of truth. The search for
justice is served in the courts by the presumption of innocence, but the
search for truth is not served by a presumption of truth. This is not the
way serious scholarly research is done.

Were we to find an ancient document that records, say, a mundane
transaction or birth, we would likely have little reason to question its

authenticity (although it very well might be false). But when an ancient text—the Torah or any other—lays claim to supernatural happenings that breach nature in miraculous ways, the burden of proof that these miraculous events really took place as the text says they did clearly lies with those who make the claims and not with the scholar who views miracles and all things supernatural with skepticism. The burden of proof lies not with you to disprove the fundamentalist claims. The burden of proof lies squarely with the fundamentalists to prove them.

To buttress his position, Hoffmeier insists, repeatedly, that minimalist historians and archeologists start out with "rejectionist" assumptions that color their approach. The interpretation of their findings becomes, therefore, a philosophical question. Perhaps. It is always a good idea to be aware that preconceived notions can inadvertently creep into one's thinking, but this possibility is hardly a justification for dismissing without further ado a mounting body of serious, scientific evidence. If you don't like the damaging evidence, dispute it scientifically. Come up with your own evidence to demonstrate that it is wrong. But don't cavalierly dismiss it out of hand, saying that the archeologists and historians who have uncovered it did so only because of their purportedly biased assumptions.

To his credit, James Hoffmeier concedes that his views that the Torah narratives are even *plausible* are at odds with those of the leading biblical archeologists of the day. Early in his book he states that "direct evidence for the events and figures of Genesis and Exodus remains elusive."[25] He also scrupulously presents extensive opposing opinions not only about the exodus, but also about the story in the book of Joshua of the conquest of Canaan. He refers to a monograph by Israel Finkelstein in 1988 as "the most thoroughly archeologically based of the recent investigations of the origins of Israel," and goes on to say that "Finkelstein's work has been received by many as authoritative and representing the state of the art on the origins of Israel . . . and his conclusions are rapidly becoming consensus."[26] But, it would appear, Hoffmeier remains unpersuaded.

At the end of the day, we have to ask ourselves what archeological evidence have the Orthodox offered us to support the conclusion— not the a priori assumption, mind you, but the reasoned conclusion— that God wrote the Torah, that the stories in the Torah, particularly the crucial episodes of the exodus and the revelation at Mount Sinai, happened as the Torah says they did, and that, therefore, the fundamentalist dogma of Orthodoxy is true. They have offered us no credible evidence at all.

On the other side of the ledger we have a rapidly growing mountain of powerful archeological evidence that directly contradicts fundamental Orthodox doctrine. The stories of the patriarchs, the sojourn in Egypt, the exodus, the revelation at Mount Sinai, the two million witnesses, the wanderings of the nation of Israel in the desert for forty years, the conquest of Canaan? All myth, fable, and legend. The Israelites were living peacefully in Canaan all along and, it now seems almost certain, started out as Canaanites themselves.

CHAPTER THREE

THE ASTROLOGER'S FALLACY

ONE OF THE BIG GUNS Orthodox Jews like to roll out to prove that their doctrines are true is that the Torah makes accurate prophecies. Only God could make such accurate predictions, they claim, so the Torah must be true. They argue that the accuracy (what they like to call the "truth") of those predictions is so extremely unlikely that it constitutes strong evidence for the truth of the Torah. Apart from the fact that the Orthodox can always produce an interpretation—no matter how much of a stretch it may seem to you and me—that will make *every* prediction in the Torah appear to have come true one way or another, there is a basic fallacy at work here, one that is not readily apparent. I call it the Astrologer's Fallacy.

Suppose an astrologer gives us a long prophecy consisting of, say, twenty-six vague and general predictions: A, B, C, . . . , X, Y, Z. As it turns out, we can construe three or four of them as correct, say, D, F, T, and W. Suppose that, after we say which came true, the astrologer notes (and let's say his estimates are correct) that the probability of each of these events is one in ten, and so the probability of all four of them coming true is

$$1/10 \times 1/10 \times 1/10 \times 1/10 = 1/10,000$$

One in ten thousand. Wow! We are flabbergasted at his ability to make such an extremely unlikely prediction. If he had hit only three of them, the probability would still be a remarkable one in one thousand.

This is amazing. It is also wrong. It is nothing more than mathematical sleight of hand. The problem is that one in one thousand or one in ten thousand is not the correct probability that the original prophecy would be *partly* successful—that three or four of the predictions would turn out correct. Assuming that each of the twenty-six events has a probability of one in ten, what is the probability that three or more of them will come true? It turns out that the probability is about one in two (.486, to be exact). The probability that four or more of them will come true is about one in four (.256).[1]

The reason for this is that there are many different ways for such a prophecy to achieve the (limited) level of accuracy required for it to be deemed partly correct. Needless to say, these are vastly higher probabilities than one in a thousand or one in ten thousand. And of course the probabilities are even greater when the individual events are more likely. For example, the probability of an ancient culture's being overrun by invaders whose language they didn't understand (one of the predictions the Orthodox single out) is a great deal higher than one in ten. Indeed, there were few ancient societies that this didn't happen to, and to many it happened more than once.

A favorite Orthodox set of prophecies is found in Deuteronomy 28–30, a description of what will happen to the Jewish people if they fail to uphold the law given to them by Moses. According to the story, both the law and the threatened consequences were delivered to the Israelites immediately before they entered the Promised Land. In *Living Up . . . to the Truth*, Rabbi Dovid Gottlieb asserts that this is a prediction that is extremely unlikely to come true, and he assigns it a probability of no more than one in sixteen thousand. This is, admittedly, a pretty low probability, assuming the estimate is correct (which, as we just saw, it isn't). But, even if we accept the estimate, keep in mind what it is that the evidence is trying to prove.

We are weighing evidence for the truth of the Torah, a text that contains many factual claims of far, far lower probabilities than this one. Remember, we are judging the credibility of a text that describes, among other things, a flood that covered the highest mountains (and a boat that carried couples of every living species), a sea that temporarily parted, clothing that didn't wear out in forty years of wandering in the desert, the sun's standing still, and so on. An event that has a one-in-sixteen-thousand chance of happening is indeed surprising. While these odds are not quite as long as the odds in winning the lottery, they are of the same order of magnitude as the odds of winning a large jackpot in Las Vegas—but it clearly does not match up to even one miraculous violation of physical laws, much less repeated violations. Using ordinary standards of belief, and even accepting the rabbi's inaccurate probability calculation, the strength of this evidence is not even in the ballpark of what we would need.

But let's set aside this important background consideration for the moment and consider the basic Orthodox claim. Does Deuteronomy 28–30 contain an unlikely prediction that has come true? If you read the entire passage, and not just those bits that the Orthodox extract, you will quickly conclude that the vast majority of the dire events predicted never came to pass. From this extensive catalogue of threats, the Orthodox choose a handful of examples and pretend that they constitute an accurate prediction of the Roman destruction of Jerusalem, the subsequent diaspora of the Jews, and their eventual return to modern Israel. The problem is, they ignore most of the relevant text.

Here is how Rabbi Gottlieb defends this practice: "Many details of Deuteronomy 28 have been omitted. There are two reasons: either the language in which they are expressed is poetical and cannot be precisely defined (and thus we cannot prove that the text means specifically what in fact happened), or they are predictions which are very likely to happen in the context of destruction and exile, so that they would not significantly lower the probability."[2] In reality, the problem is not that the ignored prophecies "would not significantly lower the probability." The problem is that they did not come true. Nor is the problem that the ignored prophecies are any more poetic or difficult to interpret than those the Orthodox like to single out. Rather, they simply choose those they can construe as fitting historical events they know to have occurred.

In any event, let's analyze one specific passage, Deuteronomy 28:49–50, that the Orthodox are fond of offering as an accurate prediction of the Roman destruction of Jerusalem. Let's see how well this prophecy lines up with the historical facts. Here is the prophecy: "The Lord* will bring a nation against you from afar, from the end of the earth, which will swoop upon you like an eagle—a nation whose language you will not understand, a ruthless nation that will show the old no regard and the young no mercy."

And here are the facts: At the time of the destruction of the Second Temple in 70 CE Rome had already ruled Judah for over 130 years, and for 70 years before that had maintained a close alliance with the [Jewish] Hasmonean rulers of Judah. The Second Temple, probably built toward the end of the sixth century BCE, was actually extensively rebuilt and refurbished during the reign of the Roman-installed dynasty under Herod the Great, who ruled from 37 to 4 BCE. This was initially a period of relative peace and prosperity, until growing religious and nationalist feelings led to the First Jewish Revolt in 66 CE. It was in response to this uprising that the Romans put down the revolt, attacked Jerusalem, and destroyed the Second Temple.[3]

So how well does the Roman conquest fit the prediction? Consider the passage point by point.

"A nation from afar, from the end of the earth"

Well, OK, Rome was in fact farther away than Greece or Babylonia. But it wasn't that much farther than Persia, which conquered the

---

* For the 2005 edition of the Plaut Torah (*The Torah: A Modern Commentary*, Revised Edition, W. Gunther Plaut, ed. [New York: URJ Press, 2005]), the text was revised to be gender neutral, so that what was "the Lord" is now "the Eternal," what was "fathers" is now "ancestors," and so on. This is the language I use throughout the book when citing Torah passages by chapter and verse. Here, however, we are dealing with a specific passage that the Orthodox use to bolster their claims. Like all fundamentalists, the Orthodox are hardly gender neutral, so in this specific instance I revert to "the Lord," as that is how the Orthodox see the text of the Torah.

Babylonian Empire (including Judah) in the sixth century BCE. One could make a case that in the ancient world Greece and Babylonia were also nations from afar. Moreover, a prediction in that age of a conqueror from afar is hardly startlingly prescient. Still, we can accept this much as a moderately accurate description of the Romans.

"Which will swoop upon you like an eagle"

This is an odd description of the two-hundred-year-long Roman presence leading up to the destruction of Jerusalem. If it was a swoop, it was a rather slow swoop. As a matter of fact, it would appear that the Romans were initially invited into Judah by the warring factions of Hasmoneans. During the occupation, there were periods in which Judah flourished, initiating massive building projects throughout the country and revitalizing the Second Temple. It was not a trouble-free time, thanks largely to the severity of Herod's rule—but Herod was not a Roman.

"A nation whose language you will not understand"

As noted earlier, the Romans controlled Judah for over 130 years before the First Revolt in 66 CE. Furthermore, there is abundant evidence that by that time Jews had been living in Rome itself for 200 years and had formed a substantial colony there as well.[4] So it is absurd to claim that the Roman language was unknown to the Jews when Jerusalem was destroyed. The prophecy is dead wrong on this point.

"A ruthless nation that will show the old no regard and the young no mercy"

Most impartial historians agree that the actual destruction of Jerusalem was an understandable political and military retaliation triggered by the actions of increasingly aggressive Zealots that culminated with the massacre of a Roman garrison in Jerusalem. As for "show[ing] the old no regard and the young no mercy," the Romans were no better and no worse than any other ancient empire in this respect—including, if we accept the Bible's story of Joshua's merciless conquest of Canaan, the Jews themselves.

Clearly, the prediction in question is not a very close match to the historical facts. The Orthodox go on to emphasize the "exile" following the destruction of Jerusalem as if it were the source of the great Jewish diaspora, which the prophecy in Deuteronomy 28–30 would seem to imply. Unfortunately, once again the Orthodox have their history a bit muddled.

In point of fact, according to the British historian Paul Johnson, in the two-hundred-year period from 750 to 550 BCE, there were six distinct deportations of the Israelites, and more left voluntarily for Egypt and other parts of the Near East. From the end of this period onward, a majority of Jews would always live outside Judah. At the time of the First Revolt of 66 CE, the Jews were already well established throughout the inhabited world. There were at least a quarter million Jews in Egypt alone (some estimates run as high as a million), and "in Alexandria, perhaps the world's greatest city after Rome itself, they formed a majority in two out of five quarters. . . . They had been in Rome for two hundred years, and from Rome they had spread all over urban Italy, into Gaul and Spain, and across the sea into northwest Africa."[5] The Jewish diaspora was not, as the Orthodox would have us believe, a massive flight from or deportation by Roman invaders.

It is hard to think of any society or people whose history could not, in broad outline, be construed as fitting many portions of the Deuteronomy 28–30 prophecy. Consider the American Indians. They were certainly attacked by a people from afar whose language they did not understand. They were dispersed from one end of the earth to the other (well, not really, but neither were the Jews). They suffered devastating illnesses (a part of the prediction, by the way, that doesn't really fit Jewish history).[6] How about the Africans during the age of slavery and colonization? Or most of Europe during the Roman conquest? Or Rome itself during the barbarian invasion? Or Mongolia, several times over? And so on down the line. The inevitable conclusion is that the probability of the Deuteronomy prophecy's being *partly* accurate is, in reality, quite high—not one in sixteen thousand, as the rabbi would have us believe. The truth of the matter is that, given all the different prophecies in the Torah, the probability that *some* of them would come true is extremely high, rather than extremely low.

Regardless of the historical facts, the Orthodox will always manage to come up with an interpretation that will prove that all of the Torah's prophecies have come true, so there is little to be gained by debating them prediction by specific prediction. We can, however, learn a great deal if we focus on the opening lines of Deuteronomy 28, as it contains one of the Torah's most fundamental overall prophecies, a prediction embodied in Leviticus 26 as well: "If you follow My laws and faithfully observe My commandments . . . I will grant peace in the land, and you shall lie down untroubled by anyone; I will give the land respite from vicious beasts, and no sword shall cross your land . . . your enemies shall fall before you by the sword."[7]

Deuteronomy 28 says pretty much the same thing: "Now, if you obey the Eternal your God, to observe faithfully all the divine commandments . . . the Eternal will put to rout before [your army] the enemies who attack you . . . [they will] flee by many roads."[8]

Both these passages are unambiguous: Obey God, observe God's law, and you will have peace, and if you don't have peace, at least you will be victorious in battle.

Tell that to Josiah, one of the last kings of Judah. Josiah, a direct descendent of King David, reigned from 639 to 609 BCE and launched the most intense moral reform in the history of Judah. And he kept going with his Yahweh crusade across the border into the kingdom of Israel to the north, where he destroyed the temple at Beth-El that King Jeroboam had established three centuries earlier to rival the centralized worship at the temple of Jerusalem in Judah.[9]

One would have thought that if ever there were a time when the predicted Torah blessings cited above were richly deserved, it was the time of good King Josiah. But, instead, the Egyptian pharaoh attacked Judah, and in the battle Josiah was killed. Decades of spiritual revival and visionary hopes—all the major themes in Deuteronomy culminated in Josiah—seemed to go down the tubes overnight. Josiah was dead, and his people, in the ultimate of ignominies, were again enslaved in Egypt.* And if this were not devastating enough, the last two decades in the history of Judah are described in the Bible as a period of continuous decline, leading to the destruction of the Judaic state.[10]

Indeed, as the biblical scholar Richard Elliott Friedman observes:

> The Deuteronomistic history looked ironic, even foolish, twenty-two years after Josiah's death. The Babylonians had destroyed Judah and exiled many of its people. The "eternal" kingdom had ended. The [Davidic] family that would "never be cut off from the throne" was cut off from the throne. The place "where Yahweh causes his name to dwell" was burned down. And the things that were said to exist "to this day" did not exist anymore.[11]

To paraphrase the old TV ad, it doesn't get any worse than this.

As should be expected, the Orthodox have a ready explanation for this seemingly inconsistent turn of events. Josiah's religious restoration, albeit worthy, was not enough to offset the sins committed by the Israelites during the reign of his grandfather, King Manasseh, so all Josiah managed to do was postpone God's punishment, not avoid it. But Orthodox casuistry aside, it is pretty obvious that what we have here is a clear-cut case where the prophecy of the blessings that were to accrue to the observant, law-abiding, and God-fearing children of Israel was not fulfilled.

In fact, just the opposite happened. Josiah's was a reign of unparalleled piety and observance, and yet he was killed (quite young), his people were subjugated by a foreign enemy, and soon thereafter his kingdom was violently and completely destroyed, all in direct contravention of the predicted blessing. A lawyer could make a pretty good case that God didn't hold up his end of the deal—or, to put it a bit more delicately, that God did not fulfill his obligations under the covenant he had made with the people of Israel.

Now fast-forward twenty-five hundred years to the creation of the

---

* The phrase "*again* enslaved in Egypt" reflects the Orthodox view of Jewish history, not my view nor that of academic historians and archeologists.

state of Israel. This is the flip side of the coin, and it represents an interesting paradox for the Orthodox position. Yes, the children of Israel did regain their homeland, not an easy task after being banished for two thousand years. But did this return fulfill the prophecy in Deuteronomy? Not in the least.

To see why, once again we have to look at the entirety of the Deuteronomy prophecy, not just the final part. Remember, this whole prophecy describes the terrible consequences that will befall the Israelites if they fail to live up to the Mosaic law. The predicted return to the Holy Land is the promised reward that will be granted only if, after ignoring the law for some period, the Jewish people, in all the countries to which God has banished them, completely and whole-heartedly regain their devotion and obedience to God. The problem is that the destruction of Jerusalem by the Romans did not coincide with a period of significant weakness of Jewish faith. I am sure there are those who would argue the contrary, but the fact remains that there is no evidence to indicate that immediately prior to the destruction of Jerusalem there was significantly less Jewish devotion than during earlier or later periods in Jewish history. Nor is there any evidence to indicate that, during the first half of the twentieth century, there was a widespread rebirth of Jewish faith or increased obedience to Mosaic law.

The facts that the Romans destroyed Jerusalem in 70 CE and that the modern state of Israel was created in 1948 do not verify the prophecy in the slightest unless we can show that (1) the first event was triggered by a widespread straying from the Mosaic law, (2) the second event was triggered by a widespread return to the Mosaic law, and (3) between these two periods there was no comparable return to devout religious observance. If (1) is not the case, then the Roman invasion was not the predicted retribution—it was simply an invasion, much like any other (although at the outset perhaps more benign than most). If (2) is not the case, then the regaining of Israel was not the predicted reward—it was perhaps an unusual historical event, but not the fulfillment of this prophecy. Finally, if (3) is not the case, then the promised reward was predicted to occur at an earlier historical period, and the fact that it did not falsifies the prophecy.

There is no historical evidence for any of these three crucial assumptions, and without all three, the entire prophecy breaks down. Of course, it is human nature to imagine that, when terrible things happen, you must have done something wrong to deserve them. Children do this all the time: The abused child grows up convinced that he or she is a terrible person. Many adults do it, too. A natural disaster destroys some homes but not others, and occupants of the former ask what they did wrong, while occupants of the latter may suffer survivor's guilt ("I didn't really deserve my good fortune . . ."). These are powerful psychological tendencies, and make it easy for the Orthodox (and for contemporary commentators) to assume that the destruction of Jerusalem was some form of divine punishment.* But, although there is ample historical evidence that the Romans did in fact assume control of Judah, there is no historical evidence that there was a marked decrease in religious observation during the period before the invasion and the subsequent destruction of Jerusalem.

On the contrary, the evidence points persuasively in the opposite direction. The destruction of Jerusalem was preceded by a period of *increasing* religious and nationalist sentiment among the Jews. Of course, this is consistent with there being other, less visible parts of the population moving away from the Mosaic law. But to believe that

---

* The destruction of New Orleans, too, it would appear. After the devastation wreaked by Hurricanes Katrina and Rita, Ron Nagin, the mayor of New Orleans, offered this explanation: "Surely God is mad at America. He sent us hurricane after hurricane, and it's destroyed and put stress on this country."[12]

When the most destructive earthquake ever recorded in the eastern United States struck Cape Ann, about thirty miles north of Boston, in 1755, the prominent minister Thomas Prince laid the blame at the doorstep of none other than Benjamin Franklin for inventing the lightning rod. "It was a widespread belief in the eighteenth century that lighting was God's instrument of choice when manifesting displeasure. . . . Lightning rods meddled with God's usual mode of reprimand, went this line of thinking, causing God to reach for another, more terrible weapon in his arsenal."[13]

I discuss the fundamentalist doctrine of divine retribution in chapter 4.

there was unprecedented disobedience to Mosaic law would be pure speculation in the face of historical evidence about the predominant sentiments of the period. The historical evidence all points to the destruction coming about as a *Roman* response to *increased* allegiance to Judaism, not as a divine response to a decreased faith.

The situation with the latter two assumptions is even worse. The nineteenth and twentieth centuries saw the growth and flourishing of various more liberal forms of Judaism, which from an Orthodox standpoint could only be interpreted as a straying from the Torah's law. And indeed that is exactly how the Orthodox viewed, and continue to view today, the liberal movement in Europe and America. In contrast, many earlier centuries witnessed a much more literalist form of Judaism, much more commonly and universally observed. The unavoidable conclusion is that assumptions (2) and (3) also are demonstrably false. The creation of the modern state of Israel is clearly not the fulfillment of the Deuteronomy prophecy. It may be a marvelous thing for the Jewish people, a justified step toward righting a tragic wrong, but it cannot logically or rationally be construed as a reward for a wholehearted return to God's law after two thousand years of straying from that law. This simply does not fit the historical facts.

One Orthodox defense against this undeniable historical reality is that the return to Israel was not a reward, but rather the result of God's taking pity on the Jewish people. They paraphrase Deuteronomy 30:3 as saying that God will have compassion on you and gather you from all the nations to which He has scattered you. This is not how I read the passage:

> When . . . you return to the Eternal your God, and you and your children heed God's command with all your heart and soul, just as I enjoin upon you this day, then the Eternal your God will restore your fortunes and take you back in love. [God] will bring you together again from all the peoples where the Eternal your God has scattered you . . . from there the Eternal your God will gather you, from there [God] will fetch you. And the Eternal will bring you to the land that your fathers possessed, and you shall possess it; and God will make you more prosperous and more numerous than your ancestors.[14]

That sounds like a classic quid pro quo to me, the promise of a specific, well-defined reward for specific, well-defined behavior. I do not see compassion as God's motive for returning the Jews to Israel. Increasing numbers of Jews in the first half of the twentieth century did *not* "heed [God's] command with all [their] heart and soul." Indeed, a strong argument can be made that there were several fifty-year periods (and some longer than that) in the prior centuries when the Jewish people were much more observant than in the fifty years leading up to the creation of the state of Israel. This being the case, there was no discernable justification under the covenant for God to bring the Jewish people back to Israel when he did.

Just as the Orthodox have a tidy explanation for the undeserved fate met by the assiduously pious King Josiah and his people, so also do they attempt to explain away the seemingly undeserved reward received by the increasingly *im*pious Jewish people in the mid-twentieth century. It is, say the Orthodox, precisely because, in the nineteenth and twentieth centuries, so many Jews strayed from God and his commandments that God visited his wrath upon the Jewish people and sent them the Holocaust as a well-deserved punishment, exactly what he said he would do close to the very end of the Torah.[15] Then, the argument goes, during and after the punishment of the Holocaust, the Jewish people saw the sins of their ways and returned to "heed [God's] command with all [their] heart and soul." So he took pity on them and gathered them into Israel.

The problem is, that isn't what happened. If anything, the reverse took place, with many Jews losing much of their faith in God. Richard Rubinstein, in his book *After Auschwitz*, holds that Auschwitz is our Sinai. Anyone who could attribute the Nazis' bestiality to God's punishment of a sinful Jewish people Rubinstein considers obscene.[16] And for what it's worth, friends, so do I.

In considering the Orthodox position—that the Torah's prophecies are proof beyond reasonable doubt that the Torah is true—we find that the preponderance of the evidence is overwhelming that their argument is irremediably flawed. Any objective reading of the prophecy, coupled with an accurate, dispassionate survey of the history in question, leads us to judge that the prophecy has *not* been fulfilled. Many more of the predicted events did not occur than did occur, and those that we can construe as having occurred did not happen at times when they should have, given the intent of the prophecy. When we read the prophecy in its entirety, and not merely brief, highly selective passages, and then look at real, documented history, the Orthodox claim—that the Torah makes accurate predictions that only God could have put there—evaporates. And with it so does their ipso facto conclusion that the Torah is God's word, reflects God's will, and, therefore, is true.

And there is something else, too. Most non-Orthodox biblical scholars believe that the prediction in Deuteronomy 31:16–18 was made after the fact. In this famous passage, when God speaks his final words to Moses, he doesn't tell Moses what terrible curses will befall the people of Israel *if* they break the covenant and turn away from him. He has already done that, amply, in previous verses in Deuteronomy. What he does here is to state unambiguously that after Moses's death the people *will* turn away from him, and, as a consequence, God *will* turn away from the people, hiding his countenance and abandoning them to their well-deserved fate.

The consensus among the leading academic biblical scholars is that this passage was written after the death of King Josiah at the hands of the Egyptians and Nebuchadnezzar's devastating conquest of Judah shortly thereafter. It was the only way to explain the calamities that struck the people of Judah at the very moment when one would have thought they were in line for all of God's blessings, not his curses. What better way to explain contemporary calamity than to demonstrate that several centuries earlier God had predicted to Moses precisely what was going to happen? Written ex post facto, of course, any prophecy will come true.

Why do people keep getting fooled by the fallacy of accurate predictions as proof that this or that religion is true? For one thing, not everyone has the math background to work through the Astrologer's

Fallacy calculations presented at the beginning of this chapter, so they tend to believe a self-styled expert who is making calculations that seem plausible enough on the surface. But more important, it is well known, and experimentally well documented, that people are easily fooled about the purported accuracy of predictions. This holds regardless of the source or nature of the prediction. There is an unshakable belief among many arthritis sufferers, for example, that they can accurately predict the weather. But a series of experiments not too long ago showed conclusively that their predictions are no more accurate than chance.

The source of the illusion of accuracy is that we tend to notice and remember the correct predictions, but overlook the occasions when the predictions are incorrect—which is why people continue to get taken in by astrologers, psychics, and fortune-tellers. Fifteen years ago Thomas Gilovich, a professor of psychology at Cornell University, wrote a fascinating book about this whole phenomenon. The title says it all: *How We Know What Isn't So.*[17]

CHAPTER FOUR

THE IMMORALITY
OF THE DOCTRINE OF
DIVINE RETRIBUTION

I T'S WORTH PAUSING FOR A MOMENT to look at the whole question of divine retribution, a good example of which we just saw in the catalogue of threats embodied in Deuteronomy 31:16–18, because it goes to the heart of what makes the Orthodox belief system so wrong. At the core of Orthodox Judaism is a morbid morality play with a recurring, circular theme:

The Jew sins.

God punishes the Jew (for his own good).

The Jew repents and asks for forgiveness.

God mercifully forgives the Jew.

The Jew sins again, is punished again, repents again, and so on, as the cycle repeats itself ad infinitum.

If one is to believe Orthodox dogma, life for the Jew comes down to this: Man is inherently bad, but God chose the Jewish people to receive his Torah, his specific instructions (his law) on how they should live. So you had better lead a moral life—defined as doing God's will, which, in turn, is defined as following the detailed instructions for living spelled out in the Torah—or God will punish you.

The idea that God's punishment is for the Jews' own good is a recurrent theme in Orthodox doctrine. After one particularly deadly suicide bombing in an Orthodox neighborhood in Jerusalem, the *New York Times* correspondent Joel Greenberg reported this reaction from one resident: "The Almighty wants to test us to see if we will continue to believe. . . . He wants to wake us up and return to the faith." Greenberg went on:

> Gathered outside the [hostel] this afternoon, yeshiva students described the attack . . . as a painful reprimand from God, like a slap from a stern father. "When someone who loves you hits you, you don't get angry," said one. A student who gave his name as Aharon said that the divine message was that Jews have to mend their ways. "We have to study and follow the Torah, keep the Sabbath, and love one another. . . . If we behave better, the troubles will end."[1]

Closer to home, an Orthodox rabbi in the United States once told me flat out: "People must have a real fear of doing the wrong thing, a fear of the consequences." Christian fundamentalists are of like mind. Three years ago the Reverend Ted Haggard, then pastor of the four-teen-thousand-member New Life Church in Colorado Springs and president of the National Association of Evangelicals, said, "The fear of God is a worthy emotion."*[2] Personally, I consider this a perverse view of human nature and of how people should lead their lives.

In the first place, I reject the Orthodox premise that man is inherently bad and leads a moral life only out of fear of the consequences. I hold with the ancient Greek philosophers, who believed that virtue should be followed because it is intrinsically worthwhile. I believe that people with character lead moral lives because it is right to do so, not because they are afraid of divine retribution should they do something

---

* Maybe so, but in 2006 the Reverend Haggard resigned both positions after the Overseer Board of the New Life Church issued this statement: "Our investigation and Pastor Haggard's public statements have proven without doubt that he has committed sexually immoral conduct."[3] It was alleged that Haggard maintained a sexual relationship with another man for three years.

wrong. They refrain from stealing not because they are afraid God (or the local authorities) will punish them, but because they know that stealing is wrong.

The Orthodox respond with this argument: "Yes, that is correct, but they know this because God established a standard of absolute morality in which stealing, among other things, is wrong, and"—this is fundamental to Orthodox doctrine—"you can't have a standard of absolute morality unless is comes from outside the human existence, unless it comes from God." This is simply not true. There is an enormous body of brilliant philosophical thought, from Plato and Aristotle down to Hume and Kant, to which all serious modern philosophers subscribe, that holds: (1) yes, there are absolute standards of morality, but (2) no, they do not necessarily have to come from God.

Second, I think the whole idea of divine punishment is grossly immoral. The Orthodox like to say that God, in his infinite wisdom, always selects a punishment appropriate for the offense. At the time of the Roman siege of Jerusalem, for example, there was apparently a lot of bickering going on among the different Jewish factions about the right approach to take with the Roman invaders. According to Orthodox doctrine, God said, in effect, "Since you can't get along, I'm going to disperse you." Which is why he caused the Jewish people to be scattered throughout the world. One has to ask, if the diaspora was an appropriate punishment for the Jewish lack of cohesion in the middle of the first century CE, what was the Holocaust appropriate punishment for in the middle of the twentieth?

The Orthodox consider the Holocaust divine retribution for the Jewish people's straying from God's law, just as God promised in Deuteronomy 31. If you think this is an unduly harsh exaggeration of their position, consider the comments of Rabbi Ovadia Yosef, the religious leader of Israel's powerful (Orthodox) Shas Party. In 2000, in one of his weekly Saturday radio sermons, Rabbi Yosef declared that the six million Jews who perished in the Holocaust died because they were "the reincarnation of earlier souls, who sinned and caused others to sin and did all sorts of forbidden acts. They returned in reincarnation to set these things right."[4] Hard to believe, I know, but this is an undeniable, recorded statement by one of Israel's most influential Orthodox religious leaders, a man who commands a huge following. Indeed, the chairman of the Shas Party said that any criticism of Yosef over these astounding remarks was unjustified.[5]

Think about this for a moment. If the Holocaust was God's just retribution for the sins of the Jewish people, doesn't that make Adolf Hitler a good guy, God's agent—a sort of latter-day Nebuchadnezzar[6]—doing God's holy work? I mean we're not talking famine, flood, or pestilence here. We're talking about a man who systematically butchered men and women and little children for no reason other than that they were Jews.

Some years ago I visited Auschwitz. The image that remains most vivid in my mind was the exhibit of the large piles of children's shoes. Were the people who murdered those little innocents instruments of God's will, following (albeit unknowingly) God's orders?

Contrast the dubious morality propounded by the Orthodox with what the liberal rabbi W. Gunther Plaut has to say about what he calls "The Problem of Retribution."

> Almost automatically [the modern reader] will question the basic assumption that virtue and piety are requited with material benefits and wickedness with material punishment. The doctrine of earthly rewards and punishment is asserted many times in the Bible with vigor and eloquence. It was challenged irresistibly in the book of Job and elsewhere; still, people continued to believe it because they wanted to believe it. But it cannot be rationally defended.
>
> As long as people thought in terms of collective responsibility, the problem could somehow be managed. For, if a nation was predominantly righteous and therefore prosperous, even the undeserving citizens might share its good fortunes. And if national wickedness entailed national disaster, some of the virtuous minority might get hurt in the general crash. . . . But morality is not the only condition for national survival, perhaps not even the decisive condition. Peaceable and culturally productive peoples have been subjugated and exterminated by nations inferior to them in every-

thing but military potential and ferocity. Who dare say that . . . the horrors of Auschwitz were punishments which the victims deserved?

Still less acceptable is the application of the doctrine to individual experience, as taught by Ezekiel. It can be upheld only by a stubborn disregard of facts. . . . The theory of mechanical retribution, moreover, is not only mistaken but actually immoral. For, if sin is regularly followed by punishment, it follows that every misfortune is a condemnation.

A few centuries after [the book of Job] was written, Jewish teachers affirmed the belief in immortality and thereby provided a new approach to the problem of retribution. In an existence beyond the grave, they taught, true justice will be meted out to the righteous and wicked alike; retribution will be spiritual rather than physical.[7] . . . [This] is an assertion of faith which can hardly be proved or disproved. But concerning the realities we can appraise here and now, at least this much may be confidently stated:

First, there is no necessary relation between a man's merits and his fortunes. Results are only possibilities; they are not guaranteed. . . .

Second, the consequences of our conduct can rarely be limited to ourselves. . . .

Third, it may be that only a world like ours—a world in which we are never sure whether we will be rewarded or punished for our actions—gives us the possibility of leading a truly moral life. For the ethical decision is the decision to do the right [thing] because it is right and not for any other advantage.[8]

These few paragraphs constitute one of the most eloquent statements I have ever read on what authentic morality is really all about.

CHAPTER FIVE

OF KOSHER HOOFS
AND CUDS

A NOTHER PIECE OF EVIDENCE the Orthodox offer to support their belief that God wrote the Torah is that it contains information that, they claim, only God could have known and put there. Who but God could have known, they ask, that among all the land animals on earth, only four—the camel, the *daman*, the hare, and the pig—either have cloven hoofs or chew a cud, but not both?[1] "Show me that this is not true," a young "modern" Orthodox rabbi once challenged me, "and you'll prove to me that God did not write the Torah." Well, it is *not* true, and that fact seriously undercuts the Orthodox argument.

In turns out that, as a matter of zoological fact, of the four animals the Torah singles out, only one, the pig, is a clear-cut case of having one or the other characteristic but not both. The pig is a cloven-hoofed animal, but it does not chew the cud. When we turn to the other three animals, however, the picture is not so clear.

The camel, which does chew the cud, has a modified structure of even toes joined together at the bottom by a pad. To say that the camel is not cloven-hoofed is, as one eminent zoologist told me, splitting hairs. But the real problem for the Orthodox is with the other two animals, the *daman* and the hare.

According to the commentary in the Plaut Torah, "the *daman* [is a] small southwest Asian animal of the hyrax family whose other members are found only in southern Africa. It looks something like a small-eared rabbit . . . earlier translations, 'cony' and 'rock badger,' are misleading. Cony is an archaic word for rabbit, and the European rock badger is nothing like the hyrax."[2] Leviticus 11:5 says "the *daman*— although it chews the cud, it has no true hoofs; it is unclean for you." But every modern zoologist knows that the *daman* does *not* chew the cud. It gives the *impression* that it does because (1) it has protrusions on its stomach, which suggest that its stomach may have compartments, as is characteristic of the ruminants,[3] and (2) it is constantly munching.

Leviticus 11:6 says exactly the same thing, word for word, about the hare: "although it chews the cud, it has no true hoofs; it is unclean for you." But here, too, every modern zoologist knows that the hare does not chew the cud either. The hare—*arnevet* in Hebrew—is actually, zoologically speaking, a lagomorph. It does not have a ruminant pattern of digestion, but gives the *impression* of being a ruminant because it munches its food so noticeably. The zoologist with whom I spoke said that the practice of coprophagy (the fancy term for an animal eating its own feces) has sometimes been mistaken for chewing a cud. Rabbits and hares do this frequently, as do many rodents. The presumed function of this behavior is to process food twice, thereby allowing the animals to extract more nutrients from everything that they eat. Another function is to recover part of the important bacterial fauna used for digesting celulose-rich food.

These two small creatures present one big problem for the Orthodox doctrine that God wrote the Torah, bigger even than the fact that history did not fulfill most of the Torah's prophecies (including the most fundamental one of all). As we stipulated, the Orthodox can always come up with an interpretation of both the Torah and history to make the latter fit the former pretty much at will. But here we are not dealing with interpretations. Here we are dealing with an unambiguous statement in the Torah that is an unmistakable error of zoological fact.

Leviticus 11:5–6 says unequivocally and in the plainest language possible that the *daman* and the hare chew the cud. It turns out, however, that they don't. The Torah is wrong. Which means that if God wrote the Torah, God made a mistake. Since God, being God, by definition cannot make a mistake—certainly not an error of zoological fact—and since the Torah contains such a clear-cut error of zoological fact, then the inescapable conclusion is that the Torah was not written by God, but by human beings like you and me, who are perfectly capable of being fooled by appearances.[4]

CHAPTER SIX

THE DELUSION
OF SCRIPTURE'S
HIDDEN CODES

ONE OF THE MORE BIZARRE ways in which the Orthodox defend their dogma that God wrote the Torah is by claiming that in the holy text you will find—if you know how to look for them—patterns and sequences that in reality are hidden codes, codes that only a divine author could have put there. In his proselytizing book *Choose Life*, Rabbi Ezriel Tauber devotes a whole section to what he calls "The Codes of Creation."[1]

In 1908 a pamphlet surfaced in Berlin entitled "The Pentateuch—A Number Edifice Discovery of a Uniformly Executed Numerical Script" and written by a Professor Oskar Goldberg. In it he listed over 120 examples throughout the Torah of key words and phrases occurring either seven times or in multiples of seven. The Documentary Hypothesis, to which just about all nonfundamentalist biblical scholars subscribe (and which is anathema to Orthodox Jews and other fundamentalists), builds a convincing case that there were four different, well-defined authors of the Torah, called J, E, P, and D, and in addition a redactor called R.* So you can imagine the elation in the Orthodox camp when Goldberg apparently discovered that the divine

---

* There is a detailed discussion of the Documentary Hypothesis in chapter 7.

names in the Torah were not randomly distributed, but occurred in patterns, usually in multiples of seven, thereby revealing an organic unity in the text that proves it was the work of a single author. Goldberg wrote this tract one hundred years ago, yet the Orthodox still dredge it up today and offer it to prospective "returnees" as iron-clad proof that God wrote the Torah.

The Orthodox also like to point to the work of a mid-twentieth-century rabbi named Michael Weissmandel, who, they say, pioneered the field of "equidistant letter sequences." These sequences, the Orthodox claim, demonstrate that the Torah's text contains many layers of encoded information that testify to a purposeful and exacting internal arrangement of words and letters. This, in turn, demonstrates that the text is a single whole written by a single, divine author, disproving the hypothesis that it was "sewn together" by several human authors over a lengthy span of time.

The Orthodox are also convinced that these hidden codes often foretell the future. A good example of that kind of thinking can be found in the story of Queen Esther, a favorite of Jewish schoolchildren everywhere. Let's leave aside for the moment the strong probability that the story itself is largely fiction (scholars believe that the book of Esther is, in reality, a Judaic version of a Persian novella about the shrewdness of harem queens). Whether or not the story really happened is beside the point. It is a captivating tale about a beautiful woman who outsmarts a cunning, evil man and saves her people.

Esther, the good (and good-looking) Jewish woman whom the Persian king, Ahasuerus (Xerxes I), chose for his queen, learns that the wicked grand vizier Haman is plotting to slaughter all the Jews in the kingdom. She convinces the king that Haman is a disloyal villain, so instead of killing the Jews, the king kills Haman, his ten sons, and his henchmen.* Ahasuerus then asks Esther what else she would like

---

* There is a lot more going on here than just the thrilling account of how Queen Esther saves her people. One of the most fundamental doctrines of Orthodox Judaism is that in the Torah the events that happened to the patriarchs set patterns that will occur at later times to the Jewish people. This doctrine is vital to the concept that God did not

him to do. She replies, "If it please the king, let it be granted to the Jews . . . to . . . let Haman's ten sons [who, by the way, according to earlier verses, have already been killed "with the stroke of the sword"] be hanged upon the gallows."[2]

An Orthodox tract I saw claims that this verse foretells the hanging of ten Nazi war criminals at Nuremberg on a particular day. "The [Nuremberg] trial ended, but the sentencing was repeatedly postponed by appeals for amnesty. Finally after the Jewish New Year's Day came and went, the sentence was pronounced: death by hanging. There were supposed to be eleven, but Göring committed suicide. In the end there were only ten. On October 16, 1946, on Hoshana Raba, they were executed."

A more recent example of the belief that the scripture's hidden codes foretell the future was described by Bill Keller in one of his op-ed pieces for the *New York Times*: "Two weeks ago a group of senior intelligence officials in the Defense Department sat for an hour listening to a briefing by a writer [Keller describes him as the author of a Nostradamus-style bestseller] who claims—I am not making this up—that messages encoded in the Hebrew text of the Old Testament provide clues to the whereabouts of Osama bin Laden."[3]

If all this sounds more than a little preposterous to you, don't

---

just wind up the world and set it in motion, but that he set life patterns. One of the most important of these life patterns is the age-old struggle between Israel and Amalek, Israel's archnemesis. Amalek is a direct descendent of Esau, and the struggle between Jacob (Israel) and Esau, Orthodox doctrine holds, is the paradigm for all subsequent generations of Jews: the fight between Jacob's descendents (the "children of Israel") and Esau's descendents, the Amalekites. So if you want to understand Jewish history, they say, you have to understand what happened to Jacob and Esau.

What the Orthodox see is a pattern—they always see a pattern—in which Esau (Amalek) is constantly trying to prevent Jacob (Israel) from returning to the Promised Land. In Genesis, Esau doesn't want to let Jacob return. In Exodus 17 the Amalekites are there to fight the Israelites after they cross into Sinai. (Joshua, in his first military engagement, won.) The next time the Jews return to Israel is after the end of the Babylonian exile, and they encounter a man whom the Orthodox call "a certain descendent of Amalek named Haman," in effect blocking the way again. The Orthodox concede that there is no proof that Haman was in fact a descendent of Amalek, but, they say, it is tradition to consider him so.

despair. It is *completely* preposterous. But bear in mind that a basic Orthodox doctrine holds that the Torah and the Talmud contain several hidden layers of meaning that only God could have put there. We are just beginning, they say, to peel away these layers and understand the deeper meaning, but you have to know how to do it or you won't see anything. It requires a lifetime of study.

The delusion that there are meaningful number patterns hidden in sacred (and not so sacred) texts is a folly as old as the hills, dating back at least twenty-five hundred years. And the delusion has a name: numerology. There is an absolutely delightful way to learn about numerology and that is to read a book called *Numerology—or What Pythagoras Wrought.*[4] The author is a serious math professor named Underwood Dudley, and he has done a masterful job of writing a book that is not only scholarly and informative, but also entertaining and often hilariously funny.

Professor Dudley takes his reader on a guided tour through the surreal world of Numerology Land. We see popping up on the landscape all the sevens, thirteens, squares, and triangles that Orthodox Jews and Christian fundamentalists have discovered running through the Bible,[5] all the fifty-sevens someone found in early American history, and all the different triangles an Englishman was able to pull out of Shakespeare's sonnets. And lots of pyramids, because no discussion of the numerologists would be complete without mention of their first cousins, the pyramidologists, who—starting in 1859 with John Taylor's *The Great Pyramid: Why Was It Built and Who Built It?*—have convinced themselves that not only was the great pyramid in Egypt put in a very special place for very special, transcendental reasons, but also that its measurements provide us with unmistakable clues to the history of mankind.

When all is said and done, of course, none of these numerical contortions proves anything—other than that if you massage any text (or any pyramid) long enough you will come up with patterns and sequences. To demonstrate this fact, Dudley extracts from Lincoln's Gettysburg Address a vast array of sevens and squares. But God didn't put them there, he observes, any more than he put them in the book of Genesis or in the Gospel according to Matthew. Nor did God make the word *Gettysburg* a perfect numerology square of 144.[6] They are all there, every single one of them, by accident.

> Picking features out of something that already exists and asking what the probability is that they exist is not playing fair. The probability is 1. What is the chance that *you* exist? When you consider the number of possible ways of combining genes, the probability of getting the combination that makes you the person you are . . . is so close to zero that you are impossible, the laws of chance say so. But there you are, not only existing but, all the more improbably, reading this.[7]

A couple of years ago the *New York Times Magazine* published an article, entitled "The Odds of That," in which contributing writer Lisa Belkin examined the tendency of people to see conspiracy when what they are really seeing is coincidence, and offered a chilling example of numerology at work:

> The numbers 9/11 (9 plus 1 plus 1) equal 11. American Airlines Flight 11 was the first to hit the twin towers. There were 92 people on board (9 plus 2). September 11 is the 254th day of the year (2 plus 5 plus 4). There are 11 letters each in "Afghanistan," "New York City," and "the Pentagon" (and, while we're counting, in George W. Bush). The World Trade towers themselves took the form of the number 11. [Yet] this seeming numerical message is not actually a pattern that exists but merely a pattern we have found.[8]

At the other end of the spectrum, sometimes the codes can get downright comical. In early 2001 thousands of Russian Orthodox priests, monks, and believers refused to accept the Russian government's new taxpayer ID numbers, claiming that the bar code on the application form contained the mark of the beast. Some priests told their parishioners they risked eternal damnation if they applied for the ID numbers. The problem was with the three pairs of parallel stripes in the bar code on the form. The stripes, which appear on any standard bar code, carry no meaning and are used to separate the beginning, middle, and end of the bar code. But some of the faithful saw in these stripes the dreaded number 666—the mark of the beast described in the book of Revelation. The head of the Movement for the Right to Live without a Taxpayer ID weighed in with this observation: "A computer decodes the separation stripes as 666, the Number of the Beast. Moreover, the principle of the bar code contains an even more elaborately coded mathematical apocalyptic equation."[9]

We can laugh at this—just as we can laugh at the biblical sevens and squares, pyramidology, and the triangulation of Shakespeare—and consider it all nonsense, which of course it is. Complete nonsense. But it was no joke to the Russian Orthodox Church (let alone to the Russian fiscal authorities, who were having a hard enough time as it was getting people to pay their taxes). The church leaders took it so seriously, in fact, that they "gathered clergy from across [Russia] in a monastery north of Moscow to debate whether the numbers [were] evil. As they struggled for a resolution, monks outside handed out leaflets denouncing the ID numbers. In the end, the church issued an appeal to its followers not to panic over the new numbers—but stopped short of urging them to file the application. In the city of Ivanovo, two hundred miles from Moscow, nine thousand people signed a petition protesting the numbers as 'satanic.' "[10]

The fact is, it can be demonstrated quite easily that a couple of simple mathematical laws make the odds of all these apparently amazing occurrences—sevens, squares, triangles, the mark of the beast, the passageways of the great pyramid, you name it—a great deal higher than one would think. The first is the Law of *Small* Numbers: Because there are so few integers to go around, coincidences will occur that can mislead. The second is the Law of *Round* Numbers: There are not enough round numbers to go around either, this shortage also creating coincidences that the numerologists pounce on and discover patterns.[11]

It is human nature that people look for patterns to explain life and its meaning. John Allen Paulos, a professor of mathematics at Temple University, says that "finding a reason or a pattern where none actually exists makes [life] less frightening, because events get placed in the realm of the logical. Believing in fate, or even conspiracy, can sometimes be more comforting than facing the fact that sometimes things just happen."[12]

Paulos is right on target. Biblical numerologists have had a fertile field to plow over the years not only because human beings are very good at seeing patterns, but also—and principally—because people *want* to find patterns. By discovering the codes of the scriptures and "peeling away" the perceived layers of meaning, they attempt to take the randomness out of life. A random walk in a random universe is not a comfortable way to view the world and one's life in it. Much better to think—as the Orthodox, indeed as all fundamentalists do—that everything is part of a grand design. That is a much more comforting, much more satisfying approach. Whether it is true, of course, is another matter.[13]

There is a ready audience for biblical numerologists because they offer the reassuring hidden proof that this sought-after grand design really does exist and that it comes from God. They refuse to believe that patterns can—and do—occur by chance. But when you strip away the cloak of mystery and look at the hard, cold facts, the numerologists' discoveries—like the "accuracy" of the prophecies we saw in chapter 3—are simply not so astounding after all.

If you want to find patterns, layers, and meaning, look hard enough and you will find them in any text, just as Underwood Dudley did in the Gettysburg Address—and as he surely would have found them just as easily had he selected instead the Magna Carta, Martin Luther King's "I Have a Dream" speech, or the New York City phone book. If, however, you are genuinely seeking the truth, then you have to agree with Professor Dudley when he concludes: "The Bible-numerists [display] the human ability to see patterns where none exist, to attribute volition where there is none, and to invest the operations of blind chance with deep meanings they do not have."[14]

When you think about it, this is an accurate description of the lens through which Orthodox Jews view the Torah and the world: They see patterns where none exist; they attribute volition where there is none; and they attach to chance events deep meanings they do not have.

The numerical patterns and sequences the Orthodox purport to have discovered in the text of the Torah offer no credible evidence of divine intervention. Indeed, *they have no significance at all.* Like all numerology, the Torah's hidden codes are just so much humbug.

CHAPTER SEVEN

WHO WROTE THE TORAH, WHEN, WHERE, AND WHY?

IN HIS "General Introduction to the Torah," Rabbi Gunther Plaut lays out in broad lines liberal Judaism's answer to this question.

> Does God have anything to do with the Torah? While God is not the author of the Torah in the fundamentalist sense, the Torah is a book about humanity's understanding of and experience with God. We believe it is possible to say: The Torah is ancient Israel's distinctive record of its search for God. The Torah tradition testifies to a people of extraordinary spiritual sensitivity. God is not the author of the text, the people are; but God's voice may be heard through theirs if we listen with open minds. Is this true for every word and verse? Not in our view.[1]

There are those who would argue that this is not true for *any* word or verse, and recently some well-known atheists have written powerful books to support their position.[2] But they can't say with complete certainty that Rabbi Plaut's hypothesis is wrong any more than he can say with certainty that theirs is wrong. Where Rabbi Plaut and the atheists do agree is that God did not write the Torah, people did.

Who were these people? When did they write the Torah? Where did they write it? And, most important of all, why did they write it?

The keys to answering these questions lie in the text of the Torah itself and its relation to the real ancient history of the Jewish people that has been uncovered by modern biblical archeology. Three facts stand out. First and foremost, there were two kingdoms—Israel to the north and Judah to the south—characterized by different geopolitical, economic, social, and religious realities. Each of the authors of the Torah was a product of, and reflected in his writings, these realities of the time and place in which he lived. Second, each also reflected his own personal position in that society, his grievances, and his ambitions. And third, the objective of each author, particularly the author of the book of Deuteronomy, was not to record history accurately, but rather to write—indeed to *create*—a history that would convey to his readers a convincing message about how they should live their lives.[3]

The best starting point to understand how, when, where, why, and by whom the Torah was written is to read *Who Wrote the Bible?* by Richard Elliott Friedman, the eminent biblical scholar whom we first met in the introduction. *Who Wrote the Bible?* is a very readable book designed for the nonscholar. However, lest anyone think Friedman's concepts are "popular" rather than scholarly, in the preface to the second edition, published close to ten years after the first, he says: "I have now assembled the data in the traditional, unblemished manner of scholarship in my entries in the *Anchor Bible Dictionary*. The entry on 'Torah,' in particular, is meant to be the largest collection of evidence to date in support of the [Documentary] Hypothesis."[4]

Friedman begins with a brief history of biblical criticism, which one can define as making a considered assessment of the sacrosanct assumption that God gave the Torah to Moses, who, in turn, gave it to the Israelites, the chosen people. Tentative doubts that Moses wrote down the whole Torah were voiced as early as the third century. Over the ensuing centuries these doubts became stronger and stronger, with the balance shifting from Moses writing down all of the Torah to most of it, to some of it, to none of it.

The first person to assert that Moses did not write most of the Torah was the seventeenth-century philosopher Thomas Hobbes, who saw inconsistencies and anachronisms in the text. Biblical criticism was dangerous business back then. The Church did not look kindly on anyone who dared question the divine authorship of the Bible. Books suggesting that Moses did not write the Pentateuch were banned and burned and their authors imprisoned until they publicly recanted their heresy. Although they had no power to imprison anyone, the Jewish religious leaders were no different. When the Jewish philosopher Baruch Spinoza reached the same conclusion as his contemporary Hobbes, and said so, he was excommunicated.

The answer of the religious establishment (Jewish as well as Christian) to observations by Hobbes, Spinoza, and others[5] of the myriad inconsistencies and contradictions in the Torah's text was that these were no more than apparent contradictions and apparent inconsistencies. The believer was admonished to study the text as a lifelong endeavor in order to learn what God really meant. This remains the view of Orthodox Jews to this day.

But the world was changing, and with these changes came serious critical scholarship that blossomed during the Enlightenment. Doubts about Moses's having written the Torah became more widespread, and biblical criticism became a legitimate field of scholarly inquiry. One of the most important contributions was the groundbreaking work in the mid-nineteenth century of the brilliant young German rabbi Abraham Geiger, considered by many to be, in effect, the founder of Reform Judaism. Geiger subjected first the Talmud and then the Hebrew Bible (the Old Testament) itself to critical scholarly analysis and concluded that neither could have been "a single unit, the product of an unchanging divine will, [but were rather] the reflection of an ongoing legal creativity ever responsive to its environment"[6] and dependent on the changing historical context in which they were written.

All this biblical criticism culminated in a model called the Documentary Hypothesis, constructed by the nineteenth-century German biblical scholar Julius Wellhausen. Briefly described, this hypothesis suggests that the Torah was not given by God to Moses on Mount Sinai in the thirteenth century BCE, but rather was the work of four distinct authors who lived several hundred years after the revelation was supposed to have taken place. Later still all their different stories were blended together into the Torah by an editor called the Redactor. Closed-minded religious opposition to legitimate scholarly inquiry into the authorship of the Bible persisted into the nineteenth century, but eventually gave way in the twentieth to the point where, according to Friedman, the Documentary Hypothesis is now almost universally accepted among nonfundamentalist biblical scholars.

Reading *Who Wrote the Bible?* is like reading a detective story with Richard Elliott Friedman as a biblical Sherlock Holmes ferreting out the different clues the Torah's text offers up which, in turn, lead him down logical paths of reasoning to solve the mystery. The same is true of the archeological detective work of Israel Finkelstein and Neil Asher Silberman in *The Bible Unearthed.*

When a text contains two different versions of essentially the same story, albeit with differences in some important details, scholars call it a doublet. It turns out that there are lots of doublets in the Torah—starting early on with different versions of the creation, the flood, and the patriarchs—which can clearly be identified as the work of two different authors, even though the two stories are often woven together into a single text.[7] The basic sources for the stories are the same myths and legends, but each author fashions his telling of these myths and legends to suit his own purposes. Each author has a distinct focus. Each reflects a different geopolitical, economic, social, and religious setting. Each emphasizes different, ostensibly historical figures. Each has his own language and writing style. Each has his own axes to grind. Each has his own conception of God. And each refers to God in a different way.

The author who always refers to God as Yahweh is called J.[8] The author who starts off calling God by the Hebrew word for God, El or Elohim, is called E. Apart from the important fact that each of the two authors writes from the perspective of the kingdom in which he lives— J in Judah, E to the north in Israel—Friedman finds almost endless sharp differences between J and E.[9] Here are just a few examples:

J emphasizes the covenant with Abraham, E emphasizes the covenant with Moses. As a result, J writes about the Ark of the Covenant, E writes about the Tabernacle. The Ark is never mentioned in E, and the Tabernacle is never mentioned in J.

The role of Joshua differs in the two stories. In E's story, Joshua is Moses's trusted right-hand man, a hero. In J's story, Joshua—who comes from the Israel tribe of Ephraim—plays no role.

The two authors reflect the antipathy Judah and Israel feel toward each other. A good example is how the kingdom of Israel acquired the city of Shechem (which became its capital). J's story is a lurid soap opera of a maiden done wrong and her family's revenge. E's story recounts a straightforward commercial transaction.

Friedman offers some well-founded theories about the reasons for such marked differences between the J and E stories. It makes for fascinating reading, but goes beyond the scope of our inquiry here. Whatever the reasons, what is important from our perspective is that modern biblical scholarship has clearly identified J and E as two different authors. Two different *human* authors.

Not only are there doublets in the text of the Torah, there are also triplets, three different versions of the same story. The Documentary Hypothesis attributes these third versions to an author called P, so named because of his emphasis on priestly matters. P's God is less personal than the God described by J and E. He is a stern, unforgiving deity who metes out justice mercilessly. Indeed, the concept of mercy, evident throughout the different stories of J and E, is not found anywhere in the P stories.[10]

But there was a lot more than theology motivating P. When E— who Friedman thinks was a Shiloh priest in Israel[11]—extolled the virtues of Moses, he often took potshots at Aaron (the famous E story of the golden calf, in which E casts Aaron as the villain, is a good example), because the supposed descendents of Aaron were the powerful priests of Judah. P—who Friedman thinks was an Aaronid priest in Judah[12]—evens the score by painting Aaron in a favorable light (there is no golden calf story in P) and diminishing the role of E's putative ancestor, Moses. The basic theme of the Aaronid priests of Judah was the centralization of religion: one God, worshipped in one place (the Temple of Jerusalem). P reflects this in his writing.

The differences between P, on the one hand, and J and E, on the other, also make for interesting reading, but again, what is important for our purposes here is that modern biblical scholarship has clearly identified a third source in the text of the Torah. A third *human* source.

The stories of J, E, and P run through the first four books of the Torah, but there is practically nothing of them in the fifth book, Deuteronomy, which was written by the fourth author, known as D.[13] In fact, the consensus of biblical scholars is that D wrote not only the book of Deuteronomy but also the next six books in the Old Testament (Joshua, Judges, 1 Samuel, 2 Samuel, 1 Kings, and 2 Kings) that comprise the grouping known as the Former Prophets. As a result, D is often referred to as the Deuteronomistic Historian, the man who recorded the Jewish people's biblical history from Moses's crucial farewell speech to the children of Israel all the way down to the Historian's own time—which all biblical scholars now place squarely in the late seventh and the early sixth century BCE, during and shortly after the reign of King Josiah.

Josiah was a direct descendent (sixteenth in the line) of King David. According to the Bible, God made an unambiguous covenant with David: As a reward for David's faith and loyalty, one of David's line would always occupy the throne of the kingdom of Judah ("Your house and your kingdom will be secure before you forever. Your throne will be established forever")[14]—as indeed they did, for close to four hundred years. Friedman calls one of his chapters "In the Court of King Josiah." The prologue of Finkelstein and Silberman's book is called "In the Days of King Josiah." It seems pretty clear that the reign of King Josiah in the seventh century BCE was a pivotal point in the biblical history of the Jewish people. The reason for this goes to the heart of what the Torah, and particularly the rest of the Deuteronomistic history, is all about.

All biblical scholars point to a couple of rather odd occurrences reported in the Bible that fasten D firmly to the period of Josiah. In the year 622 BCE, according to 2 Kings 2:28, while the Temple in Jerusalem was being renovated, a high priest named Hilkiah found a "scroll of the Torah." Biblical scholars have long known that this book was in fact Deuteronomy. At first it was thought that Moses had really written it and that Hilkiah had fortuitously come upon this long-lost holy document. It is only in the past two hundred years that biblical criticism has concluded that "Deuteronomy was written down not long before it was 'found' in the Temple, and the 'finding' was just a charade. The book was written to provide grounds for Josiah's religious reform."[15]

Then there is the unusual (to put it mildly) reference to Josiah by name—some three hundred years before he was born—in 1 Kings 13:1–2. The story tells of the arrival in the kingdom of Israel of "a man of God coming from Judah," who foretells that a descendent of David, "Josiah by name," will act as Yahweh's terrible swift sword to snuff out the unacceptable religious practices King Jeroboam I established in the kingdom of Israel to the north, also (a coincidence?) three centuries earlier. Not only does the Deuteronomistic history predict early on that much later (in 2 Kings 12:15–18) Josiah will smash the unacceptable altars at Beth-El in the "high places" in the kingdom of Israel, but also, in a burst of what can only be called literary chutzpah, it tells how this prophecy was fulfilled when Josiah does just that, and in the same specific place in Israel, Beth-El.

Unfortunately, things didn't quite work out the way D had planned. As we saw in chapter 3, the Egyptians killed young King Josiah in battle, thus ending his zealous religious cleansing. Twenty-two years later, Babylon sent its armies to conquer Judah, leaving devastation in their wake. At that point Judah—a kingdom whose dynasty had lasted for four hundred years—ceased to exist as a nation. The Temple of Jerusalem, the centralized place for authentic worship of Yahweh, was destroyed. And a good number of the people of Judah (although it now appears not nearly as many as originally thought) were marched off into exile.

The Deuteronomistic history was a shambles. What to do now? The solution was clear: rewrite it. And that is exactly what D—or another D—did. It is now widely accepted among biblical scholars that there were in fact two Ds—whom they call D_1 and D_2—the first living during the reign of King Josiah (639–609 BCE) and the second living after the fall of Josiah's kingdom. This does not necessarily mean that the two Ds were different people. In fact, Friedman suggests that they were one and the same man: Jeremiah, a Shiloh priest, whom the historian Paul Johnson calls the first Jew.

In reality, D_2's task was not all that difficult. He simply explained that the catastrophic events that had struck the people of Judah were not unexpected, because they had turned away from Yahweh to worship other gods, thus breaking the covenant they had made with God. Not only that. As we saw in chapter 3, in the self-fulfilling prophecy in Deuteronomy 31:16–18, when God speaks his last words to Moses, he doesn't tell Moses that *if* the people of Israel break the covenant he'll bring his wrath down on them. He states unequivocally that after Moses's death the people of Israel *will* break the covenant and worship other gods, and that he *will* punish them by hiding his countenance from them and abandoning them to their unhappy fate. And, of course, since it was written by D_2 after the fact, this is exactly what happened. God invoked the terrible curses he had threatened, sent the Babylonian hordes to carry them out, and then turned away, hiding his countenance. If you accept D_2's reasoning, it was the people of Judah's own fault. They got exactly what they deserved.

But why *then*, at that precise moment in time, when they were doing everything right? The answer was as clear as it was simple (and simpleminded): Josiah was good, but as good as he was, he could not undo all the evil perpetrated under his grandfather, Manasseh, who had encouraged the people of Judah to turn to other gods. So it was not surprising that God, through his agent Nebuchadnezzar, would inflict a severe punishment on the people of Judah—just as he had done a century and a half earlier in Israel, where the people also worshipped other gods, only that time God's agent was Hazael, the king of Aram-Damascus.

Orthodox doctrine holds that Hazael and Nebuchadnezzar were among the first in a long line of "God's agents of destruction" who brought calamity to the Jewish people as well-deserved punishment for perceived sins. Hitler was the most recent, although the comments by some Orthodox in Israel would lead one to believe that they consider the Palestinian suicide bombers agents of God, too. Earlier we saw that after one particularly bloody bombing, a young yeshiva student said that the divine message was that the Jews have to mend their ways. "If we behave better," he said, "the troubles will end."

D_2 said exactly the same thing. Over and over and over again D_2 makes the point that God has put the Jewish people on notice that if they fail to heed his word, he will cause terrible curses to rain down on them as punishment. But, as Friedman points out, D_2 also holds out "a channel of hope . . . emphasiz[ing] to his readers that if they would turn back to Yahweh, repent, and give up other gods, then their God would forgive them."[16]

So we now have a fourth author of the Torah. Whether he is one man or two (or more, as some scholars argue), or whether or not he is Jeremiah, as Friedman suggests, is immaterial from our perspective. What is important is that he was, like J, E, and P, a human being. God did not write Deuteronomy any more than he wrote the first four books. The Torah was written by man.

It was also *re*-written by man, and this is the last piece of the puzzle. Biblical scholars call the editor who brought it all together R, or the Redactor. Friedman, who thinks the Redactor was Ezra, the Aaronid priest and scribe who came back from exile in Babylon in 458 BCE, makes an insightful observation:

> The combination of the sources did more than just affect individual Bible stories. It had an impact on the biblical conception of God. . . . By doing that [the Redactor] formed a new balance between the personal and the transcendent qualities of the deity.

It was a picture of God as both universal and intensely personal. Yahweh was the creator of the cosmos, but also "the God of your father." The fusion was . . . theologically profound, but it was also filled with a new tension. It was now picturing human beings coming into close personal dialogue with the all-powerful master of the universe.

It was a balance that none of the individual authors had intended. But that balance . . . came to be at the heart of Judaism and Christianity. Like Jacob at Peni-El, both religions have lived and struggled with a cosmic yet personal deity. . . . Ultimate things are at stake, but, every human being is told, "The master of the universe is concerned with you." An extraordinary idea . . . not planned by any of the authors.[17]

So, not only are the four authors of the Torah human beings, the editor is, too. Whether Friedman is correct that the Redactor was Ezra is, once again, from our perspective here, unimportant. Whoever he was, he was a human being. Moreover, it is now clear that he was not the last human being to contribute to the text of what we call the Torah today.

In *The View from Nebo*, Amy Dockser Marcus cites the work of Eugene Ulrich, a professor of Hebrew Scriptures at the University of Notre Dame, who has been working on the Dead Sea Scrolls, which were discovered at Qumran, and believes that Ezra's Torah was not the final product we have today.

The scribes who copied the different books of the Bible stories at Qumran had been faithful overall to the material and the tradition they inherited. But they also . . . incorporated new material that they felt might clarify or sharpen some point for the people reading it. The scribes [believed] not only in the importance of transmitting the Torah, but in making sure it remained relevant. By Ulrich's count, the Qumran scrolls include at least four editions of Exodus and Numbers, a wide variety of Deuteronomy volumes, and two or more versions of Psalms, and he suspects there were even more editions that have not survived.[18]

Richard Elliott Friedman's detective work is based on an analysis of the texts. Israel Finkelstein's detective work is based on archeological finds. Taken together their evidence makes for an extremely persuasive case that the authors of the Torah were human beings who lived several hundred years after Orthodox dogma has Moses receiving the text from God at Mount Sinai.

This is not the only serious problem biblical scholars have found with the Orthodox view of the ancient history of the Jewish people. As we saw in chapter 2, the important archeological surveys of the past thirty years demonstrate pretty conclusively that Israel and Judah did not emerge as a result of the breakup of a united kingdom, but rather came about quite naturally in the highlands of Canaan. Indeed, the findings of modern archeology cast serious doubt on the whole idea of a united kingdom based in Jerusalem, a city that, far from the "unparalleled biblical descriptions of its grandeur, was anything more than a modest highland village in the time of David and Solomon . . . [who] were, in political terms, little more than hill-country chieftains, whose administrative reach remained on a fairly local level, restricted to the hill country."[19]

Not only that, as also noted earlier, these recent archeological discoveries have demonstrated that many of the cities heretofore assumed to have been built by Solomon were, in reality, built a hundred years later by the Omrides, leading some scholars to question whether Solomon's vast kingdom even existed and whether, as an alternative, the first true kingdom in the land of Israel was established in the north by the Omrides. The Bible portrays the Omride dynasty as a pretty nasty bunch. Remember King Ahab and his Phoenician wife Jezebel (whose name became synonymous with wickedness)? But the latest archeological findings indicate that the Omrides have gotten a bum rap. It would appear that they—and Ahab in particular— were much more capable kings, ruling over a much more developed society in Israel than were their pious counterparts in Judah. Indeed, Finkelstein and Silberman contend that "while Judah was still economically marginal and backward, Israel was booming. . . . In a sense, Judah was little more than Israel's rural hinterland."[20]

So why does the Bible knock the Israel of the Omrides and, instead, portray the Judah of David and Solomon as the apex of ancient Jewish power and splendor? By now the answer should be clear. The Deuteronomistic Historian was building a theology, not writing an authentic history. And that theology was based on three covenants that God is supposed to have made with his chosen people, Israel: (1) the covenant with Abraham the patriarch, (2) the covenant with Moses the lawgiver, and (3) the covenant with David the king. All three were, in reality, the same very straightforward deal: In exchange for their faithful devotion to God Yahweh, God Yahweh would be faithful to his chosen people. Conversely, if the people of Israel did *not* heed God's word, then the full wrath of Yahweh would come down on their heads.

The evidence keeps piling up. Specific human beings who lived in specific places at specific points in time wrote and edited the Torah, and they did so for a specific purpose. These men were products of their times and places and reflected in their writing the realities they saw around them. More important, they wrote the Torah not to accurately record a history *of* a people, but to create a history—and a theology—*for* a people.

CHAPTER EIGHT

WHY THE JEWISH PEOPLE SURVIVED

THE ORTHODOX ACE IN THE HOLE to vindicate the truth of their dogma is the fact that the Jews still exist as a people after more than three thousand years. The Orthodox claim that the survival of the Jewish people is a unique phenomenon that cannot be given a naturalistic explanation, and so can be explained only supernaturally, as the intervention of a powerful divine being with a special concern for the Jewish people. In his book *On Judaism*, Rabbi Emanuel Feldman gives us good example of this kind of thinking:

> The very fact that the Jewish people continues to exist, despite everything, says something about the mysterious relationship between this people and a transcendent force which somehow wishes us to remain alive, and which maintains our existence.
>
> By "transcendent force," of course, I mean God. Those familiar Biblical promises about the Jews being an eternal people, about our suffering and tragedies, but also about God never abandoning us— these take on tremendous meaning and power almost four thousand years after they were first uttered to Abraham. . . .
>
> Two thousand years after Abraham, as the Jews went into exile from their promised land, it may have seemed absurd. Imagine yourself as a Jew seeing Jerusalem destroyed by the Babylonians. You would surely say: "Yes, we have been kept alive since the times of Abraham; yes, we have had kings like David and Solomon, and prophets like Moses and Isaiah and Jeremiah—but all that is over

now. Our land is destroyed, our holy places pillaged, our people massacred, and here we are marching into slavery in chains. It is all over. We are history. The end!"

And yet here we are two thousand years after the slave marches, thirty-seven centuries after Abraham, and only fifty years after a third of our people were slaughtered in the twentieth century, and we are alive, vital, dynamic and flourishing. There is something very strange and mysterious about the Jewish people.

Now all this may not necessarily prove that a God exists—it may be a fluke of history, it may all have happened by chance, it could all be attributed to random occurrences—but isn't it curious that no other people had benefited from such randomness and that no other people has lived through such a history?[1]

Before examining the details of the Orthodox argument, we should be aware of an important fact. A person can believe in God, can believe that the Jewish people are God's chosen people, and can believe that Jewish survival can be explained only by God's direct intervention, without thereby having to believe that every assertion and prescription in the Torah is true and binding for modern Jews. Orthodox Judaism does not hold a patent on the claim that the Jews are God's chosen people. This claim is made by other branches of Judaism, as well as by many branches of Christianity.

It could be that God's intervention is necessary to explain Jewish survival, but suppose for a moment that his *purpose* in promoting that survival were very different from what Orthodox doctrine assumes. For example, suppose that Christianity turns out to be the true word of God, but the survival of the Jews, as the original chosen people, plays some other important role in God's plan. Who knows? This interpretation might seem preposterous in Jerusalem, but it would probably play quite well in the Vatican.

As a matter of fact, this is precisely the view of those Christian fundamentalists who believe in a literal reading of the book of Revelation. They believe that the Jews will return to their lands, whereupon they will be attacked by hosts of the anti-Christ, leading to a final showdown in the valley of Armageddon. At that point the messiah will return to take the righteous true believers up to heaven, while those Jews who have not been converted will burn for eternity. This is called the "rapture," fulfilling the prophecy in Revelation.[2] It is not for nothing that Christian fundamentalists are ardent supporters of the claims of the Orthodox Jewish settlers.[3]

Nor is the survival of the Jewish people for thousands of years the unique phenomenon the Orthodox like to claim that it is. The Basques, for example, have been around a lot longer than the Jews have. In fact, the Basque presence in the Pyrenees predates recorded history. The most recent genetic evidence suggests that they have survived in place for some forty thousand years, more than ten times the duration of an identifiable Jewish culture. And in (for them) modern times, they handily survived violent passages of Carthaginians, Romans, Moors, Franks, and Nazis.

The Parsi provide another illuminating counterexample. This ethnic group is bound together by a distinctive ancient religion, Zoroastrianism, which originated in Persia. Interestingly, it is a monotheistic religion founded by the prophet Zarathustra three thousand years ago. The Zoroastrians held the dominant position in Persia until the fourth-century BCE invasion of Alexander the Great completely destroyed their palaces and temples. Later, in the seventh century CE, Islamic armies conquered the Zoroastrians, forcing those who would not convert to flee, primarily to India, where they became known as the Parsi (after "Persia"). Zoroastrians are now dispersed throughout the world, but despite their relatively small numbers and the persecution and conquests they endured, their distinctive culture survives.

Of course, neither of these two ethnic groups, the Basques nor the Parsi, or others, such as the Armenians, who have also been around a long time, have experienced exactly the same history as any other ethnic group. Jewish history is different from Basque history, which in turn is different from Parsi history, which in turn is different from Armenian history. It is always possible to cite distinctive features of one and claim that these features are unique and in need of a special explanation.

For example, the Jews and the Basques differ in that the Jews spent much of their history dispersed in many different countries, while the Basques remained largely in one place. With clever rhetoric, we can cite this as reason to find Jewish survival even more remarkable and in need of a special explanation. How could the Jews survive when, unlike other cultures, they were scattered to the four winds, forced to live among hostile, alien cultures? Alternatively, we could adopt precisely the opposite view. A geographically compact culture is far more vulnerable to complete assimilation or annihilation. If you are dispersed among ten countries, seven of your outposts can disappear without a trace and the culture still survives. So it is not at all surprising that Jewish culture has endured, as a result of the diaspora. But how, then, could the Basques have possibly survived without the benefit of a similar diaspora? It defies naturalistic explanation. It can only be the hand of God! You see how the game is played.

The extreme parochialism of the Orthodox position is hard to overstate. Orthodox Jews rely on the fact that the people they are attempting to convince do not know a great deal about ethnographic history and, consequently, will not see through the overblown claims of uniqueness. So let's take a look at the *real* ethnographic history of the Jewish people. There is no denying that it is a remarkable and admirable history. But is it one that requires a supernatural explanation?

It is the history of a people with a common language and a distinctive religion, by far the two most important factors in the survival of a distinguishable culture. Of course, these factors do not guarantee that a people will not be assimilated, and indeed a large number of people of Jewish ancestry have been assimilated into surrounding cultures. If we assume that the Jewish population in the year 1 CE was about 3 million, a reasonable estimate, then at the rate of world population increase in the intervening two millennia, there would be 120 million Jews here today, not the 13 to 18 million according to current estimates. This means that roughly one out of every eight descendents of the ancient Jews recognizes himself or herself as Jewish. Is this a remarkably large Jewish population or remarkably small? Should we be asking how the Jewish people survived? Or should we be asking instead why so few remain?

Shorn of all the mystery, the Orthodox argument about Jewish survival relies on a very naïve view of what social scientists call "historical explanation." The basic structure of the Orthodox argument is that Jewish survival cannot be given a naturalistic explanation, and so can be explained only supernaturally, by divine intervention. Two crucial features of this seemingly simple argument deserve closer examination. The first is the claim that Jewish survival cannot be given a naturalistic explanation. The second is the jump from the alleged absence of a naturalistic explanation to the presumed presence of a supernatural cause.

The more carefully you think about the first claim, the more puzzling it seems. Historical explanations aim to explain either events, such as President Truman's decision to drop an atomic bomb, or states of affairs, such as the Democrats holding a congressional majority in 2007. So the first thing we should ask is: What is the event or state of affairs that the Orthodox are challenging us to explain? What exactly do we need to explain in order to explain the concept of Jewish survival? Presumably, it is a state of affairs, namely, the fact that now, in the first decade of the twenty-first century, there exists a substantial Jewish population in the world. Surely that is what an explanation of Jewish survival must come down to: an explanation of the fact that, at the present time, there are roughly 15 million people who share, to a greater or lesser degree, a common Jewish culture, heritage, and religion.

The Orthodox claim, then, is that this state of affairs, the present existence of a substantial Jewish community,[4] cannot be given a naturalistic explanation. The next question we need to ask is somewhat harder. Exactly what do the Orthodox *mean* when they say that this state of affairs cannot be given a naturalistic explanation? Before we can evaluate this remarkable claim, we need to understand it a bit more clearly.

Let's start with a very simple model of naturalistic explanation (and please don't be put off by the simple abbreviations S_0, S_1, and NL). Natural laws (abbreviated as NL), we shall assume, govern how the state of the world at a given time evolves into a later state. NL will denote the sum total of natural laws, those that can appear in legitimate naturalistic explanations. These will include not only the laws of physics and chemistry, but also behavioral laws such as those of psychology and sociology. A typical naturalistic explanation of an event or state of affairs (we'll call this S_1) proceeds by citing certain features of an earlier state (which we'll call S_0) plus—explicitly or implicitly—one or more natural laws (NL).

If a naturalistic explanation of this sort is possible for a state of affairs S_1 based on the earlier state S_0, we can abbreviate this as:

$$S_0 + NL \rightarrow S_1$$

We can read this abbreviation as follows: Features of the earlier state S_0, plus the natural laws in NL, explain the occurrence of the present state S_1.

For example, if you ask me why a beaker exploded when you poured water into it, I would point out that the beaker contained hydrochloric acid (the earlier state—S_0) and cite the chemical laws that determine the behavior of a powerful acid when exposed to water (the natural law—NL), causing the explosion of the beaker (the current state—S_1).

Getting back to the Orthodox argument, suppose we call the current state of the world S_{2008}, the state of the world exactly a year ago S_{2007}, the state ten years ago S_{1998}, and so on. One of the features of the current state, S_{2008}, is that there is a substantial Jewish community, a reasonably large group of people who identify themselves culturally and/or religiously as Jewish. According to the Orthodox, this fact about S_{2008} cannot be explained naturalistically. But how plausible is their claim?

Let's take it in bite-sized chunks. If we survey the events of, say, the past ten years, there is nothing particularly surprising or inexplicable about the current size or state of the Jewish community, given its size and state in 1998. Of course, much has happened since 1998, both at the macro level and at the micro level. The state of Israel experienced an unexpected change of prime minister, an unabated conflict with the Palestinians, and an inconclusive war with Hezbollah in Lebanon. Many Jewish couples, in Israel and elsewhere, have married; some have divorced. Many Jews have died, but more have been born. And so on. But it is clear that, in order to explain the current size and state of the Jewish community, given its size and state in 1998, you don't have to resort to supernatural intervention.

The existence of a substantial Jewish population in the year 2008 can be explained naturalistically in terms of facts about the state of the world in 1998—for example, the fact that there was a large Jewish population in 1998, the fact that Israel maintained a strong military throughout the ten-year period—even though, because there are many more Jews living outside Israel than inside, the survival of the state of Israel is not a determinant of the survival of the Jewish people—and so on. In other words, the Orthodox have to admit the following:

$$S_{1998} + NL \rightarrow S_{2008}$$

What this simple little formula tells us is that the existence of the Jewish community in 2008 can be explained naturalistically in terms of the state of the world in 1998.

At this point, you can begin to understand something I said earlier in this chapter. The more carefully we consider the Orthodox claim, the more puzzling it appears. Clearly, there is no need to appeal to supernatural forces to explain the events of the past ten years, to explain the existence of a substantial Jewish population in the year 2008, given the state of the world in 1998. So the question now becomes whether the existence of a substantial Jewish community in 1998 can, itself, be explained naturalistically. Again, taking a manageable chunk of time, we can translate this into the question of whether the following holds:

$$S_{1988} + NL \rightarrow S_{1998}$$

In other words, assuming the state of the world in 1988, can we explain the size and distribution of the Jewish population in 1998, or does this latter fact completely defy naturalistic explanation? When we study the history of 1988 and the events that occurred during the following ten years, do we find ourselves exclaiming that nothing could possibly explain how a substantial Jewish community existed in 1998? Of course not. That would be silly. There is nothing supernatural about how the Jewish community evolved in the ten-year period from 1988 to 1998. No amazing, inexplicable occurrence took place.

If the Orthodox claim that Jewish survival defies naturalistic explanation is to make any sense, there has to be at least one ten-year period in Jewish history—and perhaps many—for which the existence of the Jewish population at the end of the period cannot be explained in terms of its size and state at the beginning of that period and the effect of the nonsupernatural events of the period in question. Otherwise, the Orthodox would be painting themselves into a corner by arguing that each and every decade of Jewish history unfolded according to ordinary historical processes, but that the sum total of that history defies ordinary historical explanation. That would be incoherent.

So what decades should we consider? One natural candidate is the 1940s, certainly one of the most—if not *the* most—tragic decades in all of Jewish history. But even this decade does not give the Orthodox what they need for their claim. By 1940 there was a large Jewish population dispersed in many countries around the world. Most of these Jewish communities, though not unaffected by the horrible events in Europe, did not have their very existence threatened by those events. Thus, the fact that the Jewish community survived in 1950, given its size and distribution in 1940, hardly defies naturalistic explanation. It does not even qualify as unexpected.

But how about the Jewish populations in Germany and Poland? They were clearly subjected to unprecedented treatment and suffered unprecedented losses. Does the precise scope and magnitude of those losses defy naturalistic explanation? There is no evidence that it does, one way or the other. The fact that the losses were so large does not prove that there was a supernatural force bent on Jewish destruction,

nor does the fact that they were no larger prove that there was a supernatural force intent on Jewish survival. Some might find it comforting to think that the terrible history of the 1940s could not possibly
be explained by natural processes, but there is absolutely no reason to
believe that the events of the decade were ever outside human control.

The point I am making here is that Jewish survival through the
1940s was far and away the most probable outcome, given the facts at
the beginning of that decade. True genocide is almost impossible to
accomplish, even with a small, geographically compact population
such as the Kurds or the Tutsi. For a population as large and as dispersed as the Jews in 1940, it would have been far more miraculous
for the Jewish population to have disappeared by 1950 than for it to
have survived. So once again, there is no question that the existence
of the Jewish community in 1950 can be naturalistically explained
given the facts at the beginning of the decade:

$$S_{1940} + NL \rightarrow S_{1950}$$

But, the Orthodox will object, surely the creation of the state of
Israel, unlike Jewish survival, could never have been predicted at the
beginning of the decade. The answer is that this turn of events indeed
could not have been predicted, but the fact that it could not have been
predicted does not mean it cannot be given a naturalistic explanation.

Many events of the 1940s (or, for that matter, any other decade in
history) could not have been predicted in advance, since so many historical events are dependent on extraordinarily complex and unknow-
able factors. No one could have predicted, in advance, who would win
World War II, that the atomic bomb would be developed, or that the
state of Israel would be formed. But any of these events, once they have
occurred and we have uncovered the antecedent events that led to
them, can be explained by naturalistic laws and the previous state of
the world. The formation of Israel was no more an exception to this
perfectly ordinary historical process than was the bombing of Pearl
Harbor. In history, as in meteorology, being able to explain phenomena
in terms of natural laws does not necessarily give us predictability.

It is important to understand that I am not saying that the formation of the state of Israel or the development of the atomic bomb *might possibly* be explained naturalistically. I am saying they *are* so explainable, that we *have* the explanations. All you have to do is read the history books to confirm this. There you will find the explanations of how the events unfolded, of why the people involved made the decisions they made, and so on. At no point do the historians suddenly pause to proclaim: "And then the laws of nature were violated. A miracle occurred!" These events may have been unpredictable, and hence surprising to those who witnessed them, but they do not in any way signify a violation of natural law or naturalistic explanation. Thus, even with a remarkable and unpredictable event such as the formation of the state of Israel, we still have:

$$S_{1940} + NL \rightarrow S_{1950}$$

We could continue this progression back in time, looking at other difficult and not-so-difficult decades in Jewish history. But the result would always be the same. When we look at decades of Jewish prosperity, for example those in the Golden Age in Spain, we easily find explanations for how and why the Jewish population expanded and prospered. There will not, for example, be any problem explaining Jewish survival, indeed its thriving, from 1130 to 1140 (the decade of Maimonides's birth):

$$S_{1130} + NL \rightarrow S_{1140}$$

Similarly, there is no problem explaining Jewish survival during the more difficult decades, such as during the siege and destruction of Jerusalem from 60 to 70 CE. No legitimate historian would claim that the existence of a Jewish people and culture in the year 70 defies naturalistic explanation, given the size, state and location of the Jewish population in the year 60. Again, as with the 1940s, this was a tragic decade, one in which the population suffered and emerged diminished. But there is absolutely no reason to think that its survival through the decade, or its recovery during subsequent, more prosperous decades, required supernatural intervention. Indeed, when we look closely at that decade, as with the 1940s, it is clear that Jewish survival was again by far the more likely outcome:

$$S_{60} + NL \rightarrow S_{70}$$

When the Orthodox make their argument that Jewish survival for three thousand years could not have been possible without a supernatural force at the helm, they do not focus on any single decade in Jewish history, for the simple reason that their argument would be ridiculed by anyone knowledgeable about the history of the decade in question. There is not a single decade of actual Jewish history in which the existence of the Jewish community at the end of the decade, given its state at the beginning, is even surprising, much less in need of supernatural explanation. Each decade of Jewish history, when you study it carefully, has unfolded through natural historical processes, no more inexplicable than any other decade of their, or any other group's, history.

So how have the Orthodox managed to make this natural historical process seem so amazing? I began our discussion of the Orthodox argument by asserting that it relies on a naïve understanding of historical explanation. We are now in a position to diagnose and dispel that naïvete, relying on what real social scientists know about two key areas: (1) how history is explained, and (2) the probability of long chains of historical events.

How History Is Explained

If we were to look back at a long succession of explanations in Jewish history, we would discover two things. First, we would find that most of the facts and events cited have nothing to do with characteristics peculiar to the Jewish community. They are simply facts and events that had an impact on that community.

Second, and equally important, we would find that the explanatory facts that *do* have to do with the characteristics of the community will vary greatly from one period to the next. Perhaps to understand the state of the Jewish community at one time and place, it will be essential to know that the community at that time and place had become insular and separate. But to understand the state of the Jewish community at another time and place, it will be important to know that the community had become cosmopolitan and integrated, precisely the opposite characteristics. It is pretty obvious that there will be no single fact or characteristic, or even collection of characteristics, that will explain the size and state of the Jewish community in 10 CE as well as in 70 CE, as well as in 1140, as well as in 1830, as well as in 1950, and so on.

This is why it makes no sense when the Orthodox, to support their claim of supernatural intervention, say that there is no one characteristic of the Jewish people that can explain their survival. Rabbi Dovid Gottlieb's *Living Up . . . to the Truth* is a good example of the Orthodox rhetoric.[5] Over and over, the rabbi challenges us to find *the* characteristic of the Jewish community that "explains Jewish survival." Is it because they are stubborn? he asks. No, we respond, that can't be it. Is it because they were persecuted? No, we answer, that's not it either. Was it Moses's genius? No, probably not. Voilà! he says, there is simply no explanation. But of course there is. The correct response is that no one who really understands historical explanation would ever expect a single fact or characteristic—or even a hundred such characteristics—to account for two thousand years of an ethnic group's history. *That is not how history works.*

To put all this in sharper perspective, to make the point more vivid, it will be helpful to consider a comparable stretch of another ethnic group's history. At the turn of the twenty-first century, English is by far the dominant language of international commerce, and—like it or not—Anglo-American culture the most influential in the world. Who could have predicted this two thousand years ago, when the Roman emperor Hadrian ordered a wall built to sequester primitive, warlike clans to the northern reaches of their inhospitable island? Many other clans and cultures were in roughly the same state at the time of the Roman expansion. Some disappeared, some survived to the present day, but not one of them achieved a comparable influence in the modern world.

At this broad, sweeping level of description, there is no explanation for the linguistic and cultural hegemony attained by the clans of the British Isles, and not attained by, say, those in Eastern Europe or Northern Africa. If, in addition to language and secular culture, we were to add a religious component to the mix in the form of a distinctive belief system, there is no doubt that the devout would see this history as proof of divine intervention.

How else could it be explained? Was it because the Anglo-Saxon tribes were stubborn and warlike? So were the Goths and the Huns, the Turks and the Moors. Was it because they lived on an island? What about the Sicilians, the Cretans, or the Celts (who shared the very same island)? For any characteristic you might find in the primitive tribes that so annoyed Hadrian, you will find other groups with that characteristic whose subsequent history was strikingly different.

Of course, we're not inclined to read into this history any supernatural mechanism. The reason is simple. Although the huge leap from Hadrian to the present day is impossible to bridge with a simple formula, "Any culture with characteristic X will eventually achieve Y," there is no piece of history that is not perfectly understandable, perfectly explicable, when we examine it in more detail. What happened to the British in, say, the eleventh century? Quite a bit, actually. Norway invaded the island. Then William the Conqueror did. The crusaders set out and captured Jerusalem. And more. But there was no supernatural intervention; no violation of natural law. Although there is no single explanation that will get us from England in 122 CE to the present day, this is no indication of a failure of naturalistic explanation, no sign of supernatural intervention.

Now consider the Jews. Here, too, it is folly to look for a single characteristic, a single explanation that will account for two thousand years of Jewish history. That is true of any present-day state in the world, major or minor. There is still a distinctive Jewish culture. English is the dominant international language. The Basques still speak their tongue. The Armenians finally have their own, independent country. In none of these cases could we go back two thousand years, find a feature or characteristic of the population in question, and specify a single historical law that governed the subsequent history. That is not how history works.

The Probability of Long Chains of Historical Events

I have emphasized that no supernatural intervention, no violation of natural law, is required to explain the size and state of the Jewish population at any particular time—given its size and state, say, a decade before. There are only two ways for the Orthodox to respond to this. The first is to find a specific decade of Jewish history in which the laws of nature should have led inevitably to the disappearance of an identifiable Jewish community. The Orthodox cannot respond in this way, because there *is* no such decade. The second is to retreat into a probabilistic argument.

Perhaps it is true that Jewish survival was by far the most probable outcome of any given decade we might choose to look at. Nonetheless, the Orthodox say, Jewish survival over the course of two or three thousand years—two or three hundred decades—was an extremely improbable occurrence. You could never have predicted, two or three thousand years ago, that there would still be an identifiable Jewish community in the year 2005. *That* is what is amazing and in need of a supernatural explanation.

This is a bogus argument.

It is true that the actual course of Jewish history over the past two thousand years has been highly improbable. The actual course of British history has been, too. Indeed, any chain of historical events of long enough duration has an infinitesimally low probability. That's how history works. So in this respect, Jewish survival is no less explicable than Armenian survival, Basque survival, or the linguistic hegemony of the English language.

Even if the exact state of the world at the turn of each decade has a probability of .9, given its state at the start of that decade—and this is an unrealistically high estimate—then the actual chain of events over the past two hundred decades will have a probability whose magnitude is on the order of $.9^{200}$ or $.0000000007.$[6] So there is nothing surprising about the whole chain of events being extremely improbable, because any alternative succession of events would have been equally improbable.

The Orthodox claim that the survival of the Jews posits a supernatural explanation is just as fallacious as all the other claims they make to support their fundamentalist dogma. What they are doing is using a subtle trick of rhetoric called "equivocation" in which a key term of the argument is interpreted differently, thereby forcing the argument onto tracks that can lead only where the conjuror wants to lead it.

Specifically, the Orthodox equivocate on the type of explanation they are looking for. As we have seen, no plausible case can be made that Jewish survival requires anything other than the ordinary, naturalistic explanation. But the Orthodox do their best to distract us, demanding we come up with *the* reason the Jews survived for two thousand or three thousand years. This is a ruse. There *is* no *the* reason. As we have seen, history just doesn't work that way.

There is, of course, the ultimate Orthodox argument: After God made the covenant with Abraham, he has been carefully watching over the Jewish people and, at difficult-to-discern intervals, intervened in such a way that it appeared to the untrained human eye that there was nothing supernatural involved, that no laws of nature were being breached. This is a version of the old saw that God works in mysterious ways. There is no answer to this argument. You accept it on faith or you reject it on logic.

The bottom line is this: As hard as the Orthodox try, often with convoluted arguments, their fundamentalist doctrine that Jewish survival can be explained only by supernatural intervention cannot be substantiated in any way by the historical facts.

CHAPTER NINE

JUDAISM IS UNIQUE, BUT NOT UNIQUELY UNIQUE

WHEN RABBI DOVID GOTTLIEB attempts to prove by reason and logic that the dogma of Orthodox Judaism is true, he says that it is true because [Orthodox] Judaism is the only major religion that satisfies the three requirements of the scientific method: (1) that the evidence be *positive*, (2) that the evidence be *unique*, and (3) that the evidence be *true*.[1] The conditions Gottlieb calls out are laudable attributes for a theory to have, but they have absolutely nothing to do with the scientific method.

Reading the rabbi's description of the scientific method in his *Living Up . . . to the Truth* is like viewing something in a carnival mirror. There are vague similarities, but the image is distorted almost beyond recognition. His so-called scientific method—by which, among other things, he claims that if you do not have evidence for the truth of a proposition, then you may reject it without further investigation—bears very little resemblance to the actual scientific method, either as practiced by scientists or described by philosophers of science.

Gottlieb's argument is patently fallacious. This is not the scientific method, but rather the fallacy logicians call *argumentum ad ignorantium*, the appeal to ignorance. The *real* scientific method is first and foremost a set of principles governing the acquisition of empirical and experimental evidence for a theory. In particular, the method does not reject theories simply because there is no preexisting evidence. If it did, most scientific revolutions would never have occurred. Rather, the real scientific method specifies how empirical evidence should subsequently be gathered to assess those theories.

The rabbi distorts the scientific method to provide an ostensibly scientific basis for rejecting all of the other major world religions. But the same techniques of argument he uses to rule out any other major religions could be used just as easily to rule out Judaism. Of course, the resulting arguments would not be any good, but neither are they any good when Gottlieb uses them.

The fact is, even if the Orthodox claims were unique, it would make no sense to insist that this uniqueness in and of itself lends credence to their dogma. Just because nobody else claims to have happened what you claim to have happened doesn't make what you claim to have happened true. It is all very reassuring when we are told that someone's conclusions have been reached by the rigorous application of the scientific method. It sounds so, well, scientific. But there's nothing scientific about Orthodox Judaism. In fact, it's difficult to imagine anything more *un*scientific than the doctrines of religious fundamentalism.

In any event, Orthodox Judaism fails to meet the rabbi's own criteria that the evidence to support its doctrines be positive, unique, and true. Quite the contrary, the substantial amount of authoritative archeological, historical, and textual evidence we have examined thus far points us in exactly the opposite direction. It demonstrates pretty conclusively that the Orthodox doctrines are not true. If the evidence is not true, of course, it matters little whether or not it is unique. But because the Orthodox place so much emphasis on the uniqueness of their evidence, I shall give their arguments a hearing anyway.

What is so unique about the evidence the Orthodox offer? In their opinion:

- Israel's history is unique.

- The miracles and fulfilled prophecies reported in the Torah are unique.

- The impeccably accurate chain of transmission of the Torah is unique.

- Jewish survival for over three thousand years (the ethnographic history of the Jewish people) is unique.

- The contribution to the world of Jewish ideas (the intellectual history of the Jewish people) is unique.

Let's take a close look at each one of these claims to see whether or not any of them has a basis in fact.

Is Israel's history unique?

The idea that Israel's ancient history was somehow unique has pretty much been laid to rest. Early on in *The View from Nebo*, Amy Dockser Marcus sums it up nicely:

> To the Bible's writers, Israel and everything that had happened to it throughout its history were unique phenomena. But the archeological record that is now emerging demonstrates that, overall, the country was in fact subject to the same kinds of historical and environmental forces as its neighbors in the region. Israelites by and large lived very much like their contemporaries in the Middle East, an idea that biblical scribes, with their relentless focus on the creation of Israelite identity, tended either to profess disinterest in or ridicule. . . . The idea that Israel's history was unique has gradually been giving way to the notion that Israel's past can be best understood in the context of the general history of the ancient Near East.[2]

Marcus echoes the conclusion reached by Yale's William Hallo, an authority on the ancient Near East, who offers repeated, independently substantiated evidence that the history of ancient Israel was part and parcel of the customs and practices of the region and the times. Hallo observes, for instance, that the catalogue of blessings and curses in Deuteronomy bears an uncannily close connection with "the treaties or loyalty oaths imposed on their vassals by the Assyrian kings of the first millennium, most notably Esarhaddon (680–669 BCE)." He goes on:

> In numerous exemplars dated three years before his death, [Esarhaddon] adjured each of his Iranian vassals to fealty to himself and, after his demise, to his designated successor, on pain of suffering a lengthy succession of fearsome curses. Some of these curses occur in virtually identical form and even in the same order as Deuteronomy. And the efficacy of such curses was described in what has been aptly termed a striking parallel . . . between cuneiform and biblical literature.[3]

Are the miracles and prophecies in the Torah unique?

There are two big problems with the argument that Jewish miracles and prophecies are unique. The first is that the *type* of evidence is by no means unique. Many religions cite purported public miracles witnessed by whole nations as evidence for their truth. The same goes for fulfilled prophecies. So in this sense, the evidence the Orthodox are offering is far from unique.

The second problem is that even the specific miracles and predictions reported in the Torah's text are not unique to Judaism; they are also included in the sacred texts of Christianity and Islam. Rabbi Gottlieb tacitly acknowledges this when he makes this strange comment referring to the prophecies in Deuteronomy 28–30: "Of course, if someone should accept our prediction *from our sources*, then his making that prediction cannot count for him *against* us! . . . [W]hen that prediction comes true it does not give Christianity and Islam positive evidence against Judaism, since they took the prediction from us."[4]

The issue before us is whether the evidence is unique to Judaism, whether it constitutes evidence only for Judaism. The rabbi is right to say that Christians or Muslims cannot use this evidence against Judaism, but neither can it be used against Christianity or Islam. His proprietary feelings toward this text do not change the simple fact that this is not evidence unique to Judaism, evidence that favors

Judaism over these other religions. Modern physics makes many of the same predictions that classical Newtonian mechanics did, but this doesn't mean that where they agree the evidence favors Newton over Einstein. This would not change even if we imagine Newton bitterly complaining, "But they took that prediction from us!"

Is the Torah's chain of transmission unique?

Orthodox doctrine holds that God gave Moses the Torah on Mount Sinai in the thirteenth century BCE, and it has been handed down through the subsequent thirty-three hundred years completely intact without any changes. They call this the Rules of the Scribe. Even were this claim true—and, as we have seen, all the evidence points to its not being true at all—it certainly is not unique to Judaism. The work of the medieval monks was thought to be an incredibly accurate transmission of the sacred Christian texts, but we now know that it was incredibly *in*accurate. The religious in India claim that *their* sacred texts, the Vedas, were passed down faithfully by special families within the Brahmin communities for literally thousands of years. The Vedic lore, also thought to be a divine revelation, was kept in such high regard that every word was painstakingly memorized and recited with utmost fidelity.

Is Jewish survival unique?

As we saw in chapter 8, the survival of the Jewish people for over two thousand years is not the unique phenomenon the Orthodox like to claim it is. The Basques have existed as a distinctive culture for a whole lot longer than the Jews—more than forty thousand years— and the monotheistic Zoroastrians have been around just about as long as the Jews. The Armenians aren't exactly newcomers on the world scene, either. Hence, the ethnographic history of the Jewish people is not unique at all.

Ah, say the Orthodox, but those other peoples haven't made the *contribution* to the world and haven't had the impact on the world that the Jews have had. *That's* what makes Jewish survival unique. But hold on a moment. Isn't this argument yet another example of the rhetoric tactic of equivocation we saw a few pages ago? The Orthodox start out claiming that Jewish survival is unique. But when it is demonstrated—with hard, incontrovertible facts—that Jewish survival is *not* unique, they claim that it is Jewish survival plus Jewish *contribution* to the world that makes Judaism unique. Of course, these are two totally different issues. We have seen that Jewish survival per se is not unique. Let's see if the Jewish contribution to the world is unique.

Is Jewish contribution to the world of ideas unique?

I would be the last person to deny that Jewish thought has had an extraordinary influence on the modern world. This is largely because of the power of some of the central tenets of the biblical texts and the early subsumption of these tenets into the world's two largest religions, Christianity and Islam, which together claim 3.3 billion adherents, more than half the world's population. But for anyone familiar with the history of ideas, the origin, power, and persistence of the ideas found in the Old Testament are neither surprising nor unique. Comparable contributions have been made by many cultures and many individuals throughout history. The influence of Plato and Locke on modern political thought, of Aristotle and Bacon on modern scientific practice, of Euclid and al-Khwarizmi on modern mathematics,[5] or of Adam Smith on the economy of the modern world are just a few examples. And there are many, many more.

Consider four ideas the Orthodox believe to be unique to Judaism.

Monotheism

The belief in a single supreme being was certainly strikingly different from the beliefs of the predominant religions of the ancient age, and the present prevalence of monotheistic religions is indeed attributable to this important Judaic belief. To be sure, there is some archeological evidence—in the form of ancient Hebrew inscriptions referring to "Yahweh and his consort Ashereh"—that early Judaism was less unequivocally monotheistic than it became later, and there remain references in the Torah to lesser deities, subservient to Yahweh. In spite of this, the Orthodox (and liberal Jews, too) are justified in citing monotheism as a major and distinctive contribution of ancient Jewish thought.

Spirituality

The Orthodox claim that Judaism is the only ancient religion to declare that God has no physical embodiment, form, or likeness. The problem here is that, again, the Orthodox are projecting more modern Judaic doctrines back to ancient times. The incorporeality of God is actually an Aristotelian doctrine, introduced much later into Judaism. The origin of the doctrine is Greek, not Jewish—and, hence, certainly not unique to Judaism. Although the belief of the incorporeality of God was later adopted as Judaic doctrine, it is historically inaccurate to claim that it is a feature of *ancient* Judaism. Consulting a scholarly (rather than religious) translation makes it abundantly clear that the authors of the Torah held a considerably more primitive view of God's form than did later rabbinical interpreters.[6]

God as absolute

Only Judaism understands God as the creator of all that exists and completely unlimited in his power over creation. This is certainly a doctrine that becomes well articulated in later Jewish thought, but it is not clear how much it differentiates *ancient* Judaism from other ancient religions. For one thing, many ancient polytheistic religions had one god who was considered the creator of the entire universe. Indeed, the first Genesis creation story seems to be derived directly from the Babylonian version of this story. Further, there are many passages in the Torah in which Yahweh is not depicted as omnipotent and omniscient. Again, the Orthodox are artificially projecting more modern Judaic doctrines back to the ancient setting with the objective of inflating the apparent uniqueness of the ancient religion.

Morality

The Orthodox claim that morality and justice are unique concepts of ancient Judaism is, quite frankly, absurd. These concepts are present in many other religious traditions outside the Judeo-Christian tradition and were treated with unparalleled sophistication by the ancient Greek philosophers at roughly the time when the comparatively primitive Torah was first being written down. Contrary to the Orthodox claim, the treatment of moral notions in the Torah shows the direct influence of earlier ethical thought, particularly the Code of Hammurabi—dating to approximately 1750 BCE, over a thousand years before the Torah was put into writing—which is well worth comparing to the strikingly similar Deuteronomy Code. Suggesting that Judaism originated the concept of morality has no basis whatsoever in historical fact.

The only item from the list above that constitutes both a major intellectual innovation and an unequivocal feature of ancient Judaism is monotheism. It would be futile to try to compare the importance and influence of seminal ideas in widely divergent domains. One could make an argument (Max Weber likely would)[7] that monotheism has had a profound effect on the political and economic development of the world and, in effect, set the stage for modern society. But one could also make a convincing argument that monotheism has not had appreciably more influence on the character of the modern world than have the concepts of democracy, scientific method, algebra, or free enterprise

Ask yourself how different the modern world would be had monotheism never become a widespread belief, and then ask yourself what the world would be like had some of these other notions not become widespread. The answer to the first question is that the world would probably look much like modern Japan or India, where monotheistic religions have not become dominant. The answer to the second question is, in contrast, almost impossible to guess. But certainly the difference would be at least as great and, when you think about it, probably greater. This simple exercise demonstrates pretty clearly that Rabbi Gottlieb is way off base when he claims that, of all ancient conceptual contributions, "only [Orthodox] Judaism is still making contributions to the present day quality or conditions of life of world civilization as a whole."[8] This is a patently absurd declaration, totally at odds with the facts.

My intention here is not to denigrate in any way the influence of the Judeo-Christian tradition on the character of the modern world, only to put it in perspective. The Torah contains some powerful ideas that were unquestionably distinctive in the ancient world. It also contains many more ideas that were commonplace and others that were simply borrowed, sometimes with minimal modification, from surrounding religions and creeds (such as the creation stories, the Mesopotamian flood story, and the Code of Hammurabi). The originality of the ideas in the Old Testament is not extraordinary in comparison to other significant intellectual contributions made throughout history, and certainly provides no reason, in itself, to imply a source other than human authors. Nor does it seem any more surprising that the contributions that were made came from the ancient Jewish culture than that the contributions made by the Greeks, Arabs, Egyptians, and Romans came from theirs.

The Orthodox treatment of intellectual history (the history of ideas) is every bit as misleading as their treatment of ethnographic history (the history of peoples). The extreme parochialism of Gottlieb's statements in this regard is hard to overstate. The rabbi relies on his readers not knowing a great deal about either ethnographic or intellectual history and so not seeing through his overblown claims of uniqueness.

Major contributions to intellectual history have been made by a great many individuals. Perhaps Moses (if he ever really existed) was one of these. But realistically, Moses's contribution has had no greater an influence on the modern world than have the contributions of a great many other individuals, from Plato and Aristotle to Francis Bacon and Adam Smith. Is it surprising that monotheism arose from a small, Middle Eastern culture? Well, it would be surprising if a major scientific or mathematical advance had emerged from relatively primitive nomadic tribes. But I do not find the particular character of the contribution of monotheism to be especially surprising and certainly not a belief in need of a supernatural explanation.

Has the subsequent intellectual contribution of the Jewish people been unique, so out of line with those of other cultures—say the Greek, Italian, English, Dutch, or Chinese—as to suggest supernatural causes? This is impossible to quantify, but the evidence is pretty slim. Subjects with which we are intimately familiar often seem far more remarkable and distinctive to us than do subjects about which we know substantially less. A good friend of mine is a professor at one of America's leading universities. He once told me that a colleague, a professor of English there, was shocked when he found out that the university had the same number of Milton scholars as organic chemists. Mind you, he was not shocked at the abundance of Milton scholars, but rather considered it an outrage that the university devoted as many faculty positions to a narrow subfield of chemistry as it did to "the most important poet of all time."

Examples of this phenomenon are found everywhere. Our favorite novel or symphony comes to seem absolutely original and unlike any other. Every subtle nuance makes it stand apart, in our minds, from other works whose subtleties we have not taken the time to learn or appreciate. In the same way, if we know Jewish history, but not Basque or Armenian history, it is hardly surprising that the former seems remarkable to us while the latter do not.

This is not to say that there are no differences among symphonies or novels or histories beyond our familiarity with them. Some symphonies are great, some boring, some simply bad. In the same way, some ethnic groups have had relatively tranquil histories, some remarkably turbulent histories, others in between. Jewish history is unique in many senses of that term.

First, it is obviously unique in the way that individual fingerprints are unique: No other group has precisely the same history. But in that sense, the history of *every* ethnic group is unique. Second, it has made unique intellectual contributions, contributions that no other ethnic group has made—for example, the concept of monotheism[9] and the texts of the Old Testament themselves. We can hardly claim that every ethnic group has made lasting intellectual contributions. But many have. The Chinese and Greeks, for example, and others have made lasting contributions to intellectual history, of comparable—and in some cases greater—impact than those made by Jewish thinkers. Third, Jewish history has been a remarkable and turbulent history. If it were a symphony, it might be a Beethoven, certainly not a Clementi. But is it more remarkable or more turbulent than any other ethnic group's history? The more you learn about world history, the less likely you are to draw this conclusion.

Suppose Jewish history really *were* unique. Suppose we could find some dimension—say turbulence—along which Jewish history came out on top. Suppose no other ethnic group endured a comparable history of persecution and radical changes in fortune. Would this prove the Orthodox point? It's hard to see how. We learned in chapter 8 that there is no failure of naturalistic explanations when it comes to the history of the Jewish people. Their survival can be explained in terms of the same historical processes that explain any other current state of the world. There have been no supernatural discontinuities in these processes that would suggest the intervention of a divine force acting either in favor of or against the well-being of the Jewish people. So, even if that history were more turbulent than any other—a rather unlikely claim—this still would not show what the Orthodox want us to see.

Realistically, of course, it is very unlikely that Jewish history is unique along any single dimension. But we might argue that it displays a unique *combination* of characteristics. Perhaps it was not the *most* turbulent history (compared with, say, Kurdish history), and perhaps the intellectual contributions are not unsurpassed (compared with, say, Greek contributions). But how about when we combine these? Among ethnic groups with turbulent histories, are there any who have made comparable intellectual contributions? Well, certainly the Chinese. But are there any *relatively small* ethnic groups with highly turbulent histories who have made comparable intellectual contributions? Eventually, of course, the answer is going to be: No, only the Jews have all these characteristics.

But this is always possible. My friend the college professor told me that when his university hires a faculty member, the recommenders are asked whether the person under consideration is among the best in his or her academic field. The answer, he said, is almost invariably yes. However, the number of qualifiers that accompany the yes varies dramatically. One person may be described as "one of the best historians of China." Another might be "one of the best historians of *Ming-dynasty* China." Another "one of the best *political* historians of Ming-dynasty China" or "one of the best political historians of Ming-dynasty China *in his age group*," and so on. It is always possible to be among the best—even unique—if the comparison pool is defined narrowly enough. The problem is that the resulting uniqueness is more like the uniqueness of fingerprints. It does not signify a great deal, really nothing more than identifying who you are.

Jewish history is without question unique. But it is not *uniquely* unique. It is unique in the same sense in which a person's fingerprints or DNA or life history is unique: different from everyone else's. But a person's fingerprints, DNA, and life history are not uniquely unique, and neither is the ethnographic and intellectual history of the Jewish people. Nothing about that history violates natural, historical processes. There is nothing about Jewish survival that requires a supernatural explanation. The Jews may indeed be God's chosen people, but this conclusion does not follow logically from the historical evidence. If you believe that, you are taking it purely on faith. And, anyway, the Orthodox are not unique in their conviction that the Jews are God's chosen people. As we have seen, many liberal Jews—and many Christians, too—also hold this belief.

So where does all this leave Rabbi Gottlieb, who says he can prove the truth of Orthodox dogma through reason and logic? Recall that he claims that Orthodox Judaism is the only major religion that satisfies the three conditions of his so-called scientific method: (1) that the evidence be *positive*, (2) that the evidence be *unique*, and (3) that the evidence be *true*. What we have found, however, is quite the opposite:

- There is *no positive evidence*, none whatsoever, to support the dogma of Orthodox Judaism.

- The evidence the Orthodox offer to support their dogma is *not unique*.

- The evidence the Orthodox offer to support their dogma is *not true*.

CHAPTER TEN

THE FALLACY OF A SUPERIOR FUNDAMENTALIST MORALITY

FOR NON-ORTHODOX JEWS to seriously consider accepting Orthodoxy, they must first be convinced that the Orthodox lifestyle is better than their current lifestyles. But what are the criteria? The Orthodox way of life isn't more stimulating intellectually. It offers no material rewards. And it certainly isn't more fun. No, what the Orthodox—like all religious fundamentalists—are selling is a lifestyle that (they claim) is much more moral, demanding, and challenging and, as a result, much more meaningful and fulfilling than the secular Western lifestyle. To hammer this point home, they use graphic tone words to convey the desired images and create the desired mood.

Now there is nothing inherently wrong with tone words. Just as painters use tones to enhance the visual images they want to create, so, too, do writers, poets, and orators use tone words to enhance the verbal images *they* want to create. Think of the evocative tone words Dante employed in the *Divine Comedy* to convey the vivid imagery of Hell, Purgatory, and Paradise. Four centuries later the Puritan theologian Jonathan Edwards scared the hell out of his New England congregants, literally, with his frightening fire-and-brimstone sermons.

It is, however, one thing to appreciate the tone words you find in the poetry of a Tennyson or the prose of a Faulkner and quite another when you see them used by ardent advocates for a particular ideological, political, or religious position. In this setting it is essential that you focus on what these people are saying and not on how they are saying it or the mood they are attempting to create.* The key questions you must ask, always, are: Can what they are telling me be substantiated by an impartial, dispassionate assessment of the facts? *Is what they are telling me really true?*

These are precisely the questions you should put to Rabbi Emanuel Feldman, who, in his proselytizing book *On Judaism*,[1] uses a barrage of tone words to try to convince you, the reader, that Orthodox Judaism offers an antidote to the rampant moral decay he sees pervading Western, and particularly American, society. The biography on the dust jacket tells us that Rabbi Feldman "is one of the most respected and successful figures in the history of the American rabbinate. . . . He is Editor-in-Chief of *Tradition*, a scholarly quarterly, author of three [books] and of over a hundred articles in such journals as *Saturday Review* and the *New Republic;* former adjunct professor at Emory University Law School; and Senior Lecturer at Bar Ilan University. Author, editor, graceful writer, incisive thinker, and superb commentator—Rabbi Feldman distills a lifetime of accumulated wisdom and experience in this masterful book." Even allowing for publisher's hype, it is clear that we are dealing here with a prominent Orthodox leader. This is an important point to remember, because it tells us that when we listen to what Emanuel Feldman has to say, it is not the extreme fringe of Orthodox Judaism talking. It is its mainstream.

On Judaism is a dialogue between two characters that Feldman has

---

* To appreciate how tone words can color your opinion, imagine that you read an article about a boisterous political rally in which the speaker is "inspiring a cheering throng." Then you read a second article about another political rally in which *that* speaker is "inciting an unruly mob." What impressions do you draw? Both political leaders were, of course, doing exactly the same thing: haranguing a rowdy crowd of partisan supporters. But the different tone words create diametrically opposed images: happy excitement for one, danger and potential destruction for the other.

created: an Orthodox rabbi and a young man named David, who is yearning for Jewish meaning in his life.* At the outset the character David explains his current brand of Judaism to the rabbi and confesses, "I guess I'm not too proud of that."[2] Here are the rabbi's answers about the way David—in reality, the way you, the reader—should start exploring Orthodoxy. (In the following passages I have italicized all the tone words the rabbi employs to create the desired image; the italics are not in the original.)

[O]n this journey . . . you have to leave much of your *luggage* behind, by which I mean *preconceived notions* and *clichés*. . . .[3]

[David asks]

Am I going to emerge from all this an Orthodox Jew?

[The rabbi replies]

There are worse fates in life, I assure you, but I will not try to convince you or persuade you of anything. . . .[4] You'll have to start out with a *clean slate*, be willing to shed the *hackneyed prejudices, shibboleths, clichés* and *dogmas* of our day, and instead remain open to *new ideas, new modes of thinking, new experiences*. . . .[5] If you are *adventurous* and open to new things, then the search for [return] in life is a *tremendous adventure*, filled with *excitement* and *newness* and *freshness*.[6]

So here is the choice the rabbi lays out for you, the reader—whom, he insists, he is not trying to convince or persuade of anything: You can stay with your preconceived notions, clichés, hackneyed prejudices, shibboleths, and false dogmas. Or, if you are adventurous, you can cast off this burdensome baggage and enter an exciting world of fresh new ideas, new modes of thinking, and new experiences. As you

---

* The rabbi in *On Judaism* is ostensibly a literary construct, but clearly it is through him that Emanuel Feldman presents his own views to his reader. It is transparent that it is Rabbi Feldman who is doing the talking—and not to the fictitious David, but to the very real you, the reader.

can see, the rabbi's tone words have framed the choice for you very nicely.

To set the stage for his proposition that Orthodox Judaism offers a more moral, more satisfying way of life, Feldman levels a withering attack on Western society:[7]

> [W]hat I see around me: a society *profoundly materialistic*—and *profoundly miserable*. . . . We are living in a *deeply unhappy* society, and people try to *escape this sadness* and *unease* in a variety of *useless* ways, but primarily by *overindulging in various instinctual pleasures* that give *immediate but very temporary gratification*.[8]

Later he adds:

> That so-called pleasure-filled life . . . is *not that pleasurable*, or *joyous*, or *free*. On the contrary, by any objective measure, it is *miserable*. . . . [9] We live in *the ultimate no-fault society* . . . *no accountability*—just *self-indulgence* and *indolence*. Look around you at the results: *murder*, *drugs*, *crime*, *disease*, *violence*, *illegitimacy*, *lawlessness*, *bestiality*, . . . *adultery*, *greed*, *selfishness*. . . . We are in many ways *worse than animals*.[10]

Early on the rabbi claims that

> this *mad pursuit of pleasure* . . . is a barometer of the *deep sense of emptiness that pervades the lives of people*, . . .

from which he jumps to the conclusion that

> [i]t's a clear signal that within each Jew there is a yearning for something *great* and *holy*—a desire to be connected with *sanctify*, with religion, with Torah, and with God.[11]

David then tosses the rabbi a softball:

> If the inner yearning is so universal, how is it that more Jews don't reach out to return to their faith?

The rabbi replies:

Good point. I think it is because there are some special character traits which distinguish every returnee—traits that are not very common: *honesty, fortitude* and *courage.* After all, you have to be *honest* and *gutsy.* . . . Conversely, the returnees all lack other character traits: *smugness, complacency, self-satisfaction,* . . .[12]

adding, a few pages later,

That's why *I admire you* for coming in today. It required . . . *courage* . . . .[13]

And a few pages after that:

[T]oday's returnee is *truly heroic.* . . .[14]

Rabbi Feldman makes several other stark declarations early on about the state of American Jewry today:

To the vast majority of Jews, their personal Jewishness is totally irrelevant. . . . They are caught up in the *noise* and *cacophony* and *speed* and *rush* of our day. Some of them seem to be *going through life in a stupor* like robots. . . .* [15]

There is a way to behave and not to behave . . . being Jewish is serious business. If all we have to sustain us are *pap, platitudes, clichés,* and *sweet humanistic sentiments,* we will *self-destruct as a people,* or at best be left with a tiny number of *committed* Jews— while the rest of our people *fall over the edge into the black hole of ignorance, Jewish illiteracy, intermarriage, assimilation, self-indulgence,* and *Jewish nothingness.* . . .[16] [W]hat *plagues* us [today] is . . . *sheer ignorance, laziness* and *self-indulgence.*[17]

As the book proceeds, Feldman keeps up his fusillade:

---

* The non-Orthodox robots may be "going through life in a stupor," but not, apparently, the Orthodox robots. A little later in his book the rabbi admonishes, "Let's not be too harsh on people who seem to be praying like robots."[18]

Truth to tell, life without obligations is not very interesting or enjoyable . . . *such a life has no meaning.* . . . History is a *graveyard* of *once-great* cultures that *crash-landed into oblivion* because [they] lacked one essential ingredient of civilization: discipline. They consciously and willingly and with eyes wide open *allowed themselves to slide down the slippery slope* of becoming *self-indulgent animals.*[19]

And it should come as no surprise that Feldman also trains his heavy artillery on liberal Judaism:

I suspect that many of the young generation perceive in these philosophies a certain *intellectual inconsistency and flabbiness,* a kind of *consumer-oriented religion* in which the customer is always right and *contemporary fashion* rather than *eternal truths* dictate the teachings of the religion. . . . It is hard to get excited about a hybrid religion that is kind of a *half-divine centaur.* . . .[20]

Toward the end of his book, Rabbi Feldman succinctly sums up the Orthodox view of mankind:

We do believe . . . that *man is born selfish and greedy* and concerned only with his own needs, and that one of the purposes of the Torah is to wean him away from his *inborn self-centeredness.* . . .[21]

When [the Torah] becomes part of you, you are no longer tempted to *follow the mob,* and instead you learn to look objectively at the *vapid and empty silliness which pervades our existence* today.[22]

I think you've got the picture by now. Cutting through the invective and vitriolic tone words and distilling his colorful rhetoric down to its essence, what Emanuel Feldman is telling us is this:

- Western society is base and vile any way you look at it. (This, by the way, is exactly the same view of the West held by Islamic fundamentalists.)

- Man is born a selfish and greedy animal concerned only with his own physical, hedonistic needs.

- A "return" to the discipline of the Orthodox lifestyle, based on the eternal truths contained in Orthodox dogma, offers the only path to a truly meaningful Jewish life.

- Liberal Judaism is a sham, an undisciplined, worthless philosophy (not even a religion).

- The returnee possesses the desirable qualities of a heroic figure, whereas those who don't return have, by implication, undesirable qualities unfit for a hero.

Predictably, the rabbi tries to inoculate David (and the reader) against any backpedaling once he is set firmly on the road to Orthodoxy. Early on he warns:

> When a person begins to change and *grow* . . . certain conflicts inevitably arise—with a spouse, with parents, friends, society. . . . People who begin observing [kosher] or [the Sabbath], for example, may find that their mental stability is questioned by other Jews, that they are accused of having joined a cult. . . .[23]
>
> [He] often [faces] outright opposition and antagonism of family and friends. This requires a huge amount of *strength* and *conviction.*[24]

Later he adds:

> A person can always *turn back.* But the chances are that once you start out on this path, you won't want to turn back. You are *far too intelligent* for that.[25]

And toward the end of the book he reinforces his warning:

> A Jew who begins to return to Jewish *moorings,* and begins to study more and practice more, occasionally represents a challenge to those who know him—including even members of his or her own family—who are still *perfectly comfortable with their own lack of Jewish learning or living.* . . . It could make those around you uncomfortable and a bit nervous. . . .
>
> [O]ccasionally their discomfort is translated as a threat, and *you may be accused of . . . being weak-minded . . . or of having lost your mind altogether.* Returning Jews are usually *strong enough to with-*

stand such pressures and not take them seriously—were they not *strong enough to start with,* they wouldn't be seeking a *new kind of life. . . .* [26]

Let's leave aside for the moment the negative connotation of the tone words that you can always "turn back" (translation: You can always be a coward and a quitter), and the transparent flattery ("You are far too intelligent . . .") designed to appeal to the reader's vanity. Let's even leave aside that for the good Rabbi Feldman, it would appear that gaining a convert trumps keeping a family together, a cynical skewing of priorities I find both unconscionable and inexcusable. All that aside, his implication that non-Orthodox Jews are "perfectly comfortable with their lack of Jewish learning or living" is a ridiculous accusation.

The Hebrew Union College is staffed with rabbis and scholars who vigorously refute anachronistic Orthodox dogma. They are teaching a student body consisting of young men and women who have made the decision to devote their lives to Jewish learning and living. When they complete their studies they will become rabbis, who, in turn, will teach their congregants the value of Jewish learning and living, an on-going activity for children and adults alike that forms an integral part of just about every liberal synagogue everywhere.

The Orthodox response is almost guaranteed to be that the Judaism they teach at the Hebrew Union College and the Judaism that their students take back as rabbis to liberal synagogues is not really Judaism at all. Strict Orthodox observance, such as not eating pork and other "unclean" foods, and not driving on the Sabbath, constitutes as much a part of authentic Judaism as the more universal values, such as monotheism and ethical behavior. But this simply defines Judaism in such a way that any compromise of Orthodox practices is, by definition, no longer Judaism. In which case, there is no need for the Orthodox to offer any evidence as proof. It is true by definition. Of course, it also precludes any rational analysis of their argument.

Let's go back for a moment to Feldman's allegation that we in the West, lacking discipline, have "consciously and willingly and with eyes wide open allowed [our]selves to slide down the slippery slope of becoming self-indulgent animals." The slippery slope is an alliteration that has a nice ring to it and calls up a vivid image: If you give up or question any tenet or practice, however minor, you will find yourself on a greased slide where next you cannot help but question the more important ones, and so on down the line until finally there will be none left. But this argument is a well-known fallacy.

The slippery slope fallacy is a general-purpose technique for arguing against any act or change that can be associated in one's mind with other changes that would be patently undesirable. It works by inflating the importance of what may be a minor decision by associating it with more consequential changes that are alleged to be inevitable or likely results of the decision in question. Remember the domino theory? It was the justification for the Vietnam war. If we let Vietnam fall, it would inevitably lead to communism in all the countries of Southeast Asia. Similarly, it is used by the Islamic regime in Iran to combat the growing signs in a restive populace of a desire, especially among its young people, for liberalization and Westernization. If you allow women to appear in public without the prescribed head covering, next thing you know the whole society will become degenerate. On the other side of the political spectrum, it is an argument sometimes used in defense of hate speech or hard-core pornography as important forms of free speech that we must protect.

The slippery slope is a favorite form of argument among religious fundamentalists, because it allows them to appeal directly to firmly held beliefs and values of a more moderate audience in support of their own extreme views. But it is also a fallacy. It is a point of view that may appear to make sense—until you recognize that it has no basis in fact. The Orthodox, indeed all religious fundamentalists, use this fallacious line of reasoning all the time when they argue their position. Rabbi Dovid Gottlieb employs the slippery slope fallacy early on in *Living Up . . . to the Truth*. He states that "cultural compromise" inevitably results in "cultural failure, complete cultural disintegration." He doesn't offer any facts to substantiate this categorical position. He simply asserts that it is a lesson of history, "in particular Jewish history."[27]

What Feldman and Gottlieb are doing here is pretty obvious. They are attempting to capitalize on the general, vague belief that a loosening of religious standards inevitably leads to a loosening of moral standards. There are two serious defects with this tactic. First, one can make a strong argument—and shortly I do—that strict religious standards often involve practices that many would call highly immoral. I am not referring to the devout believer who goes astray. I am talking about immoral beliefs and practices that are embedded in the religious doctrines themselves.

Second, the evidence does not support the assertion. Listen to what Gottlieb has to say:

> Everyone wants to live with as little crime as possible. Again, [Orthodox Judaism] is very proud that within Torah communities, crime, violent crime in particular, is almost unknown. Imagine interviewing the presiding police officer in a precinct in Williamsburg, Brooklyn, Borough Park, Flatbush, Monsey, Monroe, or any place where you have large concentrations of [Orthodox] Jews. Ask him how many times he is called out on a murder charge, rape, assault and battery, mugging, child abuse, etc. The incidence of these sorts of crimes in Orthodox communities is very low.[28]

I'm sure it is. Much lower than in other precincts in Brooklyn where crime rates are higher. But is it lower than in the thriving liberal Jewish communities of Newton, Massachusetts, or Palo Alto, California, or the hundreds of others in between? I doubt it.

How plausible is Gottlieb's claim that cultural compromise inevitably results in "complete cultural disintegration"? More precisely, does cultural compromise weaken the value system of a society and thereby impair the well-being of the individuals and families that constitute this society? In the specific context of the doctrines of Orthodox Judaism, do you really think that compromise on certain practices—for example, eating a ham sandwich or driving (even to the synagogue) on the Sabbath—inevitably leads to the abandonment of the core values of Judaism, such as honesty, moral excellence, and a reverence for life?

Can the Orthodox prove the alleged inevitability of "complete cultural disintegration"? A convincing argument might produce evidence that there are no examples of individuals or families or communities who maintain the core values of Judaism without also maintaining the fundamentalist practices in question. But this is clearly false. So all they are left with is the fallacy of the slippery slope.

Every advance in what we call civilization has always been labeled by the doomsayers as a step backward for mankind. I'm not just talking about American socialists, such as Upton Sinclair, who wrote popular proletarian novels decrying capitalist greed. Jean-Jacques Rousseau, in the middle of the Enlightenment, wrote *Discourse on the Sciences and the Arts*, in which he attacked both as corrupting influences that serve the rich. In 1930 Sinclair Lewis became the first American to win the Nobel Prize for Literature. His novels were aimed at puncturing American complacency with broadly drawn satirical pictures of the crass values, emotional shallowness, and spiritual emptiness in American life—essentially the same criticism the Orthodox level at American society today, seventy-five years later.

In the silent film classic *Modern Times*, Charlie Chaplin portrayed a worker who goes berserk from the monotonous repetition he faces day in and day out on an unforgiving assembly line. The fact that the assembly line made it possible for working people to have automobiles—which enriched their lives beyond measure by giving them a mobility they had never thought possible—didn't come across in the movie. Nor did the fact that the autoworkers were making more money than they had ever dreamed of, so they could even think about sending their children to college. But that's all right, because in a free society social criticism has an important role to play. Such criticism often leads to improvement in people's lives. Today we hear how computers are leading to an increased "dehumanization" of society. And so it goes.

When you look at the other side of the coin, however, don't you find it highly significant that the United States is one of the world's largest agricultural producers and yet there has never been an American peasant class? Think for a minute about what this means, not only materially, but also psychologically and, if you will, spiritually. I wonder if Emanuel Feldman, when he is standing in the kosher section of his local supermarket, to which he refers in his book, ever takes a moment to reflect on how Western (and particularly American) inventiveness in farm mechanization, food distribution, and retail self-service has made it possible for people to buy much more and much more varied food for much less cost per hour of their work. All this—and this is but one example—was made possible by the free, democratic society whose moral profile the rabbi trashes mercilessly.

Are there serious problems in Western society today? Yes, of course there are. Very serious problems. Are these problems so pervasive that the moral fiber of the West is disintegrating, as the Orthodox—and all fundamentalists—would have us believe? No, they are not. Margaret Thatcher put all this in proper perspective when she said that England's and America's greatest asset is their democracy, which she defines as a free society, imbued with the love of liberty, governed by the rule of a law developed through the ages on the basis of equity and fairness for all their citizens.[29] This is the society, she said, that in the past century triumphed over the scourges of Nazism, Fascism, and Communism. And, I would add, it has also gone a long way toward triumphing over disease and poverty.

With all its warts, Western society is still the place where people—women as well as men—enjoy the most personal freedom, have the most upward social and economic mobility, and also make the most contributions to the betterment of mankind. When you stop to think about it, that is a pretty good yardstick against which to measure a society's morality in the aggregate.

There are two basic differences between Western society and Orthodox society. First, the prime coordinate for the West is personal freedom. For Orthodox Judaism the prime coordinate is strict, unquestioning, and unwavering submission to what is claimed to be God-given law. Second, Western society looks forward, whereas Orthodox society looks backward (and as a result, not surprisingly, *is* backward). A forward-looking orientation has enabled the West not only to achieve the great scientific advances that have so improved people's lives, but also eventually to correct injustices that have no place in a democratic society. The backward-looking orientation of Orthodox society simply keeps people in a tight box with the lid clamped firmly down.

A perfect example of the Orthodox flight from freedom is what everyone considered a landmark ruling handed down in 2001 by Israel's Supreme Court, that the government must register as Jews those Israeli citizens converted in Israel by non-Orthodox rabbis. Even the fact that such a ruling could be labeled "landmark" should tell you something. Here is the ruling, eloquent in its simplicity, written by the Chief Justice, Aharon Barak: "Israel is the state of the Jewish people. There are different streams in Judaism active in Israel and abroad. Every stream acts according to its own views. Every Jew in Israel—like every person who is not Jewish—is entitled to freedom of religion, conscience and organization. Our basic concepts grant every individual the freedom to decide whether he will belong to one stream or another."[30]

Do you have any doubt what the Orthodox reaction was? Eli Yishai, then the interior minister and a member of the Shas Party, had this to say: "This is a scandalous, difficult and disastrous decision for the Jewish people."[31] Zevulun Orlev, a National Religious Party member of the Knesset, likened the court's decision—in classic Orthodox rhetoric—to "a terrorist attack on the [Jewish] people's unity."[32] In one respect, Orlev was right. Individual freedom does subvert the doctrines of Orthodoxy.

Orthodox Judaism's claim to a superior morality is undercut not only by the fact that Western society is not the decadent den of iniquity the Orthodox claim it to be, but also because there are serious moral problems with Orthodox doctrine itself.

A few years ago I had a fascinating conversation with a "modern" Orthodox rabbi that extended over a period of a few months.* He insisted that the Torah provides Jews with their only valid standard of moral conduct. What he said can be distilled down to the following four theological and philosophical claims:

- True morality is absolute. To think otherwise is to embrace the fallacy of moral relativism.

- Only God can establish an absolute morality.

- To be moral is to do God's will (as defined in the Torah).

- God wrote the Torah for the express purpose of giving mankind a guide for proper moral behavior.

This is what the rabbi told me:

What is goodness? What does it mean to be good? The answer to this question is why God wrote the Torah. Without some kind of extra-human document, we would have no basis for determining that something is absolutely good or absolutely evil. How does one know what's good and what's bad? We need an external document not dependent on society. Morality has to be true.

Now if we knew exactly what God wanted, then any moral choice would come down to doing what God wants (moral) versus going against God's will (immoral). Therefore, if it were God's will for us to murder, then that would be moral. I don't believe it is God's will for us to murder. I am only using this example to make a point. But it is important to acknowledge that the only reason murder is immoral is because it is contrary to God's will. Morality is defined by God's will. We refrain from murder because we have internalized God's will. Values that are not guided by divine morality (even indirectly) are mere convention and are not absolute.

---

* I want to assure the reader that this was a real conversation with a real live Orthodox rabbi, not a contrived conversation with a fictitious character (like Rabbi Feldman's "David") created to act as a foil for my line of reasoning. I took extensive notes on our face-to-face discussions, and parts of our extended conversation took place by e-mail. Everything is fully documented.

In the finite universe, we are merely images projected on a movie screen. It is just one light, although there are many images. The whole movie depends on that light continuing to shine. If the light is ever turned off or blocked, then the movie would stop. Our finite existence is no more real than the images on the screen. The reality is that God (the light) is there, but we don't see it. We see it as real images. Light is a very good metaphor, like when it shines into a prism. You see seven colors coming out the other side of the prism, but it is an illusion that there are multiple lights. In reality, there is only one light. This is why everything one has is a gift from God. The relevance of this is that we can never have an absolute source of goodness unless we have a source of that information that is not dependent on the current mores of one's society. And that source, that light, is of course the Torah.

We have to be careful not to let the Orthodox sidetrack us into a sterile argument about absolutism versus relativism. Religious conservatives of every stripe are always citing relativism as the antithesis of truth. But this is a straw man, because the indisputable fact is that there are no relativists among the significant figures in the history of philosophy. Plato and Aristotle were not relativists and neither was Kant or Hume. They all believed that, yes, there is an absolute morality but, no, it doesn't have to come from God.

And while it is doubtless true that we inherently recognize that murder is wrong, this does not allow us to claim, as the rabbi does, that the only reason it is immoral is because it is contrary to God's will, or to jump to the conclusion that the reason we refrain from murder is because we have internalized God's will that murder is wrong. This is mere speculation. It might very well be one of Jung's archetypes. Or maybe the Harvard biologist Marc Hauser is right when he says that our moral judgments evolved over millions of years.[33] Or there might be some other explanation.

As for the rabbi's colorful metaphor, all it really does is restate the basic Orthodox position that without God there is no absolute morality and without the Torah we don't know what it is. Of course, if it turns out that God did *not* write the Torah, then the metaphor is hollow and completely irrelevant, and the basic foundation on which the

Orthodox build their edifice of absolute morality crumbles to the ground. But even leaving this fundamental question aside, the Orthodox argument that the Torah is our timeless guide to absolute morality collapses of its own accord.

In his latest book, *The God Delusion,* Richard Dawkins, the English biologist, atheist, and latter-day Thomas Aikenhead,* argues that the Old Testament is not only not the timeless guide to absolute morality that the fundamentalists claim it to be, but that it is a positively immoral document. To buttress his position Dawkins takes on God (who orders Abraham to murder his son, Isaac, to test his faith), Abraham (who poses as Sarah's brother and, out of fear for his own life, offers his wife into Pharaoh's harem), and the Torah-sanctioned ethnic cleansing, starting with Moses's ordering the merciless massacre of the Midianites and culminating with Joshua's bloodthirsty slaughter of the Canaanites. The fact that none of this ever really happened, Dawkins says, is immaterial.

> The point is that, whether true or not, the Bible is held up to us as a source of our morality. And the Bible story of Joshua's destruction of Jericho, and the invasion of the Promised Land in general, is morally indistinguishable from Hitler's invasion of Poland or Saddam Hussein's massacres of the Kurds and Marsh Arabs. The Bible may be an arresting and poetic work of fiction, but it is not the sort of book you should give your children to form their morals.[34]

The Orthodox dismiss Dawkins out of hand, of course, claiming that he completely misses the point. I don't think he misses the point at all. But more important, even if you leave aside Dawkins's disturbing references (and many others that are similar), the Orthodox assertion that the Torah is our timeless guide to absolute morality cannot stand up to intellectual scrutiny.

---

*The aptly named Aikenhead was the hapless young Scot we met in the preface (see note 2 on page 227), who was hanged in 1697 for poking fun at the doctrines of Christianity. Fortunately for Dawkins, humorous blasphemy is no longer a capital crime in the West. For Muslims, however, it would appear that blaspheming Islam still can mean a death sentence, as the recently knighted Salman Rushdie can attest.[35]

Consider the question of slavery. In America we had slavery in the southern states before the Civil War. In that place and at that time, the practice of slavery was considered perfectly moral behavior. Moreover, the clergy often used scripture not only to defend the practice as moral, but also—following the Orthodox logic that morality is defined as doing God's will—to justify it as divinely ordained. And I'm not talking only of Christian clergy. In the days leading up to the Civil War, two prominent Orthodox rabbis, Morris Raphael and Bernard Illowy, cited scripture to defend the practice of slavery.[36]

We have to ask an important question here. Does the absolute standard of morality that the Orthodox claim God gave the Jewish people in the Torah say—or indirectly imply—that it is perfectly acceptable for one human being to own another as his or her personal property? If it does—and because, by the Orthodox definition, God-given morality is absolute, immutable, timeless, and placeless— then Rabbi Raphael and Rabbi Illowy were certainly behaving morally when they made their public declarations in support of slavery. Taking this position one step further, one must ask: if the Torah says or implies that slavery is acceptable, then the Torah's statement of absolute morality—again, by the Orthodox definition, not relative to a particular society in a particular time in a particular place—makes slavery morally acceptable behavior today, too. This being the case, there would be no reason for any Jew to criticize as immoral the de facto slavery in Sudan.

So what does the Torah actually say? It says that slavery is a perfectly acceptable practice and that slaves are property like any other asset an Israelite could own. The Torah couldn't have put it more explicitly than its declaration in Leviticus 25:45–46: "These [slaves] shall become your property: you may keep them as a possession for your children after you, for them to inherit as property for all time." Of course, like every other practice, slavery was something to be strictly regulated, so Exodus 21:1–11 sets out very specific rules for slavery, including rules for when a man sells his daughter as a slave.

The Torah makes no categorical statement that it is morally wrong for one human being to own another as chattel. Talmudic scholars may attempt to mitigate this position, pointing out that the Torah stipulates that a slave must be freed after six years unless the slave himself opts to stay with his master (Exodus 21:2), that in the fiftieth year all slaves are to go free, that an escaped slave is not to be returned to his master (Deuteronomy 23:16), and that no Israelite should be condemned to permanent servitude (Leviticus 25:42–43). But *mitigating* is not *prohibiting* or even *condemning* the practice of slavery. It is merely saying that there are certain rules and guidelines for the good Israelite slave owner to follow. Furthermore—and this is rather revealing about the Torah's double standard of morality—the same passage in Leviticus goes on to permit Israelites to make slaves of the Canaanites around them.

The rabbis of the Talmud may have been made uncomfortable by the practice of slavery, but they did not believe they could entirely abrogate the laws of the Torah and abolish its practice, so instead they tried to alleviate the lot of the slave. Maimonides took a similar view several centuries later when he said in his legal code that it is allowed to work a slave hard, but the Israelite master should be just and merciful. One would have hoped that the rabbis of the Talmud—or at least the brilliant Maimonides—could have brought themselves to recognize that slavery was a grossly immoral practice and come out strongly and categorically against it. But they didn't, because to have done so would have been to declare that the Torah, the God-given guide for man's absolute morality, was not on solid moral ground, and that would have presented a problem a whole lot bigger (for them, not for the slaves, of course) than the question of slavery. So they resolved the dilemma in classic Talmudic fashion, getting around the text without denying its validity outright, by trying to ameliorate the slave's condition. And they did it in the context of the moral climate of their day, when the practice of slavery was accepted custom and practice. Which, by the Orthodox definition, sort of makes these Talmudic rabbis moral relativists themselves, doesn't it?

To my way of thinking, the fact that the Torah condones the

practice of slavery and makes no categorical, crystal-clear statement that it is completely unacceptable, indeed unconscionable moral behavior, invalidates and renders totally indefensible the Orthodox claim that the Torah is the source of absolute morality. This concrete example also offers an excellent illustration of why the great philosophers of the past like Hume and Kant knew—and why all serious philosophers today also know—that absolute morality is indeed possible without its having to have been given to us by God. I would say that it is quite a challenge for the Orthodox to try to explain how God could have written a timeless guide for moral human behavior that sanctions the unquestionably immoral practice of slavery. Or the equally unquestionably immoral practice of blatant discrimination against women.

The Orthodox, even Orthodox women themselves, deny that Orthodox Judaism discriminates against women. But to any impartial observer their denials fly in the face of the facts. Just walk into any Orthodox synagogue and you'll find those women who are there segregated from the men. The Orthodox say that Judaism envisions different roles for men and women. A fair response to that dictum would be a couple of simple questions: Who made the rules? And who assigned the roles?

The Orthodox attitude toward women was made manifest in an interview that Deborah Sontag, then the Israel correspondent for the *New York Times*, conducted in 2000 with Rabbi Menachem Mendel Taub, the "rebbe of Kaliv." She reported that the interview was conducted "through his personal secretary. The rabbi does not take questions from a woman; his secretary posed the questions. His assistants placed a large picture frame between the rabbi and this reporter so that his view would be blocked. He talked to the ceiling. . . ."[37]

No serious person denies that there are differences between men and women. But this doesn't mean that such differences should result in the deeply ingrained—and, in my view, deeply immoral—discrimination against women embodied in the doctrines of Orthodox Judaism. One of the prayers that Orthodox men recite each morning is a blessing thanking God *sheh lo-asani isha,* which means "for not making me a woman." Women recite a blessing thanking God *sheh asani kirtzono,* which means "who has made me according to his will." With classic casuistry, the Orthodox attempt to explain this away by saying that men have more *mitzvoth*[*] to fulfill. Because women are exempt from several, the men are thanking God for the privilege of performing more *mitzvoth.* What they neglect to mention is that the men also recite blessings thanking God for not making them a slave.

To put the meaning of this delightful little prayer into sharper perspective, consider the following incident, reported in the *New York Times,* that took place in Israel in 1999:

> The topic for the day in an Israeli Army classroom was the status of women in Judaism, part of an education series where attendance was mandatory. The instructor, a young lieutenant, began by citing [the aforementioned blessing]. One young soldier, the daughter of a reform rabbi, raised her hand to challenge him. Not all Jews say that, she said. Some use an alternative blessing, which thanks God for making people as they are. According to Israeli Army records, the lieutenant, who is Orthodox, replied: "The Reform and Conservative are not Jews to me." When the teenager stood to leave, he followed her, continuing: "The Reform and Conservative caused the assimilation of eight million Jews, and this was worse than the Holocaust in which only six million were killed."
>
> One week later the Israeli Defense Force (IDF) suspended the lieutenant and said he would be discharged from the military. He apologized for the reference to the Holocaust, but remained steadfast in his view that liberal Judaism had caused more damage than the Nazis to the future of the Jewish people. [The response of] a spokesman for the Orthodox media center [was that while] "Holocaust metaphors should be out of bounds," [they] did not consider his statements on assimilation to be "extreme."
>
> [The comment of the Israeli Army was that the lieutenant] "doesn't understand what the Jewish people is, what the state of Israel is, or what the IDF stands for."[37]

In 2000 a controversial French-Israeli film called *Kadosh* opened with a scene of the protagonist, an Orthodox Jewish man, offering the

---

[*] Literally "blessings," but in this context, "obligations."

daily morning blessing I have just described, thanking God for not having made him a woman. One reviewer said he *should* give thanks—lots of it—as the film depicts a woman's lot in Jerusalem's Orthodox community as pretty close to what one usually associates with Islamic fundamentalism. Orthodox Jews are not as extreme in their treatment of women as are the Islamic fundamentalists,[39] but in essence what they are doing is exactly the same thing. It is only a matter of degree. When the Taliban were running Afghanistan, they, too, sincerely believed with complete certainty (as they still do) that they were doing God's will when they denied women and young girls any formal education and forced them to live in degrading, dehumanizing conditions. Can any objective person believe that such unabashed discrimination—whether by Islamic fundamentalists or by Jewish fundamentalists—is really God's word and God's will? I doubt it. I think any objective person could not help but conclude that what we have here is nothing more than a convenient (from the male point of view) holdover from an earlier, less enlightened age.

It is evident—it is impossible to deny it—that the position of women in Judaism described in the Torah and the Talmud is a reflection of the totally male-dominated biblical times. Men had several wives, who served to bear them children and do their bidding without question. Over the centuries their lot improved, but not as much as it should have, and certainly not anywhere close to the point where Orthodox women are full-fledged partners. At best they are minority partners and, until relatively recently, not even that. Today the Orthodox attitude toward women is a sexist anachronism and, as such, immoral in the extreme.

Of course, Orthodox Jews were not the only ones to discriminate against women. Just about every society did. But the Western societies evolved,* and with this evolution they even managed to pull

---

* Not everywhere, unfortunately. In 1984 a woman named Kelly Sisson became the first woman to preach in the chapel at New Orleans Theological Seminary, one of six graduate schools run by the Southern Baptist Convention. The following Sunday, a local pastor pronounced the chapel's pulpit "demonically possessed" because a woman had

Continued on following page

Orthodox Jews—kicking and screaming, to be sure—along with them to a somewhat more equitable treatment of women. In the twentieth century Orthodox Jewish women gained certain rights, most notably that of receiving a full-scale Jewish education. Almost certainly, however, the change from the mid-nineteenth to the mid-twentieth century was an unacknowledged response to the liberal Jews' previous insistence on breaking with traditional Jewish practice in this regard. Rabbi Eugene Borowitz sums it up this way: "As so often happens in human history, what an orthodoxy first proclaims as alien and heretical is later cautiously accepted, and finally claimed to be what the institution had really stood for all along."[40]

The partial emancipation of some Orthodox Jewish women raises an interesting question. The only authority the Orthodox recognize as a proper standard of moral behavior is the Torah, the same Torah they claim God gave to Moses at Mount Sinai and which, they also claim, has been handed down intact, without change, to the present day. But if this is so, then, logically, what was correct behavior for women in, say, 1808, should also be correct behavior for women in 2008. Sadly, for some Orthodox Jewish women it probably is.

But for other Orthodox women, a group of rabbis decided that now it was all right to loosen the leash somewhat. This decision required a more liberal reinterpretation of the Torah's restrictions, one that allowed women more freedom than prior interpretations had allowed. But who was responsible for this new interpretation, and on what authority did they make it? Whoever they were, they created a

----

preached there. Shortly thereafter, delegates, or "messengers," at the annual meeting of the Southern Baptist Convention passed a resolution discouraging the ordination of women for "pastoral functions and leadership roles."

Things haven't changed. "In 2000, the information officer [a minister] for the Nashville-based convention's executive committee, said that 'there's nothing new here. . . .' Most Southern Baptists, he said, support the Apostle Paul's assertion: 'I suffer not a woman to teach, not to usurp authority over the man, but to be in silence.' He continued, 'We believe the office of pastor is reserved to men as qualified by Scripture.'"[41]

A few years later the *Wall Street Journal* ran this item in the page-one news summary: "Southern Baptist missionaries were told they must swear by May 5 that they believe in wives' submission to husbands and oppose female pastors" (April 17, 2003).

conundrum for the Orthodox: Either the Torah is divine, immutable law or it isn't. They can't have it both ways.

Not a problem, says Rabbi Emanuel Feldman:

The written Torah itself has its own mechanism which allows for the Torah to be applied to every generation and to every new and changing situation. This is done by duly qualified sages and scholars who are empowered to apply the principles of the Torah to every conceivable scenario. Deuteronomy 17:11 specifically says that we are to follow their decisions. . . .

David, Feldman's fictitious interlocutor, asks:

Does every rabbi today have the right to make his own interpretations?

The rabbi replies:

Not at all. Only those world-class scholars who are universally recognized for their learning, piety, and unimpeachable integrity, who devote their entire lives to the study of both the Written and Oral Torah, who are loyal to its precepts, who are profoundly familiar with its principles of *halachic* interpretation,* who are intellectually brilliant, and who are spiritual giants, have the authority in every generation to rule on fundamental matters of Jewish law and Jewish practice . . . [Feldman identifies Maimonides and four other rabbis as meeting this qualification and says that they are] universally recognized by world-class Torah scholars as being a kind of unofficial Jewish Supreme Court. These . . . sages were given the right by that verse in Deuteronomy 17 to apply and interpret the laws of the Torah.[42]

Rather than accepting Feldman's claims at face value, let's stop for a moment and ask the two questions you should always ask when the Orthodox make one of their broad and seemingly authoritative assertions. First: *Is what he is telling us true?* And second: *Does what he is telling us make any sense?* Because the rabbi claims that the Torah commands us to "follow [the] decisions" of "qualified sages and scholars," the best place to start is with his specific Torah reference, Deuteronomy 17:11, to see if the text really says what the rabbi says it says.

---

* *Halacha* is Jewish law.

It doesn't look that way to me. The way I read the text, Deuteronomy 17:2–7 is a detailed (and rather bloodthirsty) legal procedure for adjudicating the capital crime of idolatry; 17:8–13 is a legal procedure for handling both crimes and civil disputes; and 17:14–20 deals with the question of monarchy. When you actually read the text of this passage,[43] you see that what 17:11 really says is not at all what Rabbi Feldman claims it says. The instructions to which 17:11 refers have nothing to do with applying the Torah to "every generation and every new and changing situation," as the rabbi would have us believe. Rather, they refer to the carrying out of the decisions handed down by priests and/or magistrates brought before them involving (1) the capital religious crime of idolatry, (2) criminal cases, such as homicide and assault, and (3) civil disputes.

What we are seeing here is a crude legal apparatus indicative of a sociological transformation of the Israelite society at a given point in time. In the commentary in the Plaut Torah, the passage in Deuteronomy from 16:18 to 18:8 is described as showing "that the original tribal system had developed into a centralized one . . . and how an older wilderness-bred people, geared for war, had become a settled society with a civic organization."[44] What it certainly is not is carte blanche authorization for "world-class" sages and scholars or anyone else down through the ensuing ages into the twenty-first century to interpret for us what the Torah means, and much less a divine command that we believe the interpretation they hand us.

The fact of the matter is, as Rabbi Borowitz observes, that liberal Jews see "the slow if grudging acknowledgment" by some Orthodox rabbis "that a Jewish woman is entitled to be a person in her own right, as another vindication of the liberal view that conscientious" behavior today, not behavior based on "a previous generation's" outdated "law or custom, should set the standard for authentic, moral Jewish life."[45]

The Orthodox view of the proper role of women is simply one more log on the fire of Orthodox antipathy toward liberal Western society and its mores. Listen to the ideas of a major orthodox figure as described in a 2003 cover story in the *New York Times Magazine*:

> On women's role in society . . . he understood quite clearly that, in a liberal society, women were free to consult their own hearts and to pursue careers in quest of material wealth. But from his point of view, this could only mean that women had shucked their responsibility to shape the human character, through child-rearing. The Western notion of women's freedom could only mean that God and the natural order of life had been set aside in favor of a belief in other sources of authority, like one's own heart.
>
> But what did it mean to recognize the existence of more than one source of authority? It meant paganism—a backward step, into the heathen primitivism of the past. It meant a life without reference to God—a life with no prospect of being satisfactory or fulfilling. And why had the liberal societies of the West lost sight of the natural harmony of gender roles and of women's place in the family and in the home? This was because of the "hideous schizophrenia" of modern life—the Western outlook that led people to picture God's domain in one place and the ordinary business of daily life in some other place.[46]

That is a succinct statement of the position of Orthodox Judaism on the subjects of both the status of women and liberal Western values.* The writer, however, was not describing the thinking of an Orthodox Jew but that of a twentieth-century Muslim scholar, Sayyid Qutb, the founder of the fundamentalist sect that murdered Anwar Sadat, and the author of a vast commentary on the Koran called *In the Shade of the Qur'an*. The article, a penetrating analysis by Paul Berman, is called "The Philosopher of Islamic Terror."

It is well worth taking a look at some of Qutb's other thoughts, as their similarity to Orthodox Jewish doctrine is uncanny.

In the Muslim fashion, Qutb looked on the teachings of Judaism as being divinely revealed by God to Moses and the other prophets. Judaism instructed man to worship one God and to for-

---

* Stated unambiguously by Rabbi Emanuel Feldman: "The Jewish genius lies in . . . its perception that religion and God-consciousness are not merely one compartment of life, but are in fact the summation and totality of all of life."[47]

swear all others. Judaism instructed man on how to behave in every sphere of life—how to live a worldly existence that was also a life at one with God. This could be done by obeying a system of divinely mandated laws, the code of Moses. . . .

The old code of Moses, with its laws for diet, dress, marriage, sex and everything else, had enfolded the divine and the worldly into a single concept, which was the worship of God. But Christianity divided these things into two. . . . Christianity's modern legacy . . . was the liberal idea that religion should stay in one corner and secular life in another corner. . . .

[Qutb] complained about . . . America's loss of moral values. . . . He opposed the United States because it was a liberal society. . . . The truly dangerous element lay in America's separation of church and state—the modern political legacy of Christianity's ancient division between the sacred and the secular. This was not a political criticism. This was theological. . . .

People with liberal ideas were mounting a gigantic campaign against Islam. . . . The secular reformers were already at work, throughout the Muslim world. . . . It is an effort to exterminate this religion as even a basic creed and to replace it with secular conceptions having their own implications, values, institutions and organizations. . . . The assault from inside was conducted by Muslims, but who polluted the Muslim world with incompatible ideas derived from elsewhere. . . .

To live in the shade of the Qur'an is a great blessing which can only be appreciated by those who experience it. It is a rich experience that gives meaning to life and makes it worth living. . . .

He wanted the true Muslims to engage in a lifelong study of the Koran.[48]

In the fourth paragraph, substitute "Judaism" for "Islam," "Jewish" for "Muslim," and "Jews" for "Muslims," and you have exactly what the Orthodox think that liberal Judaism is doing to what they define as authentic Judaism. And in the fourth and fifth paragraphs, substitute "Torah" for "Qur'an" and "Jews" for "Muslims," and again you have the Orthodox position.

Qutb hates the West—and let's not kid ourselves, hate is exactly what it is—precisely because it is made up of liberal societies that don't follow a strict religious code of laws that trumps the inherent individualism and personal freedom that, by definition, characterize a liberal society. If you have any doubt about the reason Islamic fundamentalists despise Western values, recall that, in January 2005, one week before the national election in Iraq, an audiotape was posted on the Internet by a speaker identifying himself as Abu Musab al-Zarqawi, at the time the leader of al-Qaeda in Iraq. This was his candid message: "We have declared a fierce war on this evil principle of democracy and those who follow this wrong ideology." The Associated Press described al-Zarqawi's diatribe: "He railed against democracy for supplanting the rule of God with the rule of man and the majority, saying it was based on un-Islamic beliefs and behaviors such as freedom of religion, freedom of expression, separation of religion and state and forming political parties."[49]

A year later the Iranian president Mahmoud Ahmadinejad said essentially the same thing, albeit with a softer tone, in a strange letter he sent to President Bush: "Those with insight can already hear the sounds of the shattering of the liberal democratic systems. We increasingly see that people around the world are flocking toward a main focal point—that is the Almighty God."[50]

Now think back to what Rabbi Emanuel Feldman had to say earlier about contemporary Western values. For Qutb, al-Zarqawi, and Ahmadinejad, the fundamentalist Muslims, and for Feldman, the fundamentalist Jew, the solution to this unhappy state of affairs is for you to give up much of the immense freedom you enjoy within the framework of democratically enacted laws in a liberal democracy, and instead submit to a strict, God-given law. For the Orthodox rabbi, it is the 613 commandments in the Torah (or, if not the whole enchilada, at least a goodly number of them). For Qutb, it is *shariah*, the Muslim legal code. Many of the rules under *shariah* are pretty severe (as they are in the Torah), and the punishments called for in the Koran are notoriously harsh (as they are in the Torah, too, except that capital and corporal punishment are no longer tolerated). But Qutb didn't see it that way:

> Qutb refused to regard these punishments as barbarous or primitive. *Shariah*, in his view, meant liberation. Other societies, draw-

ing on non-Koranic principles, forced people to obey . . . man-made law. . . . Under *shariah*, no one was going to be forced to obey mere humans. *Shariah*, in Qutb's view, meant "the abolition of man-made laws." . . . [But] it was an impossible vision—a vision that was plainly going to require a total dictatorship in order to enforce; a vision that, by claiming not to rely on man-made laws, was going to have to rely, instead, on theocrats, who would inter-pret God's laws to the masses.[51]

And that, of course, is exactly what happened in the Islamic state the Taliban created in Afghanistan. They carried out Qutb's vision by fusing the religious and the secular spheres into one, dominated by the religious. It was in fact a total theocratic dictatorship. They applied *shariah* to the letter of the law, without pity. And, to put it mildly, they envisioned different roles for men and women.

Iran espouses a somewhat less extreme version of Qutb's funda-mentalist vision, but like all nations with an Islamic government, Iran also forces women into shrouded subservience. A few years ago the first vignette in a powerful Iranian film called *The Day I Became a Woman*, told the story of a little girl on the day she turns nine.

> This isn't just any birthday but the end of childhood, according to Islamic law. Beginning at noon, she must cloak herself in a chador. The days of innocent fun and games with male playmates are over forever.
>
> Until the noon deadline, however, the stubborn, spirited girl is determined to play on the beach with a boy her own age. But because he has homework to do, he is forbidden to go outside, and she must converse with him through a barred window of his home. To mark the time, [she] inserts a stick in the sand to measure the sun's shadow. But when the appointed moment arrives, her mother and severe grandmother appear carrying the chador that symbol-izes her transition into young womanhood. . . .
>
> The movie's three vignettes are all meditations on the near-impossibility of escaping the assigned female role in a fundamental-ist Muslim state.[52]

Is this different from the way Orthodox Jews treat women in their society? It is. But, if one is honest, it is really only a matter of degree. For example, in 2001 the *New York Times* reported that "the rigorously

Orthodox Shas Party . . . boycotted the rally tonight 'for reasons of modesty.' Women artists were scheduled to perform, and . . . [there is] a theological prohibition on men listening to women sing."[53] This is the same Orthodox Shas Party whose political leader, Aryeh Deri, was convicted of graft and corruption and sentenced to jail. I think it fair to ask, which is the more immoral act: listening to a woman sing or taking bribes? It is also fair to ask, who in his right mind thinks it is immoral for a man to listen to a woman sing?

Let's go back now to what the "modern" Orthodox rabbi told me. "If it were God's will for us to murder," he said, "then that would be moral." And his disclaimer, "I don't believe it is God's will for us to murder. I am only using this example to make a point." This rabbi does not believe that murder is God's will, but other Orthodox Jews *do* believe it, and they believe deeply enough to commit murderous acts precisely because they know they are doing God's will. It is quite understandable that they should think so, given the Torah's description of Moses's command to ruthlessly kill the Midianites and Joshua's slaughter of the idolatrous Canaanites—women and children along with the men.

Yigal Amir, the young Orthodox Jew who assassinated Yitzhak Rabin in 1995, remains unrepentant to this day. Rabin was a husband, a father, and a grandfather as well as Israel's prime minister, but that made no difference at all to the Orthodox murderer. For him—and he still believes this—killing Rabin was a moral act because "Rabin's peace efforts put him into the Talmudic category of one who may be freely executed because he is in the act of killing Jews."[54] A year earlier a physician named Baruch Goldstein, whose life had been dedicated to healing people, one day walked into a mosque in Hebron and there he calmly and methodically gunned down twenty-nine peaceful Muslims at prayer. Does anyone have the slightest doubt that he, too, believed he was acting in God's name and doing God's will? And by the way, both Amir and Goldstein were "modern" Orthodox.[55]

If you think these heinous crimes were perpetrated by deranged individuals outside the mainstream of Orthodox Judaism, think again.

Consider what Rabbi Ovadia Yosef, the spiritual leader of the Shas Party in Israel, whose incredible explanation of the Holocaust I cited earlier, had to say in 2000 about the then minister of education, Yossi Sarid. Apparently the rabbi was upset that Sarid wanted more oversight of Shas schools because of what could politely be called "irregularities." Yosef was also riled because Aryeh Deri, the Shas political leader, had been indicted on charges of graft and corruption.

Now when Ovadia Yosef speaks, to paraphrase the old TV ad, a large segment of Israel's religious community listens, watching satellite broadcasts of his commanding weekly sermons on screens set up throughout the country. From a synagogue in Jerusalem, the rabbi called Sarid "Satan," and said that just as God "extirpated Amalek, so may he extirpate Sarid. . . . Just as he showed us in killing Haman and the vengeance done to Haman, so will vengeance be done to Sarid." He then led his congregation in a chant of: "Accursed is Haman. Accursed is Sarid."[56]

I don't know about you, but this sure sounds to me like the rabbi was putting out a contract on Israel's minister of education and blessing it with the assurance that the hit man would be doing God's will. It appeared that way to Israel's attorney general, too, who was prepared to start a criminal investigation of Rabbi Yosef's remarks as an incitement to violence. Rabin's assassination was still fresh in people's minds, and many Israelis believed that it was precisely such verbal violence on the part of the Orthodox clergy against Rabin's peace efforts that incited his killer to action. But, because Rabbi Yosef (who, to the best of my knowledge, has never retracted his statements) holds such a substantial part of the Israeli religious population in his sway, he was politically untouchable, and the incident was allowed to fade away.

There are still many in the Orthodox community in Israel who believe Baruch Goldstein was a good man doing God's will. To rationalize his crime, some Orthodox settlers claim that he acted to prevent a planned Arab massacre of Jews. This hollow accusation has never been substantiated by anyone, and it was left unexplained how the killing of all those people praying in a mosque—none of whom was ever identified by anyone as an Arab militant, let alone as a terrorist—prevented this supposed massacre.

Goldstein was buried, appropriately, in a park named after Rabbi Meir Kahane, another religious zealot convinced he was doing God's will, in his case by aggressively spewing out anti-Arab hate and provoking confrontation. The Orthodox faithful built a shrine around Goldstein's grave, and it soon became a pilgrimage site. Orthodox admirers from Israel and abroad would come and pray, kneeling and kissing the tombstone. Around the tombstone there was built a stone plaza that contained benches and lights, a prayer book case, a stand for memorial candles, faucets for ritual hand washing and (of course) a collection box. On the Sabbath Orthodox settler children were encouraged to pray over his tomb. In the epitaph on the tombstone Goldstein was described as a "martyr" with "clean hands and a pure heart. . . . He gave his life for the people of Israel, its Torah and land." This is the same guy who, without the slightest provocation and without mercy, slaughtered twenty-nine innocent people kneeling at prayer.

Eventually, as a result of legislation passed by the Knesset, the Israeli army demolished the shrine because it was a symbol of terrorism. This is what the then minister of trade, Ran Cohen, a member of the liberal Meretz Party, who sponsored the bill, had to say: "This is a very important day in the struggle over the moral image of Israeli society. A great disgrace has been wiped from our face. The other half of the stain will be removed when the shameful inscription is erased. This monument symbolized everything that is anti-Jewish, anti-Israeli, and anti-human. It was a site of incitement and education for murder."[57]

Contrast these sentiments with Rabbi Yosef's words. Or with the words of those Orthodox faithful present when the army bulldozed the shrine. "He was a righteous man. He gave his life to sanctify God's name." Or another, shouting at the soldiers, "God will take his revenge on you. God willing, you won't make it through the year, and we'll have the privilege of dancing on your blood." But for me the most telling comment of all, as reported by Joel Greenberg in the *New*

York Times, was this by a young woman: "I knew him as a doctor. He was a very good person."[58] And he probably was. A good person, a good doctor, and a good Orthodox Jew, absolutely convinced—as still are a lot of other good Orthodox Jews—that he was doing God's will and, therefore, was acting 100 percent morally when he methodically killed all those innocent people in the Hebron mosque.

I think it is fair to ask: Who is the more moral person? Dr. Goldstein, an observant Orthodox Jew who didn't drive on the Sabbath, ate only kosher food, prayed three times a day—and in the name of his God murdered twenty-nine people peacefully praying to *their* God? Or Ran Cohen, a man whom the Orthodox would disdainfully call "secular," who considers the Orthodox veneration of Goldstein and his murderous action anti-Jewish and anti-human?

Such fanaticism among the Orthodox faithful is, unfortunately, still alive and well in Israel (and probably elsewhere, too). In 2004 Shimon Perez, the long-time leader of the Labor Party and formerly a prime minister of Israel, warned: "I fear that someone will try to assassinate the prime minister."[59] The same year Jeffrey Goldberg wrote a chilling op-ed piece for the *New York Times* entitled "Protect Sharon from the Right." Among other things, he recounted his conversation with an Orthodox girl in her late teens, married and pregnant, a resident of a settlement in the West Bank. "I asked her if she thought Amalek was alive today.* 'Of course,' she said, and pointed toward an Arab village. 'The Amalekite spirit is everywhere. It's not just the Arabs.' Who else, then? 'Sharon isn't Amalek,' she said, 'but he works for Amalek.' I asked her if she would like to kill [Sharon]. 'It's not for me to do. If the rabbis say it, then someone will do it. He is working against God.'"

Goldberg went on to say:

Over the past year I've heard of at least fourteen young Orthodox settlers express with vehemence a desire to murder Prime Minister

---

* According to Orthodox doctrine, the Amalekites, descended from Amalek and Esau, are the eternal archenemy of the Jews. For a detailed explanation, please see the footnote on p. 70.

Ariel Sharon and his men, in particular the deputy prime minister, Ehud Olmert, and the defense minister, Shaul Mofaz. . . . The threat of the radical right has become a matter of terrible urgency in the Israeli government. Avi Dichter, the chief of the Israeli internal security service, told a Knesset committee [in July 2004] that his agents believe there are 130 to 200 settlers hoping to kill Mr. Sharon.

In the summer of 1995, Yitzhak Rabin, the man who led the Israeli Army to victory in the Six-Day War—making possible the settler movement in the first place—was called a Nazi at public rallies; radical Orthodox rabbis cursed him; and much of world Jewry was silent. Today, once again, the atmosphere is one of tolerance for murder.

And to put this scary picture into even sharper focus, Goldberg also tells us: "The extremist yeshivas that give rise to fundamentalist thuggery are financed in part by Orthodox Jews in America. Several Orthodox rabbis in America took the lead in demonizing Mr. Rabin."[60]

How is this different from the Islamic fundamentalism being taught in the madrassas across the Muslim world, financed in large measure by wealthy Arab institutions and fomenting Islamic terror and suicide bombers? The short answer is that in essence there is no difference at all. It is only a matter of scale.

The Orthodox rabbi with whom I was speaking emphasized: "The bottom line is this: Embracing Torah Judaism is not to be regarded as simply a lifestyle choice. We believe that it is a moral imperative. We believe that it is real and true. We really do believe this. Someone who really believes that God wants him to keep kosher would have to be crazy not to do so."* Following this line of reasoning, if someone really believes that God wants him to murder an Israeli prime minister—that it is his moral imperative—he would have to be crazy not to do so. To my way of thinking, the two murder cases I have just cited, together with the real threat to the life of Ariel Sharon while he was

---

* The liberal Jewish position is that this is so much nonsense, an anachronism embedded in Orthodox dogma—along with so many others—that can and should be discarded.

still in office, demonstrate that what is crazy—really crazy—is this whole fundamentalist mind-set.

The root of the problem is that all religious fundamentalists, Orthodox Jews included, believe with all their heart that it is they, and they alone, who are in sole and certain possession of the truth. There is an old Portuguese saying that no one is the owner of the truth. The fundamentalist would vigorously dispute this dictum. He believes with complete certainty that he does in fact own a patent on the truth.

It is a sad fact of history that massive numbers of innocent people have died as a direct result of someone or other knowing that he or she was in sole and certain possession of God's truth. History is replete with incidents of mass murder in the name of God: the Spanish Inquisition, all the religious wars in Europe, Cortés in Mexico and Pizarro in Peru (they were plunderers, but the Catholic Church was right there along with them, justifying the slaughter of the Indians as God's will), the brutal massacre in southwestern Utah in 1887 of 140 "infidel" men, women, and children by Mormon zealots (an event that the historian Geoffrey Ward has called "the most hideous example of the human cost exacted by religious fanaticism in American history until 9/11"),[61] to name but a very, very few. Every one of those incidents was characterized by an unshakable conviction on the part of the perpetrators that they were doing God's will. How did they know this? Because they were in sole and certain possession of the absolute truth—and it came to them directly from God.

Big numbers in the abstract, while impressive, are often not as effective in getting a message across as a more personalized example. That is why the *Diary of Anne Frank* hit home more powerfully than did the gruesome statistics of the Holocaust. In 2001 Judith Miller, a reporter for the *New York Times*, interviewed a young man whom she described as a "polite, soft-spoken twenty-six-year-old Pakistani [who] thinks he has killed at least one hundred people. Maybe more; he isn't really sure. 'My goal was not to kill,' he said. 'But I had a line to follow, an Islamic ideal.' Having decided 'to consecrate my life to jihad' while studying law at Punjab University in Lahore, he said, he joined a Pakistani militant group." This young man eventually joined up with the Taliban in Afghanistan and was captured by rebels fighting in the north. The reporter asked him whether, if asked to do so, he would go to London, Paris, or New York and blow up women and children for Islam. "'Yes, I would do it,' he said quietly, without hesitation."[62]

This young Islamic fundamentalist and Baruch Goldstein, the Jewish fundamentalist, were cut from the same cloth. They both were acting on what they knew with absolute certainty was what God wanted them to do—even if it meant cold-blooded murder. They were doing God's will as they understood it, and therefore, according to their warped fundamentalist logic, they were behaving morally. I'm sure the young Pakistani considered his actions completely consistent with his beliefs, which themselves were internally consistent—just like Orthodox Judaism.

Religious fundamentalism is not limited to Orthodox Jews and Islamic fundamentalists. Other groups, with their own fundamentalist belief systems and doctrines, know it is *they* who are in sole and certain possession of the truth and, hence, exemplars of a divinely ordained moral behavior. Here is a smattering of some examples I came across in the press:

- In the early 1990s there was a protracted struggle in the Southern Baptist Convention,* and, when the dust settled, a conservative group displaced a theologically moderate group from control. This is what the leader of that conservative group (who subsequently became the president of the Southern Baptists) had to say when some rabbis criticized them for trying to convert Jews: "Our expressed mandate from Jesus is to take the gospel to the whole world. Jewish people are part of the world. . . . [In John 14:6] Jesus says that He is the way, the truth and the life; no one comes to the father except through me. If Jesus was telling the

---

* These are the same people whom we met earlier in this chapter (see footnote on p. 139), who admonished women not to teach, but to remain in silence.

truth, He's the Lord and we have to do what he says."[63] In other words, they are doing God's will.

• In 2001, after a long international manhunt, the antiabortionist who was suspected of murdering an obstetrician in Buffalo, New York, in 1988 (by shooting him through a window in his home with a high-powered rifle) was captured in France. But there is more to this story. The police finally caught up with him because he had contacted an organization that supports antiabortion activities and activists who have been convicted and are serving jail sentences. In early 2001 there was a fund-raiser in Bowie, Maryland, called the White Rose Banquet. Its founder (a Protestant clergyman) said that the annual event recognized those who were serving prison time for antiabortion activity. He said a feature of the banquet was an auction to raise money for the imprisoned. Paul Hill, for example (convicted for killing a doctor who performed abortions in Florida), sent a letter listing the Ten Commandments.[64] Another guy's contribution to the auction was the watch he used as a timing device in a bombing attempt in the 1980s.[65] These people, too, are sincerely convinced they are God's agents.

• In 2000 a white Episcopal priest and his 760-member middle-class congregation of St. Andrew's-by-the-Sea, in the Gulf Coast city of Destin, Florida, voted to sever ties with the Episcopal Church and place themselves under the authority of the head of the Anglican Church in Rwanda. In doing so, St. Andrew's became one of about twenty conservative congregations seeking spiritual harbor by way of Africa. Despite vast geographical and cultural differences, the breakaway congregations and the East African bishops shared a conservative reading of scripture, an evangelical zealousness, and an abiding suspicion that some Episcopal leaders did not quite hold to their convictions. In an interview, the priest had this to say: "I think the demonic targets the church from time to time. If you don't know you're at war, the enemy has a great advantage. That can sound real strange and esoteric, but I believe it. I think [the breakaway] was part of God's perfect plan to prepare us, without our knowledge it was coming."[66]

I do agree. It does sound real strange and esoteric.*

• The Trappist monks, of all people, hired a publicity woman in 2001 to market monasticism to young men who, as they put it, might feel led toward a life of religious service. "We are using a system of marketing that has been very effective in business," she said. The pitch was to bring them in to experience monastic life for three days; a sort of "Try it, you'll like it!" PR campaign. The young men were to follow the monks' schedule, a rhythm of communal prayers, meals, and labor intended to engage the spirit and the body. The leaders of the Trappists summed it up thus: "You learn about truths."[67]

• Could anything be more immoral than the Indian caste system? India's Untouchables, as described in a heartrending article in *National Geographic,* are "branded as impure from the moment of their birth . . . victims of a religion that judges them as subhuman and a rural society that exploits them practically as slaves." The writer describes the pathetic plight of one man: "One morning, for reasons he himself is not sure of, Bairwa decided to bathe in the village pond, off-limits to Untouchables. That evening a mob surrounded his house and threatened to kill him. . . . 'I am clean. I don't smoke or drink or eat meat. I work hard. I do everything right. Why am I Untouchable?' Because he was born one. One hundred and sixty million Indians serve this life sentence."[69] The Indian government is trying to ameliorate their predicament, but

---

* But it is not unique. Toward the end of 2006 several Episcopal parishes in northern Virginia voted to secede from the United States Episcopal Church and to affiliate themselves with a more conservative diocese in Nigeria. The leader of the Nigerian diocese is the Anglican Bishop Peter Akinola, "who has called the growing acceptance of gay relationships a 'satanic attack' on the church."[68]

as we continue to see almost daily on the subcontinent, government policy is one thing and religious fanaticism is another.

• Consider the fundamentalist Mormon practice of arranged marriages involving child brides. Five years ago the *New York Times* published an article that started out: "At the age of fifteen, Lu Ann Kingston was ready for marriage, or so her family elders decreed. They arranged for her to wed a twenty-three-year-old distant relative, and she became his fourth wife, quickly bearing him two children. Five years later . . . [she] gathered the children, called for a police escort and left. . . . Now twenty-three, Ms. Kingston said . . . that teenage brides from fundamentalist Mormon homes are often told, as she was: 'This is what the heavenly father wants, and they're at an age they can't run away because there is nowhere to go. There's no way out.'"[70]

• In 2001 the pastor of a church in Georgia and four church leaders were charged with cruelty to children. Apparently it was standard practice for parents and church leaders to beat their children, severely, under the direction of the pastor. The judge said that the children, who had been placed in foster care, could go home if their parents agreed to spank them only with their hands, and by themselves, at home. Incredibly, the parents refused. "We're going to raise our children according to the Bible," one parent said at the hearing.[71]

• And then there are the Taliban. They *really* know with complete certainty exactly what God wants them to do. Among other things, God wanted them to destroy all pre-Islamic relics, including priceless two-thousand-year-old massive Buddhist statues. The Taliban leader, Mullah Mohammed Omar, issued an edict ruling that the relics were idolatrous and against the tenets of Islam. The Vatican called the order the "crazy" result of "fanatic extremism" (perhaps forgetting that the Church took a similar position on pre-Columbian culture, also in the name of God). Mullah Omar told the Afghan people, "It has given praise to

God that we have destroyed them."[72] While the destruction of priceless relics was senseless, what the Taliban do to Afghan women, also in the name of God, is nothing short of monstrous.

The Orthodox will no doubt argue that these examples are different from Judaism for all sorts of reasons. First, because they are extreme. Yes, they are at the extreme, but it is the fundamentalist who takes his religious fervor to the extreme.[73] A moderate extremist would be an oxymoron. However you classify the examples cited above, how is the attempt by Southern Baptists to gain converts any different from the Orthodox practice of approaching young men at the Wall in Jerusalem with the intent to gain converts? The Orthodox will respond that what they are doing is different because they are targeting only non-Orthodox Jews. But is there really any difference? Both the Southern Baptists and the Orthodox Jews are seeking converts to "save their souls," and both sects believe with all their heart that by so doing they are acting morally, doing God's will.

The Orthodox will also argue that the examples I listed above are different from Judaism because God wrote the Torah and that really *is* the truth for Jews. But this is nothing more than the same old question-begging assumption we have encountered time and time again in the Orthodox argument: If you assume that God wrote the Torah, you can conclude that what it says is the word of God and, hence, true. But what we're assessing here is precisely whether or not what the Torah says about how human beings should behave is evidence that God did in fact write the Torah.

The Orthodox insist that the standard of moral conduct the Torah spells out for us—a theological text for behavior today—is consistent with the claim that God wrote the Torah. But the Torah's blithe acceptance of slavery is not at all consistent with the claim that God wrote the Torah. Neither is the Torah's blatant discrimination against women. Therefore, one would be hard pressed to defend the proposition that Orthodox Jews are, at root, any different from any of these other religious zealots.

But now let's move away from the extremes and take a look at the morality of mainstream Orthodox Judaism in the United States. I am not going to dwell on those Orthodox Jews who are immoral people in the (nonreligious) sense of what we normally call immoral. There are bad apples in every barrel. But a few cases do deserve a brief mention, because one would think there should be a complete disconnect between pious Orthodox observance and outright immoral, indeed criminal, behavior.

I have already briefly touched on the case of Aryeh Deri, the leader of the Orthodox Shas political party in Israel, who was tried and convicted of bribery. After a protracted appeals process, Israel's Supreme Court upheld the lower court's judgment that Deri was guilty of graft and corruption and its decision to send him to prison for his crimes. When he went to jail, large crowds of Orthodox supporters outside the prison gates boisterously demonstrated against his "martyrdom at the hands of the secular elite." Balancing this demonstration, a poll showed that 70 percent of Israelis felt that Deri was a crook and was getting his just desserts.[74]

In the last few days before he left office in 2001, President Clinton made headlines by issuing an unusually large number of presidential pardons. Here is how the *New York Times* described four of them:

> President Clinton commuted the prison sentences of four Hasidic men from New York last week after he and his wife, Hillary Rodham Clinton, met at the White House with supporters of the men, whose religious sect overwhelmingly backed Mrs. Clinton in her victorious Senate campaign. . . . Mrs. Clinton and her aides acknowledged that the supporters, who included the grand rabbi of their sect, made pleas for leniency during the meeting in late December. . . .
>
> The four men . . . were convicted after prosecutors charged they had invented a fictitious religious school in the 1980s and used it to attract millions of dollars in government aid. . . . The men were accused of keeping some of the money for themselves and giving the rest to other residents of the town and its yeshiva. . . .
>
> The office of the United States Attorney . . . opposed the commutations for the four men. . . .

The deceit came to light, prosecutors said, through inconsistencies in audits and the presence of state and federal grant program inspectors who left scratching their heads after meetings with the men or visits to the bogus facilities they had set up. Few rushed to suspect the Hasidim of anything untoward; hard questions came with difficulty, "especially," [the prosecutor] told the jury, "when the people seeking the funding present themselves as deeply religious, pious people."[75]

There is an understandable inclination to believe that religious people, and especially religious leaders, have higher moral standards than the average person does. But they are not necessarily holier than thou, a fact attested to by the unsavory spectacle of Catholic priests all over the country who were found to have molested so many young children over the course of so many years—and, what is infinitely worse, of their superiors who covered up these immoral, criminal acts.

And then we have that pillar of the Orthodox community, Jack Abramoff. In a national scandal of massive proportions that is still playing out,[76] Abramoff, a powerful Washington lobbyist, pleaded guilty in January 2006 to swindling Indian tribes out of tens of millions of dollars, suborning government officials, and evading taxes.[77] The *New York Times* also reported that, in a separate action in March 2006, a Florida court sentenced Abramoff to close to six years in prison for "defrauding lenders in a gambling ship line that [he and a partner] bought in 2000 for $147.5 million. . . . The two men [also] agreed to make a total of $20.7 million in restitution as a result of the [Florida] fraud, which involved faking documents to get a $60 million loan to buy the Sun-Cruz fleet of gambling ships." The *Times* also picked up a puzzling angle of this story: "A lingering mystery in the Florida case is why the former owner of Sun-Cruz, Konstantinos Boulis, also known as Gus, was gunned down in a gangland-style ambush in February 2001 in the midst of an angry post-sale dispute with the company's new buyers."[78]

The intriguing question is how Abramoff, the four Hasidic men convicted of blatant fraud, and others could continue to be, for all intents and purposes, observant Orthodox Jews, keeping the Sabbath, keeping kosher, offering all the prescribed blessings, going the whole nine yards of Orthodox belief, while engaging in such blatantly immoral and criminal behavior. The Orthodox answer? "[T]hat person by definition is simply not a religious person," says Emanuel Feldman.[79] But isn't this answer just another example of the old rhetoric trick of truth by definition that we've seen before?

More disturbing than the immoral acts of some individual observant Orthodox Jews is the behavior of the Union of Orthodox Jewish Congregations, commonly known as the Orthodox Union. In 2000 the *New York Times* ran an illuminating article about an in-depth piece published earlier that year by the *Jewish Week*, the largest Jewish newspaper in America, under the headline "Stolen Innocence." The article documented accusations that a "brilliant, charismatic and dynamic" rabbi in New Jersey had abused teenagers in his charge, emotionally, sexually, and physically. But that's not my point. As I said, there are bad apples in every barrel, including clergymen. What I found much more disturbing was that, according to the *Times* article, this rabbi had been shielded for decades by his superiors in the Orthodox Union, one of the most important national organizations of Orthodox Judaism. The rabbi disputed many of the charges, either denying them or claiming he did not recall. But on the day that the article appeared, his resignation was accepted by the Orthodox Union.

There is yet another angle to this story that is also disconcerting. For some of the ninety thousand subscribers to the *Jewish Week*, the real villains were not the rabbi or the Orthodox Union, but the newspaper and its editors who ran the story. One letter to the editor chastised: "You are giving the families of teens from nonobservant homes the opportunity to completely remove their children from anything that has to do with Torah." This irrational, kill-the-messenger mentality shows, once again, how fervent religious convictions can cloud people's thinking and judgment.* The newspaper's editor commented,

---

* And not only the thinking and judgment of simple people. In the midst of the uproar over the way in which the Catholic Church had kept a lid on the incidence of priests molesting young children—so many priests, so many children, over so many years—

"If you read the Jewish press, Jews are perfect people. They never do drugs. They never beat their wives. . . . I did a cover story on these Orthodox teens—how they were heavily into Ecstasy and all kinds of drugs. I was told that if the story runs, you will become persona non grata in the Orthodox community."[80]

It turns out that the editor's experience—the hostile reaction of the Orthodox community to the revelation of immoral behavior on the part of Orthodox Jews—was not unique. For the *Chicago Jewish News*, the flash point was an article on money laundering at a kosher restaurant. And in 1996 the Jewish Telegraphic Agency, a news service to which nearly one hundred Jewish newspapers subscribe, published a five-part series on sexual misconduct, entitled "When Rabbis Go Astray." The typical response, according to the editor of the news service, was: "How could you be writing about such a terrible thing?" As if sweeping it under the rug would make it not true, or at least make the truth go away.

Getting back to the New Jersey rabbi and the Orthodox Union, the article in the *Jewish Week* quoted by name ten people, most in their thirties and forties, who said that, as teenagers, they had experienced either the rabbi's violence or his sexually aggressive behavior. This is certainly bad enough. But far worse, in my opinion, is the absence of action by the Orthodox Union. It is nothing less than a shameful cover-up, no different from the way the Catholic Church for years covered up the sexual misconduct of a staggering number of its priests.

In February 2004 advisors to the United States Conference of Catholic Bishops reported on the problem of sexual abuse by the clergy and "concluded that some church leaders had been more concerned with shielding priests and avoiding scandal than with helping victims

---

until the scandal burst out into the open, Reuters reported that *Avvenire* (the newspaper of Italy's bishops) published a full-page article entitled "USA—A Country in the Hands of Lawyers," in which the writer pointed to America's "lawsuit culture" as being partly to blame for the scandal. As described by Reuters, the writer was attempting to portray the predatory priests and the dioceses that covered up the immoral—and illegal—behavior as victims of an unduly aggressive legal system.

and weeding out abusers." Robert Bennett, an attorney who helped draft the report, summed it up succinctly: "Knowingly allowing evil to continue is cooperation with evil."[81] The same can be said about the leaders of the Orthodox Union, who were apparently perfectly willing to engage in a long-term cover-up of a rabbi's alleged sexual abuse of children.

What are we to make of this whole sordid episode? First, if the accusations are to be believed, and they seem pretty convincing,[82] then, for all his piety, for all his observant Orthodoxy, the rabbi in question is clearly an immoral man. Second, and much more important, by covering up the rabbi's misconduct the Orthodox Union behaved—over an extended period of time—in a totally indefensible, totally inexcusable, and grossly immoral manner. What happened to the God-given absolute moral standard the Orthodox are always talking about?

What we have here is nothing less than the Machiavellian maxim that the end justifies the means. The bottom line for the Orthodox Union, that paragon of virtue responsible for keeping unclean food from the lips of the faithful, was that protecting its own image took precedence over protecting unsuspecting children from abuse.* It is hard to think of anything more immoral and hypocritical. These are the same people who claim to be the official guardians of God's will. Can any thinking person doubt that protecting innocent children from abuse is a lot more important a moral mission for the Orthodox Union than putting its kosher label on a jar of gefilte fish?

The Orthodox have presented us with no credible evidence, none whatsoever, that Orthodox Judaism offers a more moral way of life than liberal Judaism—or than any other system of belief, or, for that matter, than no religious belief at all. Say what they will, it simply does

---

* Ellen Goodman, a writer for the *Boston Globe,* said pretty much the same thing over five years ago about the Catholic Church: "Throughout this sorry tale, one thing has dismayed loyal Catholics the most: The realization that the hierarchy defended the institution instead of defending the children. The church hunkered down to protect its moral reputation. And lost its moral authority."[83]

not follow that the Orthodox Jew is a more moral person for embracing the dogma of Orthodoxy. In the final analysis, Orthodox Jews, like religious fundamentalists everywhere, are no more moral than anyone else. Some are moral people, like an old rabbi I knew when I was growing up, who would gently admonish me for mowing the lawn on Saturday as he walked by my house on his way back from the synagogue. Others, like the leaders of the Orthodox Union who covered up a rabbi's alleged sexual abuse of children for so many years, are to my mind extremely *im*moral people. But their morality, or their lack of morality, has absolutely nothing to do with their Orthodoxy.

Moral people do the right thing not because it is what God demands, nor because they are afraid that God (or the civil authorities) will punish them if they do not. Moral people do the right thing *because it is the right thing to do.*

CHAPTER ELEVEN

THE FUNDAMENTALISTS' LAST LINES OF DEFENSE

W E HAVE SEEN THAT in spite of strenuous efforts, not a shred of credible evidence has been found to corroborate any aspect of the Exodus story, from Egypt to Mount Sinai to Canaan. Unable to offer a convincing positive argument drawn from archeology and history, the Orthodox make equally strenuous efforts to explain away or counteract various forms of evidence derived from the historical and archeological record. Their goal is to insulate themselves—and us—against the increasing weight of solid evidence that disproves their claim that the Torah is both an accurate account of the ancient history of the Jewish people and a God-given guide for proper moral behavior today.

In 2002 a new Conservative[1] Torah was published with commentaries that, "incorporating the latest findings from archeology, philology, anthropology and the study of ancient cultures," propose that the Bible was a "human rather than divine document," that Noah never existed, that the story of the Flood was in all likelihood borrowed from the Mesopotamian myth of Gilgamesh, that the patriarchs never existed, that even Moses probably never existed and that, in any event, the Jews were never in Egypt in any significant numbers, and, hence, the exodus—the cornerstone of Orthodox Jewish belief—never happened. Furthermore, "Jericho was unwalled and uninhabited, and

David was not the fearless king who built Jerusalem into a mighty capital, but more likely a provincial leader whose reputation was later magnified to provide a rallying point for a fledgling nation."[2]

The Orthodox reaction was not long in coming: "Ah, but you haven't proved that God didn't give Moses the Torah on Mount Sinai. All you've shown is that you can't find anything to prove that these people did exist and that the Exodus did happen." Then one Orthodox interlocutor briefly let down his guard with a candid comment that says volumes about their insular approach to everything: "Anyway, these commentaries are at the back of the book, and most synagogue-goers won't even see them."[3]

The Orthodox are so determined to maintain their fundamentalist position that they effectively inoculate themselves against the facts, building an impregnable fortress that defies logic and empirical evidence. And they can finesse the hard scientific facts quite easily. Because they view God as omnipotent, they conclude that he can easily adjust the evidence however he pleases. Here are a few examples of their line of reasoning:

- When archeologists uncovered conclusive evidence that Jericho had no walls to come tumblin' down, why should we care? Perhaps they were there, but after the trumpets sounded God made them fall and disintegrate into dust. It was a miracle, after all.

- When archeologists and historians find no evidence whatsoever of any significant Jewish presence in Egypt, why should we care? Perhaps God erased all the evidence for good reasons, reasons we humans cannot understand yet.

- When respected academic scholars of the ancient Near East point out that crucial parts of the Torah were very close—in some cases almost identical—to earlier or contemporary writings from other civilizations,[4] all that proves is that God gave the Jewish people his commandments in a context they would understand, so the fact that much of the Torah appears to be borrowed from other contemporary ancient societies is no evidence that God didn't write it.

• When historians offer a perfectly natural explanation for the survival of the Jewish people for over three thousand years, it proves nothing. Perhaps God wanted it to appear that there was a rational, natural explanation for what, in reality, was divinely orchestrated by his hidden hand.

To put this denial in its proper perspective, consider the legend of Bigfoot (or Sasquatch). A few years ago the truth finally came to light. It turned out to be a monumental hoax, perpetrated by a man named Ray L. Wallace. Wallace created this modern myth by stomping a track of oversized footprints in a northern Californian logging camp in 1958, using carved wooden feet. After Wallace died in 2001, his children announced that Bigfoot was a prank, and their father was the prankster. "This wasn't a well-planned plot or anything," one of his sons said. "It's weird because it was just a joke, and then it took on such a life of its own that even now we can't stop it."[5]

It *is* weird. Even in the face of hard evidence that they have been victims of a hoax, there are still a lot of people who continue to deny it. For them, Bigfoot is still real. "All it means is that Ray Wallace is dead, not Bigfoot," said one die-hard believer, a retired zoologist who has been trying to prove by DNA analysis of hair samples that Bigfoot is a species heretofore unknown to science. To date he has come up empty handed.[6] And in March 2007 a member of the Canadian Parliament seriously petitioned the House of Commons "to establish immediate, comprehensive legislation to effect immediate protection of Bigfoot."[7] Because they want to believe, the zoologist, the Canadian MP, and other Bigfoot believers have inoculated themselves against the facts.

Sometimes the refusal to face reality can be hilarious. Five years ago the *New York Times* ran an article that started out:

And so it came to pass that a talking carp, shouting in Hebrew, shattered the calm of the New Square [New York] Fish Market and created what many here are calling a miracle. . . .

The story goes that a twenty-pound carp about to be slaughtered and made into gefilte fish for Sabbath dinner began speaking in Hebrew, shouting apocalyptic warnings and claiming to be the troubled soul of a revered community elder who recently died. Many here believe that it was God revealing himself that day. . . . Some people say the story is as credible as the Bible's account of the burning bush. . . . [One New Square resident said] "it is very rare that God reminds people he exists in this modern world. But when he does, you cannot ignore it. . . ." [The story] jibes with the belief of some Hasidic sects that righteous people can be reincarnated as fish. . . .

[According to] a local lawyer, "If people say God talks to them, we recommend a psychiatrist, but this is different. . . . This is one of those historical times when God reveals himself for a reason. It has sent spiritual shock waves throughout the Jewish community worldwide and will be talked about throughout the ages."[8]

Yes, indeed. If people want to believe, they will believe.

A second line of defense of Orthodox dogma is that if something doesn't make any sense, the meaning is hidden from us (such as the reason there is no archeological evidence for the truth of the Torah). How can you argue against that? You can't, of course, which makes it the ideal fallback position for the Orthodox when they find themselves cornered. The Orthodox resort to the hidden-meaning gambit all the time. Not only is it a move that by its very nature is impossible to counter, but it also provides subtle support for the fundamentalist concept of revealed truth. If God has hidden the meaning from us, we shall never discover this meaning until God decides to reveal it to us. Until that time, we must take it on faith.

Remember our friend, David, Rabbi Emanuel Feldman's fictitious young man searching for meaning in life? The following exchange between David and the rabbi offers a good example of the hidden-meaning gambit:

David: "Will we ever understand?"

Rabbi: "Perhaps some day. Because there are answers, but they are beyond our present understanding."

David: "But why can't we see God as clearly as the people in the Bible did?"

Rabbi: "Simply because we are not on their level of perception. They were granted the gifts of prophecy and revelation so they could accept the Torah and develop the legacy that they would pass on to future generations. . . ."

David: "[H]ow long will His hiddenness . . . last? . . . Will things ever get a little clearer, or at least a bit less murky?"

Rabbi: "Those are difficult questions. The best way to strip away the veil is to attach ourselves to His teachings, to the study of His Torah, and to prayer. . . . Then we realize that there are aspects of life which reason alone cannot comprehend."[9]

Feldman continues along the same line a little further on with another exchange between David and the rabbi:

David: "Those . . . [commandments] we don't understand—am I expected to perform something that makes no sense?"

Rabbi: "When we deal with the Torah, we are dealing with God's will, which is beyond our comprehension. . . . [E]ven if we . . . do not understand, we are nevertheless bound to observe the commandments—because ultimately they are God's will and contain Divine secrets which are beyond human comprehension."[10]

Think for a moment. You read things in the Torah that make no sense to you. Perhaps they did to a primitive people in a simpler age, but to you, today, in the twenty-first century, they make no sense at all. What the rabbi is telling you is not to bother looking for answers, because you'll never find them. God has hidden them from us and will reveal them to us only when he chooses to do so. In the meantime, your best course of action is to accept without question that the Torah is true and that the Orthodox lifestyle is the proper, moral way to live that truth—and your life.

Rabbi Ezriel Tauber echoes the same sentiments and offers the same prescription. At a number of different points in his book *Choose Life* he frames the issue for *his* fictitious character, also named David and also a young man searching for meaning in *his* life:

What, specifically, is G-d's purpose in creation that Abraham grasped and dedicated his life to? The truth is we cannot know G-d's true purpose in the ultimate sense. However . . . [a] human being's highest purpose is to live completely for G-d's purpose. . . .[11]

The real goal is to serve G-d through filling the world with the knowledge of G-d, to reveal G-d through the very essence of our life. . . .[12]

Each of the commandments in the Torah points us to blessing, life and eternity. Exactly how is eating kosher . . . a choice of eternity? That we don't necessarily see right away.* We are 'computer operators' extending back in a long line to the first computer operator, Abraham. . . . All we know is that we have the instructions in front of us. The instructions are the commandments of the Torah; they are the screen prompts which tell the operator which key to push next. As long as we push the right keys, even if the act is totally meaningless to us, it produces its desired effect.[13]

We work in a secretive assembly line. What are we accomplishing [by following the detailed instructions]? We don't really know. All we know is . . . when we get there, we will see it.[14]

Tauber attempts to give the Orthodox doctrines a modern tone when he tells us that we're all computer operators who don't know how a computer works, but who get the desired results as long as we follow the screen prompts. The rabbi works this analogy pretty hard. In part 2 of his book, chapter 3 is entitled "World History in a Nutshell," and successive sections are called The Software of Creation, The Codes of Creation, and The Hardware of Creation. Here's how he explains things:

> G-d had a desire. Exactly what that desire is, no one knows—at least not yet. The Messiah is not here. And we cannot truly understand G-d's desire . . . until the coming of the Messiah. . . . The next stage entailed mapping out that desire in full; in other words, writing the software. The Torah is the software. . . . If we would have the spiritual microscope to penetrate into the depths of the mystery of the

---

* No we don't—and neither does the comedian Jon Stewart, who, it is said, once offered this comment in one of his old stand-up routines: "Thou shalt not kill. Thou shalt not commit adultery. Don't eat pork. I'm sorry, what was that last one? Don't eat pork? Is that the word of God, or is that pigs trying to outsmart everybody?"

Torah, we would find everything. As it is, only the Master Programmer knows all the intimate details and how everything fits—only the One who wrote the software can see it clearly.[15]

When Tauber tells us (echoing the eighteenth-century Talmudic sage known as the Vilna Gaon)[16] that everything is in the Torah software package, that's exactly what he means, and he says so in no uncertain terms: "When I say everything, I mean everything—as our Sages said: 'There is nothing missing from the Torah.' Not only the universe and the planet Earth, but every human being who was, is and will be; his birth, his death, his family, his job; his height, weight, hair color, eye color—everything, even his telephone number and social security number. All are in the Torah!"[17] The rabbi offers us an image that we are all just life's computer operators working with a software package (the Torah) written by that Great Programmer in the Sky. As mere mortals, we are incapable of understanding the software, so we should just accept it and follow its screen prompts (the commandments) to live the proper moral life.

Before we get too carried away with the rabbi's homey computer analogy, let's bring the discussion back to reality. It is true that people operating computers don't need to understand the science that makes their computers work, and that most simply follow the instruction manual and/or screen prompts to achieve the desired results. But there *are* people who *do* know how computers work. Lots of them. Thousands upon thousands of computer scientists—the people who design the computers and write the code—and even many technicians understand hardware and software down to the minutest detail.

If for any reason computer operators do want to know how the hardware and/or software works, they are not going to be satisfied with being told that there is an explanation but it is hidden from them. They are going to get an explanation based on fact, science, and logic, either from a computer scientist or from books written by computer scientists or technical writers. Nothing is hidden from the computer operators. It's all there for them to see if they are so inclined. Nor are they going to be satisfied with the silly explanation that they are working on a "secret assembly line," not knowing what they are actually doing—but not to worry, they'll "see it when [they] get there."

The fact is, the hidden-meaning gambit is a very weak move. I can't explain something that doesn't make any sense to you, so I'll tell you that there is an explanation, but we can't see it because it is hidden from us. Nobody can argue with this statement. If you *want* to believe, you accept it on faith. Otherwise, you reject it on logic.

If the hidden-meaning gambit doesn't work, the Orthodox have one last card to play: If you can't see The Truth, it's your fault, not ours. A good example is provided in the foreword to Rabbi Gottlieb's *Living Up . . . to the Truth,* in which the reader is told, in essence, that if he buys the rabbi's argument he has an open mind, and if he doesn't buy it he has a closed mind. "Apparent deficiencies in [Rabbi Gottlieb's] arguments can often be resolved by simple introspection on the part of you, the reader."[18] What the Orthodox are really doing here is employing one of the standard devices used by cultists in tracts aimed at the indoctrination of initiates: warning the reader that if he doesn't see the truth of what is written, it is not the fault of the argument, but rather a failure on the part of the reader.

This tactic is reminiscent of a technique often used by stage hypnotists in their heyday. After getting a group from the audience up on stage, the hypnotist would explain that hypnosis had been proven to work with almost all people, and that the more intelligent a person is, the more susceptible he or she is to hypnosis. The volunteers are then faced with the decision whether to cooperate with the hypnotist or be judged to be of less than average intelligence by the audience.

The less we know about a phenomenon, the more amazing and inexplicable it seems. This is obviously true of natural phenomena the underlying processes of which we don't understand—fire to the earliest human beings, gunpowder to the early Native Americans, impressive chemical reactions to the high school chemistry student. But it is equally true of historical phenomena the fundamental processes of which may be easily understood, but not the detailed unfolding.

When the Orthodox rabbis offer us proof that the text of the Torah, miracles and all, is an accurate history of the ancient Jewish people written by God—and hence a divine guide for our moral behavior—it calls to mind the shaman igniting a torch in front of an astonished tribe. Neither of these performances—not the shaman's, not the Orthodox rabbis'—is evidence of supernatural forces at work.

And if anyone tells you that apparent glaring deficiencies in the Orthodox claims can be resolved by introspection on your part, thank him politely for the keen insight—and try very hard not to laugh.

CHAPTER TWELVE

JUDGMENT DAY

THE JESUITS USED TO SAY that if you gave them a child until he was seven, they would give you a lifelong Christian. When religious stories and doctrines are learned at an early enough age, they become perceived as common knowledge. That is why Orthodox doctrine would not be convincing to an adult raised in the Hindu tradition (and, conversely, why the Hindu sacred texts would rarely convince an adult raised in the Jewish or Christian traditions). The variety of subtle ways in which the Orthodox arguments beg the question are far more transparent to a person raised outside the tradition than they are to a person raised within it.

One reason that begging the question—the fallacy of assuming, directly or indirectly, the conclusion to be proven—is such a seductive trap in a discussion of biblical texts is that the stories in those texts are so familiar that we easily mistake them for common knowledge. Everyone knows that Jericho was a great walled city before it was conquered by the Israelites. That *must* be historical fact, recorded somewhere else besides the Bible. So, given this ostensible fact, how can we possibly account for the city's conquest by a primitive, untested army unless it was with God's miraculous intervention? Doesn't this give us proof, or at least strong evidence, that an actual miracle occurred? The answer, of course, is no.

We easily overlook the undeniable fact that, when it comes to all the events described in the Torah's texts that are crucial to Orthodox dogma, we have only one source of evidence for those events, and that is the Torah's texts themselves. We overlook this in part because such an abundance of material has subsequently been written about those events and texts. There is an enormous amount of Judaic scholarship, Christian scholarship, and Islamic scholarship, all presenting the "authentic" interpretation of the texts and elaborating on the doctrines contained therein. Armies of rabbis, priests, and mullahs are proclaiming the truth of those texts, albeit with very different interpretations. How much weight should we give to these secondary sources? How much should we defer to one or the other of these theological traditions? If our concern is with the truth, the answer is very little, if at all.

Distilled to its essence, what the Orthodox have done is to pose a factual question about the historical accuracy of the Torah's texts. To answer this question, should we give more weight to the conclusions of rabbinical scholars in past centuries, all basing their scholarship on exactly the same collection of ancient texts? Or should we give more weight to modern biblical scholars, who have the advantage of being able to avail themselves of the wealth of real historical and archeological evidence uncovered in the past quarter century? The exponential increase in human knowledge forces us to discount heavily the conclusions of even the most brilliant thinkers of the past. Aristotle may well have been the most brilliant scientist ever. Yet, if we need to build a bridge or treat a sickness today, there is no question that we are much better off listening to a qualified, albeit less brilliant, modern engineer or doctor than referring back to Aristotle's scientific treatises.

If we *assume* a priori that most of the Torah is a historically accurate description of ancient Jewish history, then it is a good bet that we would be able to come up with internal arguments to "verify" a few of the events in the rest. This is the question-begging methodology that religious believers often rely on. But this methodology can *at best* show the internal consistency of the document (that is, after the more obvious inconsistencies are explained away through selective reconstruction of the text). And the fact is, internal consistency is no proof at all of the truth of anything. The internal consistency of *Mein Kampf* is not proof that Nazi dogma is true. The internal consistency of *Das Kapital* is not proof that communist dogma is true. And the internal consistency of the Torah—if indeed it *is* internally consistent—is not proof that the dogma of Orthodox Judaism is true.

If we are genuinely in search of the truth, it is incumbent on us to seek out credible, independent sources of evidence. And, as we have seen, what the objective evidence tells us, and tells us very convincingly, is this:

- The story of the patriarchs is pure myth and legend.

- The real history of ancient Israel was pretty much the same as that of the other contemporary cultures in the ancient Near East, subject to the same kinds of historical and environmental forces as its neighbors.

- At most there was only a handful of Israelites in Egypt in the thirteenth century BCE, and they were there as part of the normal migratory ebbs and flows caused by the impact of climate on the food supply.

- The exodus described in the Torah never happened.

- There was no "nation of Israel" wandering in the Sinai desert for forty years.

- There was no revelation at Mount Sinai witnessed by two million people.

- There was no conquest of Canaan. The Israelites were living peacefully in Canaan all along and, indeed, were Canaanites themselves.

- The so-called united kingdom of David and Solomon had little of the grandeur ascribed to it in the Bible.

- The two kingdoms of Israel and Judah did not result from the breakup of a united kingdom. There were always two kingdoms: a flourishing Israel in the north and an economically backward Judah, with Jerusalem as its capital, in the south.

- Most of the events predicted in the famous prophecy in Deuteronomy 28–30 did not come to pass, including the most fundamental prophecy of all.

- The Torah contains unambiguous errors of zoological fact.

- The Torah's so-called hidden codes are just so much humbug.

- Jewish survival can be explained naturally, without recourse to divine intervention.

- The Torah was written by human beings and reflected the sociopolitical realities of the places and times where and when it was written.

Are we being too tough on the Orthodox? Are we requiring too much, imposing the impossible standard of irrefutable proof? I'll let you judge that for yourself by examining a famous biblical passage. The Assyrian siege of Jerusalem (which would have taken place around 700 BCE) is described thus in 2 Kings 18: The Assyrian general tries to convince the defenders of Jerusalem to give up or die. But that night an angel of the Lord kills one hundred and eighty-five thousand Assyrian soldiers in their camp. The Assyrian king Sennacherib then retreats to his capital of Nineveh and soon thereafter is killed by his own sons. It is a captivating tale of the power of faith, where God delivers the pious Hezekiah and his city from the invaders.

The Assyrians, however, tell quite a different story. The Annals of Sennacherib (as translated by Luckenbill in 1927, and still the best edition we have) describe how Sennacherib "shut [King Hezekiah] up in Jerusalem, his royal city, like a caged bird," but otherwise laid waste to the entire kingdom in Judah. Sennacherib does not claim that he captured Jerusalem in this campaign, but the Assyrian texts clearly reflect the massive Assyrian defeat of the kingdom of Judah.

Rabbi Dovid Gottlieb, in *Living Up . . . to the Truth,* claims that just because the Bible disagrees with another ancient source, we should not assume that it is the Bible that is wrong—and that, if we do, we are being unfair and harboring "a hidden prejudice against the Bible."[1]

Of the two accounts, the archeological record supports the Assyrian version. Amy Dockser Marcus, in her book *The View from Nebo,* adds the following comment:

> It's not important that the Assyrian account of the campaign, which mentions that Jerusalem was put under siege and avoids destruction only because Hezekiah agrees to become an Assyrian vassal and pay tribute to Sennacherib, doesn't match the Bible's description. Or that Assyrian records indicate that Sennacherib apparently lived for another twenty years after the war in Judah, and wasn't killed immediately after his return from Jerusalem, as the Bible implies. These points don't matter because [the Bible] is a theological narrative, concerned with Jerusalem's miraculous deliverance.[2]

Gottlieb is quite correct in saying, "When there is a contradiction between the Bible and [other] ancient sources, then the question has to be raised: How can we best understand the nature of the contradiction, and which source do we rely upon?"[3] Well, in the sharp contradiction described above, which source *do* we rely on? The Bible story, in which an angel of the Lord slays one hundred and eighty-five thousand Assyrian soldiers and saves the day for the righteous King Hezekiah? Or the Annals of Sennacherib, which, according to Finkelstein and Silberman (writing in *The Bible Unearthed*), "mesh perfectly with the grim archeological remains of the devastating Assyrian conquest of Judah?"[4]

The fact is, we are not demanding irrefutable proof of what the Orthodox claim is true. We would be if the alternative scenarios were wild and unlikely hypotheses we had dreamt up out of whole cloth. But the alternative scenarios that the Orthodox either ignore or disparage were not dreamt up at all. On the contrary, they constitute the

very best judgments of the community of objective academic authorities (including eminent liberal Jewish authorities) on the ancient history of the Jews. If we are weighing objective evidence, these alternative hypotheses are considerably more likely to be true than are those
that the Orthodox presuppose in their question-begging assumptions.
Surely, paying attention to the judgments of serious, highly qualified
academic historians and archeologists is not setting the bar too high.

We have now, quite literally, reached the moment of truth.

The Orthodox try their best to undercut all the evidence against
their fundamentalist dogma by saying that, because the Torah contains its own set of values, if we try to assess those values by means of
any external standard—such as the standard of Western scholarship,
which is rational logic applied to as much credible empirical evidence
as we can amass—then we have already decided not to treat the Torah
as true. But this is an incoherent argument. It confuses assessment—
the attempt to determine the correctness or incorrectness of a body of
doctrine—with one possible result of that assessment.

The preponderance of evidence—*the overwhelming preponderance
of compelling empirical evidence*—leads us to the inescapable conclusion
that the Torah is not the work of God, but of human beings—human
beings, who wrote the Torah not to record an accurate history *of* a
people but to create a history and a theology *for* a people. As such, the
Torah's stories are not history but a mix of myth, fable, and legend.
Nor are its commandments the divine, immutable law binding on all
Jews for all time that the Orthodox claim them to be.

Now, if you are sufficiently determined to maintain the fundamentalist position, you can inoculate yourself against the facts, severing all
ties to logic and evidence, and adopt a stance that says, in effect,
"Don't confuse me with facts, my mind's made up. I believe!" But my
own view is that reason is the most reliable—perhaps our only—
access to the truth. If we are genuinely in search of the truth, it is
incumbent on us to seek out the best current evidence uncovered by
objective, impartial scholars. And then to make up our own minds
about what the evidence tells us.

What the evidence tells us is that *the Orthodox arguments are baseless*. The fact is, there is no credible, objective evidence whatsoever that supports the fundamentalist Orthodox claims (1) that God wrote the Torah, (2) that the Torah is an accurate history of the ancient Jewish people, or (3) that the Torah is God's instruction manual on the proper way to lead a moral life. You may reach this conclusion by a leap of faith, or by the warped logic in Dovid Gottlieb's tract. But you will never get there from the empirical evidence and legitimate principles of reasoning.

* * * * *

Writing about Islamic fundamentalists, George Melloan, the insightful columnist for the *Wall Street Journal*, observed:

> Over the centuries, individuals given a real choice between personal freedom and strict adherence to religious law have usually chosen freedom. . . . The march of civilization toward better-educated polities and a greater trust in science over superstition . . . favors the liberal democracies. Islamic [fundamentalism] is an effort to turn the clock back toward pious ignorance.[5]

So is Orthodox Judaism, an effort to turn the clock back toward pious ignorance.

What infuriates all religious fundamentalists about Western society is precisely this marked preference for personal freedom over the enforced discipline of strict religious law. I have never been a big believer in the theory that enforced discipline—not *self*-discipline, but the unquestioning obedience demanded by an outside authority—purifies the soul and makes for a better person. Unquestioning obedience is essential to the armed forces for their task of fighting wars, but it doesn't make children grow into better citizens, it didn't make priests who flagellated themselves bloody better Christians, and it doesn't make Jews who submit to all the strict Orthodox rules and regulations better Jews. I disagree with the proposition that holds that subjecting yourself to a series of morally unnecessary restrictions toughens you up spiritually and makes you a better person or, in the case of Orthodoxy, a better Jew.

I am not suggesting we do away with all limits on our behavior. Our code of democratically enacted laws allows us to live in harmony with others in our society. We are not permitted to harm other people, and we, in turn, are protected from other people harming us. Traffic laws requiring us to stop at red lights are designed to allow us all to drive on the roads in a safe and orderly fashion. But this clearly is very different from laws that demand we eat only a certain type of food served only on certain types of dishes (all other food and dishes being labeled "unclean"), that require us to wear a hat on our head, that forbid us from driving or even carrying anything—including a child—outside of the home or synagogue on the Sabbath, that tell us we can't shave with a razor blade, and on and on and on.

"Obeying an order was the most important thing for me. It could be that is the nature of the German." So said Adolf Eichmann early on in his memoirs published in 1999 by the German newspaper *Die Welt*. From the outset, in attempting to explain his role in the Holocaust, Eichmann strikes the overarching theme of unquestioning obedience (emphasis mine).

> My father raised me in a strict manner. I was an obedient boy. . . .
> From my childhood, obedience was something I could not get out of my system. When I entered the armed services at the age of twenty-seven, I found being obedient not a bit more difficult than it had been during my life to that point. . . . Now that I look back, I realize that a life predicated on being obedient and taking orders is a very comfortable life. *Living in such a way reduces to a minimum one's own need to think.*[6]

Yes, it does. It certainly does.

As the year 1999 was drawing to a close, the *Economist* published one of its signature in-depth pieces, a survey of the twentieth century called "Freedom's Journey." With great clarity the writer framed the fundamental issue of individual freedom versus strict adherence to religious law (emphasis mine):

The more telling pressure imposed by globalization is for the increasing adoption not of American products or ways, but of three American characteristics: freedom, equality and adaptability. . . .

Isaiah Berlin, an émigré Jew from Latvia and then an eminent political theorist at Oxford, gave the best summary of the century's basic issue in his 1958 essay on "Two Concepts of Liberty." This contrasted [real] liberty—individuals' freedom to make their own choices—with [false liberty,] the notion that people should be helped, or forced to do what was deemed to be in their best interests. The moral case against [the latter] is easy to see. The practical case against it is that those doing the deeming, even when well meaning, *are claiming a knowledge and certainty which they do not— and cannot—have.*

The extremes of [this] were seen in the false claims of communism. But they are also inherent in attempts, whether by conservatives, socialists or anyone else, to *force people to live in particular ways.*

We should take with us into the twenty-first century an awareness of the many acts of man that threaten our liberties and our freedom of choice, that are liable through *false claims of certainty* to send us in dangerous directions.

Let the final words belong to Thomas Jefferson: "The price of liberty," he wrote, is "eternal vigilance."[7]

PART II

UNDERSTANDING THE RELIGIOUS EXPERIENCE

CHAPTER THIRTEEN

ESCAPE FROM BONDAGE

I F I WERE TO ASK YOU which city had the largest Jewish community in America in the early nineteenth century, what would you answer? New York? Boston? Philadelphia? You'll probably be surprised to learn, as was I, that it was Charleston, South Carolina. In 1750 the Jews of Charleston had formed Beth Elohim, the fifth American Jewish congregation.

In 1824, cognizant of the reform of Orthodox doctrine and practices in Europe, several of the congregants of Beth Elohim no longer wanted to worship "as slaves of bigotry and priestcraft," but as part of the "enlightened world." They petitioned the rabbinical authorities to permit them to enact certain modest reforms to allow, as they put it in the document, "the free citizens of America to worship God in an enlightened fashion."[1] When their petition was, not surprisingly, rebuffed, in 1825 they formed the Reformed Society of Israelites. The Society's constitution couldn't have been plainer: "The great cause of many calamities with which mankind have been so often visited resulted from blind observance of ceremonial law, to the neglect of the essential spirit of [the] religion."[2] The society "equated Talmudic rabbis with the medieval monks and priests whose power and prejudice had held back the progress of civilization. Not only had the rabbis made false claims as to the authority of revelation, they had plunged Israel into a 'bondage of the mind deeper than Egyptian darkness.'"[3]

This declaration calls to mind Thomas Jefferson when he decried oppressive religion, swearing "eternal hostility against every form of tyranny over the mind of man."[4]

Indeed, in contrast to their European brethren, the men of the Reformed Society thought of themselves not as American Jews, Jews living in America, but as Jewish Americans. Michael A. Meyer, in his first-rate book *Response to Modernity* (a comprehensive, easy-to-read history of liberal Judaism), recounts an anecdote that forcefully illustrates this important distinction.

> In 1816, when Secretary of State James Monroe dismissed a man named Mordecai Noah from his post as U.S. consul in Tunis partly on religious grounds, Isaac Harby [whom Meyer calls the outstanding intellectual of the Society] wrote Monroe a letter in which he reminded him that in America, Jews were not, as in Europe, a tolerated sect, but rather a "portion of the people" and that it was on the basis of equal, unalienable constitutional rights that Jews were appointed to or elected to office. Of course, religious ties continued to exist in America, but they were less important than the political ones which united everyone: "I am not only Mr. Noah's *co-religion-aire*," [Harby] wrote, "I am his *fellow citizen*. The latter relation is in my mind infinitely stronger than the former."[5]

Orthodox Jews take a diametrically opposite position. In his book *On Judaism,* Rabbi Emanuel Feldman admits this important distinction with unusual candor. One of the basic tenets of Orthodox Judaism is that Jews should be "separate and apart." In fact, the Hebrew word *kadosh,* found throughout the Torah, usually translated as "holy," also means "separate and apart."[6] "Modern" Orthodox Jews don't like to emphasize this, as it smacks of self-imposed segregation—which, of course, is exactly what it is. Feldman is to be commended not only for not denying it, but also for unabashedly calling attention to it. At one point David (the fictional character he has created) declares: "[O]ne clear pattern is beginning to emerge. I detect one underlying motif beneath many of the [commandments], and that is an effort to ensure that Jews remain different and separate from the rest of the world. For example, our food laws certainly keep us apart from other people. As you yourself said, If we can't eat with others, that severely limits our interaction with them."[7] Yes, it does—and it is one of the most objectionable parts of Orthodox doctrine, one that gave powerful impetus to the liberal movement.

In 1885 a small group of liberal American rabbis met in Pittsburgh to formulate the first organized statement of the beliefs of the Reform movement in America. The result was a document called the Pittsburgh Platform of 1885. More than a hundred years later, the Central Conference of American Rabbis met, also in Pittsburgh, and issued a new set of guidelines, the Pittsburgh Principles of 1999. In the fall 2001 issue of the *CCAR Journal: A Reform Jewish Quarterly*, David H. Aaron contributed a penetrating essay* in which he argues that the Platform of 1885 is a more accurate reflection of liberal Judaism in America today than are the Principles of 1999, and in clear, concise language he explains what liberal Judaism is all about:

> Since the enlightenment, many Jews, including the forerunners of the Reform Movement, rejected the notion of Torah as a divinely revealed, eternally relevant document. Rather, as the 1885 framers wrote, Jews will continue to do what they have always done: to conceptualize Torah as myth, laws, and customs of the ancient era. . . .
>
> The writers of Pittsburgh 1885 rejected outright customs that offended their moral, their aesthetic, and their enlightened humanistic sensitivities . . . not only did Pittsburgh 1885 reject *ideas* they regarded as obsolete, they also rejected *practices* [such as dietary laws] contingent upon those discarded ideas. Such practices were the primitive products of antiquity and not integral to the eternally valid and progressive aspects of the Israelite religion that the early Reformers took up as central to their cause. . . .[8]
>
> Reform Judaism's critical doubts regarding life after death, the revealed nature of the Torah, and the efficacy of a whole gamut of ancient practices . . . have ultimately served to free it from falsehoods and ancient practices that have no place in the modern world.[9]

The Pittsburgh Platform of 1885 was ratified by the Columbus Platform of 1937 and again in 1976 at the San Francisco Centenary

---

* "The First Loose Plank—On the Rejection of Reason in the Pittsburgh Principles of 1999."

Perspective, where the Central Conference of American Rabbis made the following declaration. "It now seems self-evident to most Jews: that our tradition should interact with modern culture; that its forms ought to reflect a contemporary aesthetic; that its scholarship needs to be conducted by modern, critical methods; and that change has been and must continue to be a fundamental reality in Jewish life."[10] "In this very brief passage," Aaron concludes, "we find summarized the attitudes of Reform Judaism as it had been lived during the previous century."[11]

Rejecting the dogma of Orthodox Judaism does not mean that you are rejecting Judaism. The Orthodox, of course, claim that you are, because they define Judaism as Orthodox Judaism—or, as they like to say to camouflage their fundamentalism, "traditional" Judaism. But that's just the old rhetoric trick of truth by definition we saw earlier. Orthodox Judaism is not Judaism. It is *Orthodox* Judaism. You don't have to be Orthodox to be a Jew, any more than you have to be an evangelical to be a Christian.

Rabbi Bernard Bamberger's introductory essay for the Plaut Torah, "The Torah and the Jewish People," contains a subsection, The Torah and the Modern Jew, about which he says (emphasis mine):

> The last three centuries have seen a great upheaval in the religious thinking of Western man, in general, and of the Jew, in particular. The development of natural science has undermined belief in the supernatural and miraculous and, thus, brought into question the authority of all sacred scriptures. Philological analysis and historical criticism make it impossible to explain away errors of fact and, to us, unacceptable theological apprehensions and moral injunctions. All of these must be understood in their own context and their own time . . . we no longer feel the need to rationalize or justify *those things in the Torah which intellect forbids us to accept as true or conscience will not let us defend.*[12]

There are innumerable differences between the liberal and the fundamentalist brands of Judaism, such as how each views miracles, divine retribution, religious pluralism, gender equality, and prayer for God to grant personal wishes.* But the most important distinction by far, the one that underlies everything else, is the question of authority. Orthodox Judaism is grounded in God's revelation of the written and oral Torah. Whenever an Orthodox Jew is pressed for the source of authority for any action, ultimately the answer is, "God said so." An Orthodox young man I knew, a recent "returnee," explained it this way to an incredulous friend: "Let's face it. We're all slaves of God."

For the liberal Jew, by contrast, authority is vested in personal autonomy, in each individual's conscience. Religion is not only a matter of tradition. It is also a matter of individual choice. People have the right to choose for themselves how they will live.[13] That personal autonomy is anathema to the Orthodox should come as no surprise. Rabbi Eugene Borowitz succinctly frames the dichotomy:

> [Orthodox] Judaism does not allow individual Jewish conscience to determine which provisions of the law remain binding and which may be set aside. In Orthodoxy, the *halachah* [Jewish law] sets the limits of personal autonomy. [Liberal Judaism] holds that authentic Judaism does not require the acceptance of God's law as revealed to the prophets and interpreted by the rabbis, but may be derived from our present-day human understanding of what God demands of us as members of the covenant people. [For the liberal Jew,] personal autonomy determines the effective bounds of Jewish "law."[14]

The question of ultimate authority is not limited to Jews. The conservative columnist George Will noted that, as they watch the turmoil taking place in the Episcopalian Church, "Roman Catholics must be saying: 'We told you so.' For almost five centuries they have been warning that Protestantism has an incurable problem of doctrinal

---

* Rabbi Emanuel Feldman says: "Petitionary prayer is perfectly legitimate, and God welcomes it."[15] Rabbi Ezriel Tauber explains how Orthodox petitionary prayer works in practice: [The businessman] "comes to the office and gets a phone call. It is a prospective customer. Immediately he turns to G-d and prays: 'G-d, please let him accept my terms.'"[16] One is tempted to speculate what would happen if the guy on the other end of the line also happened to be an Orthodox Jew, who, before making the phone call, prayed: "God, please let him give me better terms."

instability. They say Protestantism lacks an authoritative, final voice on arguments about faith and morals."[17]

Liberal Judaism rejects such an authoritative, final voice on arguments about faith and morals, asserting, on the contrary, that a self-legislating ethos constitutes a major sign of proper human dignity. I commented earlier that the men of the Reformed Society of Israelites in early nineteenth-century South Carolina felt a strong connection to America. Professor Meyer makes this insightful observation, which to a large degree explains why liberal Judaism found a more congenial environment in America than in Europe:

> Individual authority in religious matters was the very hallmark of Reform, an ideal that could not flourish where it was thought suspect, if not dangerous. By contrast, individualism by the middle of the nineteenth century had become a fundamental component of Americanism. As propagated by Ralph Waldo Emerson, the doctrine meant a willingness to break sharply with the past, to rely on the sovereign self and almost never on tradition. The sublime, Emerson held, lay not in ritual, but in the moral nature of humanity, redemption not in the church but in the individual soul. . . . America would be different from Europe because it would reach forward, not back. America, Emerson said, "has no past, all has an outward and prospective look. . . ."
>
> Most Americans [of Emerson's era] possessed an inveterate optimism that held that their country would succeed where Europe had failed. Its new institutions would make possible the realization of human potential, which the Old World, trapped under the burden of its past, could never hope to achieve. Religion would, of course, play a role. But it would have to be the free man's faith, not imposed but self-chosen, more the product of individual experience than of inherited law and tenet.[18]

I am convinced that when a non-Orthodox Jew embraces Orthodoxy today, one of the strongest motivating factors is just the opposite of Emersonian individuality and courage. It is rather a terrifying fear of personal autonomy. The same is true of the Islamic fundamentalist. Remember Sayyid Qutb, the author of *In the Shade of the Qur'an*, whom we met earlier? He took much the same position. Qutb detested the West because its freedom and personal autonomy led, in his mind, to a libertine society hostile to the teachings of Islam. Much better to live in the protective shade of the Koran.

The Orthodox offer the shade of the Torah, a protection against Western freedom and personal autonomy that, in their minds, leads to a libertine society hostile to the teachings of Orthodox Judaism. Hence (as we saw so vividly in chapter 10) their blistering diatribes against the perceived evils of Western civilization. By scrupulously observing the law, which regulates every aspect of the way he lives—from morning to night, every day of the year, every year of his life—the Orthodox Jew willingly makes a trade-off: In exchange for giving up his individual authority, his personal autonomy of choice, and his freedom, he gets "protection" from what he perceives to be a secular environment that is wicked or, more likely, both wicked and perilous. But even in the extreme, even when, in addition to the perceived wickedness, hostility, and peril, an individual also feels personally alienated and lonely, when he has experienced a loss of self-esteem and the collapse of his humanistic values and wants to "recover" his Jewish identity, where is it written that this must be done by donning the straightjacket of Orthodoxy? In the Torah? As we have seen over and over again, that depends on how you read it.

It is true that by basing the legitimacy of religious authority on personal autonomy and individual choice, liberal Judaism does not offer the psychic security blanket of an unquestioning faith. But a strong case can be made that liberal Judaism offers the thinking Jew the best combination of universal moral aspiration and intellectual honesty, drawn from inside the Jewish heritage, with Jewish religious faith and ethnic loyalty. Further, this approach bespeaks a central religious intuition of modern Jewry: The deghettoization of the Jewish community must be accompanied by a deghettoization of Judaism. Modern Jews "know that leaving the ghetto was the right thing to do and . . . they are not going back there."[19]

This is why the essence of liberal Judaism is not mindless ritual. The fourth principle enunciated in the Pittsburgh Platform of 1885 states this position explicitly: "We hold that all such Mosaic and rabbinical laws as regulate diet, priestly purity and dress originated in ages and under the influence of ideas altogether foreign to our present mental and spiritual state. Their observance in our days is apt rather to obstruct than to further modern spiritual elevation."[20]

But lately there has been some backsliding in "official" Reform Judaism. Perhaps this is because some liberal Jewish leaders are seeking to provide a little more emotional security in what they perceive to be a more complex, more troubled and, hence, more insecure time. Whatever the reason, the Pittsburgh Principles of 1999 seemed to have adopted a more literal reading of the Torah and a return to rituals that the Pittsburgh Platform of 1885 had rejected more than a hundred years earlier.

In his *CCAR Journal* essay, Professor Aaron delivers a scathing rebuke of these new principles:

- There are no grounds for sustaining a belief in a divinely given Torah, nor is there a legitimate basis for preserving the (originally Greek) notion of an afterlife. . . . Of course, one is free to believe in such things, just as one is free to believe in creationism, or that the world is flat, but Reform Judaism has no reason to teach such ideas or to tolerate belief in them.

- If belief in immortality can be called scientific, rational and believable,[21] then the general position of the liberal Jewish community is being forced to regress to pre-Enlightenment standards of critical inquiry. Far from serving as liberation, this attitude constitutes an enslavement, one that entails shackling rational discourse to the superstitions and ignorance of pre-modern societies.

- The Torah is a work of ideology, not a neutral record of history. Mount Sinai is not a historical reality; it is an ideological reality, just as Jesus' resurrection is an ideological reality. . . . The ideology expressed [in the Principles] is precisely the ideology pursued by right-wing religionists in Israel and elsewhere, who argue that Jews have a God-given right to the Land of Israel, thereby discrediting automatically all conflicting claims.[22]

- To return Reform Jews to the pre-Kantian notion that the foundation of our sense of ethical obligation is derived from God is nothing other than reactionary.

- [We should] give up on vague, nostalgic principles of revelation, while insisting upon critical approaches to history and literature—approaches that will allow us, with integrity, to celebrate with joy the deep mythological and ideological origins that accompany our people's ongoing development and creativity.[23]

Aaron sums it up when he says that what's at stake is whether Reform Jews today accept "the irrationalism of this document or the rationalism celebrated by previous platforms."[24]

My own view is that Aaron's concept of liberal Judaism—with its unequivocal commitment to modernity, pluralism, and democracy—is much more the rule for the modern Jew than are the aberrations promoted by the framers of the Pittsburgh Principles of 1999.

When the great American writer William Faulkner went to Stockholm to receive the Nobel Prize for Literature in 1949, he gave a brief but memorable acceptance speech, which he closed with an eloquent message of hope for mankind. He said that man will not merely endure, he will *prevail*.

To my way of thinking, the Orthodox Jew endures, the liberal Jew prevails. I think the Americans who founded the Reformed Society of Israelites close to two hundred years ago would agree.

CHAPTER FOURTEEN

VOX POPULI VOX DEI

The voice of the people is the voice of God.

$\mathbb{M}$ORDECAI KAPLAN, who took liberal Jewish thinking to a new level, was brought to the United States from Lithuania in 1889 as a boy of eight. The son of an Orthodox rabbi, young Kaplan was captivated by the provocative ideas of Arnold Ehrlich, one of the most erudite Bible critics of the time. As Kaplan put it, Ehrlich wanted every intellectually responsible Jew to "penetrate through the vast layers of traditional commentaries to the rock-bottom intent of the biblical authors."[1] But Ehrlich was not the only contributor to Mordecai Kaplan's out-of-the-box thinking. A number of other noted scholars played a role in developing the ideas that would ultimately gain expression in his magnum opus, *Judaism as a Civilization.*[2]

At Columbia University, under the tutelage of Nicholas Murray Butler, an eminent scholar in anthropology and sociology, Kaplan began to see religious texts as cultural artifacts, pieces of literature that were best viewed as attempts to give expression to the deepest seated human need: the need for a substantive social solidarity that would provide each member of a community with a sense of belonging, warmth, and acceptance.

Gustav LeBon, the French social scientist and pioneer in the field of collective psychology, believed that religious feelings are fundamentally expressions of the need that individuals have for meaningful involvement in a community of like-minded compatriots. For LeBon, the specter of loneliness triggers in all people the desire to reach out to others, to join a community, and to make a meaningful contribution to it.

Already committed to systematically integrating the influences of group psychology into his theological views, Kaplan found his thinking reinforced and profoundly influenced by the work of John Dewey. It was Dewey's pragmatism that helped Kaplan conceptualize religious practices as requiring contextual, historical analysis if they were to be adequately understood.

William James's thinking reinforced Kaplan's ideas that the content and utility of religious practices can be evaluated only in relation to the complex historical matrix in which they unfold. More important, James's work was filled with one of the cardinal ideas that occupied Kaplan for his entire life: the critical importance of this-worldly salvation over the fantasy of eternal bliss secured from a benevolent, but ultimately distant, deity.

But the person to whom Kaplan owed the most was, unquestionably, Emile Durkheim. To understand the Judaism of Mordecai Kaplan, you must first understand the atheism of Emile Durkheim.

Emile Durkheim

Emile Durkheim, a French Jew (ironically, from a rabbinical family) whose life bracketed the end of the nineteenth and the beginning of the twentieth century, is generally recognized as one of the founders of modern sociology. In his landmark book *The Elementary Forms of Religious Life,* Durkheim put forth the powerful and iconoclastic theory that serves as the starting point for Mordecai Kaplan's theology: *A people precedes its religion.*

For Durkheim, religion is fundamentally a form of social organization. Or, put another way, religion is legitimate if its core practices and beliefs serve a valuable social function.[3] The earliest religious practices had the effect of fostering—perhaps were even designed to foster—efficient, stable social organization. Religion also plays an important *psychological* role in the lives of community members. It provides them with a symbol—a totem—that they can identify with and relate to.[4] Durkheim claimed that the need for a god, or more accurately the need for a totem, emerged as a result of the pressure for individuals, who were living in social groups without sharply delineated borders—and who were without science as an intermediary between them and their world—to unify themselves and provide a worldview from which everyday social life and adventure could be undertaken and understood. "Since neither man nor nature is inherently sacred," Durkheim concluded, "this quality of sacredness must come from another source. Outside the human individual and the physical world, then, there must be some other reality in which the kind of delirium that characterizes all religion, in a sense, takes on meaning and objective value."[5] That other "reality" is the totem and what the totem represents.

Durkheim made a compelling case that a people is prior to its religion. His step-by-step logic works like this:

1. In human prehistory, there was a desperate need for social solidarity and community organization. People had—and have—a deep need for social cohesion, and they prefer a coherent, comprehensive view of the world.

2. In most primitive societies, our best empirical evidence strongly suggests the need for cohesion, and a stable worldview became manifest through totemic forms of religious practice. Primitives identified with totems because they had a basic psychological tendency to do so, given their limited scientific knowledge and deep need for social cohesion.

3. So it is logical to conclude that the earliest forms of religion were based on collective desires and tendencies.

4. The totems later morphed into polytheistic and, then, monotheistic deities.

5. Therefore—and this is the crux of Durkheim's thinking—*our*

varied conceptions of God are created by natural processes and are real
only in the restricted sense that we created them.

Durkheim defined religious activity as the collective feelings and
ideas that both constitute a society's unity and personality and are
indispensable in helping people make moral choices. The scientific
method, after all, is not equipped to help individuals make moral
choices. However, even if one accepts the idea that there is a timeless,
universal need for any given society to unify itself through collective
feelings and ideas, why must we think that these feelings and ideas
need to be religious ones? Durkheim's short answer is that religious
feelings and ideas are distinctive. While other types of social glue
might tend to produce solidarity, religion does so by describing and
explaining the world, somewhat in the same general vein that science
does. Religion unifies through describing the world in a satisfactory
fashion, and that is what makes it unique.

Durkheim was an atheist,[6] so as far as he was concerned certain
kinds of religion—those based upon traditional conceptions of God
as a transcendental, omnipotent being—leave too large a role for non-
scientific (that is, supernatural) explanations of natural phenomena to
be viable in an enlightened world. In an oft-quoted passage, he
asserts: "One can affirm nothing that science denies, deny nothing
that it affirms, establish nothing that does not rest, directly or indirectly, on the principles borrowed from it. From then on, faith no
longer exerts the same hegemony as before over a system of ideas that
we can continue to call religious."[7] In other words, science—in the
business of describing and explaining the natural world—sets the
agenda that religious thinking must respect.

But, unlike many of his contemporaries, Durkheim did not believe
that science and religion were necessarily at variance with each other,
at least not in the sense that scientific methodology invalidates the
reality of religious belief and experience. Religion and science spring
from the same basic human desire: the general need to understand the
world and the specific, pragmatic need to be able to predict the
world's most important processes. But, with the advance of science,

the supernatural ideas generated by previous religious traditions are no longer necessary to promote social cohesion.

For Durkheim, the essence of religious activity is its social element. Religion unifies. Religion creates common interests and helps them to flourish. And, most important, religion helps preempt the anarchy that would threaten the very stability necessary for scientific inquiry and progress. What this means is that religion, as Durkheim broadly defines it, does not itself chafe against science (although specific religious beliefs certainly do), so the essence of religion is not threatened by science, nor will it be supplanted by science. This is because the essence of religion is really a complex form of social solidarity, which has historically required religious totems to facilitate group unification.

Durkheim's bottom line is this: Yes, human societies do create their particular religions in response to their deep sociological and psychological needs. Nonetheless, certain aspects of traditional religious beliefs are worth preserving in a modern world dominated by science—precisely so that they can continue to provide a vehicle for fulfilling some of humanity's most basic needs. Mordecai Kaplan reached exactly the same conclusion, but for different reasons. And it took him in a different direction.

Mordecai Kaplan

Emile Durkheim's basic thesis that a people precedes its religion constituted the foundation on which Mordecai Kaplan built his theology. But Kaplan was much less interested in dwelling on the philosophical and sociological implications of this revolutionary principle than in applying it to the American Jewish community he saw in the first third of the twentieth century. Durkheim provided (ironically, as he himself was an atheist) a detached philosophical defense of the continued relevance of religion in modern times. Kaplan was much more adept at illustrating the human concerns and interests at stake in the context of a living, breathing culture—or, as he himself might have put it, a civilization.

Kaplan faced distinctive challenges that Durkheim did not. As an activist leader in the American Jewish community, he felt a strong responsibility for articulating a new vision of Judaism. He did not think it necessary to create a grand narrative attesting to the reality and importance of God. Indeed, Kaplan was infamous for arousing the enmity of the Orthodox by arguing that their standard narrative was a bankrupt, dogmatic story that could not effectively speak to, much less guide, modern Jews.

It should come as no surprise that the Orthodox considered—and still consider—Kaplan's ideas to be a heretical rejection of Judaism. After all, they excommunicated him. But it should also come as no surprise that, as has always been the case when the Orthodox have been faced with any true innovation in Jewish thought or practice, they were dead wrong. Kaplan's objective was to revitalize Judaism, not to expose it as a bundle of practices and beliefs that could be summarily discarded.

In Judaism as a Civilization, Kaplan's principal concern was how the Jewish community could be reinvented, renewed, and remade—in a word, reconstructed. Emile Durkheim offered a new, sociological way to understand religion as a complex mélange of collective practices, a unifying social force, an association that brings people together by making explicit their common values, mores, and interests. Mordecai Kaplan shared this view (although not Durkheim's atheism), and he did something with it. He articulated a new religious vision for the Jewish people, a more modern, more dynamic, more realistic, and ultimately more ethical vision. On the basis of this vision he founded a new religious movement, Reconstructionist Judaism.

Both Durkheim and Kaplan were, broadly speaking, naturalists. Rejecting supernaturalism, they shared the belief that religion should not try to explain things that science is better equipped to account for or to endeavor to promote attitudes or practices that are at variance with science. In *Choices in Modern Jewish Thought,* Rabbi Eugene Borowitz explains that Kaplan's naturalism was an outgrowth of nationalism:

For Kaplan . . . the concept of society as divinely ordained—and hence unchangeable—gave way to that of a secular state founded on a social contract. . . . Nationalism brought the Jews emancipation, the end of ghetto existence, both physically and spiritually. After centuries of segregation, full participation in the life of the country entailed a radical change in their accustomed way of life and their manner of thinking about it. . . .

Kaplan uses the term *naturalism* to identify the way people in secular states think about the world. . . . Moderns limit their thought to this world and structure it in terms of the natural order. . . . Naturalist religious thinking focuses on people and their welfare rather than God or God's purposes.

[Kaplan's] theological humanism revolutionizes the classic religious emphasis on supernatural revelation, miracles, and otherworldly salvation. Not just God's word, but God, too, must be found in, not above, the natural order; miracles are dismissed as unscientific, and this world, the only one human beings can know, must be the place in which they seek salvation.[8]

Where does God fit into Kaplan's thinking? Because both Kaplan and Durkheim were naturalists, much of what Kaplan says is consistent with Durkheim's logic of the evolution of the concept of the totemic God. But the two present very different conceptions of God. Durkheim believed that our substantive conceptions of God are fantasies of our collective imagination, that we made God up to suit our social needs. Kaplan concedes that our specific conceptions of God may be nonsense, but at the same time he insists that the basic urge to project and respond appropriately to humanity's sundry conceptions of God is natural, healthy, and legitimate.

Kaplan's God is an umbrella term for the bundle of emotions and dispositions bound up in the community's will to live, a projection that human beings can legitimately believe in, the force that is "immanently manifest" in a given social group. This abstract conception of God is one of the driving themes in *Judaism as a Civilization,* and in it Kaplan thought he had found a totem that was scientifically respectable and, at the same time, capable of unifying the Jewish people if they chose to recognize its power.

In *The Meaning of God in Modern Jewish Religion*,[9] Kaplan further explains that, in accepting the abstract conception of God (as community will) outlined in *Judaism as a Civilization*, Jews would be able to achieve what many would now call self-realization. However, this would require them to revise the belief that they are God's "chosen people," a belief to which many Jews were (and many still remain) deeply wedded.

Kaplan holds that the traditional doctrine of election (the Jews as God's chosen people) is so absurd on its face that it could never be sustained in the modern world. There are simply too many educated Jews who would never accept it. Instead, he advocates a new doctrine of election, one based on moral excellence. He argues that, because cultural difference is not to be valued for its own sake, Jews must understand that effectively fostering group solidarity requires living "up to a higher ethical standard than the average." After all, "no other justification for our remaining an identifiable minority will avail."[10]

In a post-Enlightenment world, Kaplan asserts, social solidarity has to come with a price for any group that seeks it, and the Jews are no exception. Social solidarity has to be built upon a strong foundation, and since the traditional doctrine of the Jews as God's chosen people has proven itself unstable, what will take its place is the desire for moral excellence.

In this sense Kaplan is perfectly aligned with other liberal Jewish thinkers of that general era. Kaufmann Kohler, one of the framers of the Pittsburgh Platform of 1885, took the position that Judaism is not to be understood as law, but as the eternal moral idea. For Hermann Cohen, often called the Jewish Kant, ethical monotheism is the heart of Judaism. Where Kaplan differs from Kohler, Cohen, and the other liberal Jewish thinkers of that era is in his view that Judaism is the Jewish people's *civilization*. For Kaplan, an evolving civilization is characterized by the social forms through which the folk expresses itself. And one of the most important forms of expression in any civilization is the relationship of the people to the law. Borowitz explains how Kaplan views this relationship as it pertains to the Jewish people and to Jewish law (emphasis mine):

> In pre-modern days Judaism's major folk acts were authorized as religious duties . . . commandments given by God. But in a democratic society, Jewish law must be the community's participatory legislation of its standards. The law is not the creator of the people. The folk creates "law" as another facet of its civilization to serve the needs of the people. Thus construed, the law can be changed as needed or created as deemed fitting . . . rather than limiting change to what the traditional processes of the law might allow (which is often retrograde). . . . Where [Orthodox] Judaism spoke of God giving the Torah, thereby constituting the people of Israel, Kaplan argued it was the other way around, that *the Jewish folk created its culture, its Torah and its religion, climaxed by its idea of God.*[11]

There is some irony in the fact that Kaplan, a theologian who eschews traditional religious practices that make little or no sense, takes ritual to be an important part of modern Judaism. How could ritual be so important in the view of someone who wants to excise practices that are backward, who wants to do away with religious activities that don't seem to belong in the modern world? Because, Kaplan claims, ritual allows individuals to identify with Judaism and to reinforce the social and communal structures necessary for the survival and flourishing of the renascent Judaism that Kaplan intended to nurture.

Interestingly—and unlike Durkheim, who holds that what is meaningful and significant about religious ritual is its content—Kaplan believes that the content of religious beliefs and ritual is pretty irrelevant, going so far as to say, "The recital of the *Shema Yisrael* is traditionally one of the most dramatically meaningful practices of Judaism, not because of the abstract idea of absolute monotheism which it is supposed to express, but simply because it provides an occasion for experiencing the thrill of being a Jew."[12] "Thrill" may be a bit much, but what Kaplan is saying here is that Jews value religious practices not for the specific words they are reciting, but because those practices are accompanied by certain agreeable feelings, in some cases intensely emotional agreeable feelings, that bind them to the Jewish community past and present. In other words, what is important is not what you say or what you do, but what you *feel* when you say or do it. Kaplan's insight in this regard has important biological implications that I shall examine in the next chapter.

This thesis is quite consistent with Kaplan's Reconstructionism. For although it is true that he was interested in undermining Orthodox Judaism because it is completely incongruent with science, he was really much more concerned with finding a form of Judaism that would address the spiritual needs of modern Jews without rubbing science the wrong way. To be workable, this theology must be faithful to the distinctive aspects of the Jewish religious culture, broadly consistent with a scientific worldview, and congruent with religious pluralism. But this is not enough. You also have to distribute the new, reconstructed theology to its adherents effectively—and this effective distribution is the role played by ritual and religious ceremony.

Yes, but *how much* ritual is enough to achieve this objective? According to Kaplan, a lot. More, in fact, than Reform Judaism calls for. Much more than I, for one, am willing to accept. And this is why, although I am a great admirer of Mordecai Kaplan, I get off his train before it reaches the Reconstructionist station.

Emile Durkheim's great insight was that a people precedes its religion, that religion is a natural phenomenon, sociological in nature, created because it is necessary to meet both the deep-seated psychological needs of the individual and the pragmatic social needs of the group. These are principles that probably have atheistic or at least agnostic connotations for most people, but Kaplan used them to develop a complete Jewish theology for a rapidly changing world.

You have to admire Mordecai Kaplan. We may find it a little hard to grasp his abstract conception of God. We may object to his insistence on a great deal of ritual. And although Reconstructionist Judaism is alive and well, it never came close to fulfilling Kaplan's vision of unifying Jewish culture completely and comprehensively. Be all that as it may, the fact remains that close to three-quarters of a century before modern archeology would prove him right beyond a shadow of a doubt, Mordecai Kaplan courageously took the unpopular position that the doctrines of Orthodox Judaism are false. In fact, he turned Orthodoxy completely on its head. The Jewish people don't serve the law, as the Orthodox would have us believe. *The law serves the people*. Even more basic, Judaism did not create the Jewish people, as the Orthodox would also have us believe. *The Jewish people created Judaism*.

CHAPTER FIFTEEN

UNDERSTANDING THE RELIGIOUS EXPERIENCE

The human mind evolved to believe in the gods . . . [not] in biology.
—E. O. Wilson

HERE ARE TWO STATEMENTS that were reported in the press. See if you can guess what they are describing:

> She felt a palpable sense of God's presence and an absorption of her self into his being.

> You can feel his presence here. . . . I don't understand the phenomenon myself, but you feel it.

The first statement is a description of what a Franciscan nun felt during the most intensely religious moments of a forty-five-minute prayer.[1] The second statement was made by a middle-aged woman who is a frequent visitor to Graceland, and the presence she felt was that of the late Elvis Presley. She went on to say, "As many times as I've been here, I've never really lost that feeling." A man who had accompanied his mother to Graceland added, "It's like its own kind of religion." And a British tourist: "It's a bit scary. . . . He's their God, isn't he."[2]

I mean no disrespect to the nun, nor am I equating her devout Catholicism with the reverence in which the visitor to Graceland holds the departed Elvis. All I am doing is comparing what these two

people—who on the surface could probably not be more different—
felt at a particular moment, because what they both felt may offer us
a clue to a crucial aspect of religious belief: the biological makeup of
the human brain.

In the last two chapters we examined the sociological and psychological bases of religion in general (Emile Durkheim) and of Judaism
in particular (Mordecai Kaplan) and the philosophical basis for
Judaism—moral excellence—developed over the past 150 years by a
number of liberal Jewish thinkers, Kaplan included. Let us now turn,
in this final chapter, to the idea that the sociological, psychological,
and philosophical development of a religion—any religion—has as its
necessary underpinning a *biological* component, a human brain that is
"wired" to accept spirituality.

Harvard's E. O. Wilson, whose provocative observation I cited at
the top of the chapter, is one of the world's leading zoologists. He is
also a pioneer in the new field of sociobiology. In 1998 Wilson wrote
a book called *Consilience* in which he expounds on two central ideas:

- Science and the humanities should be unified and should convey
  their respective truths in the same tongue, with essentially the
  same vocabulary.

- Epigenesis should guide us in attempting to understand the natural world and our place in it.

Epigenesis, a concept drawn from evolutionary biology, refers to the
innate operations in the sensory system and brain that allow organisms
to find rapid solutions to problems encountered in the environment.
Wilson explains epigenesis this way: "With epigenetic rules, we see a
rainbow in four basic colors and not in a continuum of light frequen-
cies. We avoid mating with a sibling, speak in grammatically correct
sentences, smile at friends, and when alone fear strangers in first
encounters. Typically emotion-driven, epigenetic rules in all categories
of behavior direct the individual toward those relatively quick and accurate responses most likely to ensure survival and reproduction."[3]

Science and the humanities are indeed under increasing pressure to provide complementary explanations of specific kinds of phenomena. But is Wilson carrying this drive to reconcile the harder, empirical sciences and the softer, interpretive sciences too far when he asserts that the best epigenetically informed explanation of religion we have is that we are biologically hardwired for religion's characteristic tendencies and beliefs? Is a certain configuration of the brain necessary for religious experience? Has the human mind evolved to believe in the gods? In God?

While his term *hardwired* might not be the most accurate shorthand description, recent scientific findings indicate that Wilson could well be on the right track. In 2001 Dr. Andrew Newberg, of the University of Pennsylvania, and his late colleague, Eugene d'Aquili, wrote a book on the neurobiology of religion and spirituality. In this book, called *Why God Won't Go Away: Brain Science and the Biology of Belief*,[4] and in a paper published the same year in the scientific journal *Psychiatry Research*,[5] Newberg provides solid evidence for the view that identifiable neural activity is associated with religious or meditative experience. Newberg's key finding is that, regardless of the specific religion, the human brain has evolved to treat spirituality exactly the same way. This finding lends scientific support to Wilson's thesis that spirituality and religion—all religions—have a basic biological foundation common to every human being.

This is not to say—and Wilson is not saying it (neither is Newberg)—that just because a religious experience can be traced to neurobiological roots it is not an authentic experience. The fact that romantic love may also have an important neurobiological component doesn't detract in the slightest from the genuine emotions of those experiencing it or make their experience any less valid. What Wilson is saying is that the evolutionary process of natural selection has configured our brains to be especially receptive to spirituality.

It should come as no surprise that natural selection—often called Darwinian evolution, or simply evolution—is anathema to all religious fundamentalists, Orthodox Jews included. Whenever the Orthodox are confronted with the unavoidable scientific reality of natural selection and biology, they become very defensive, because to accept evolution is to accept Darwin's naturalist maxims, (1) that all life springs from earlier life in an unbroken tree of life, (2) that everything is accomplished by natural forces, and (3) that there is no credible evidence that supernatural breaches of nature ever took place. The Orthodox become defensive for the simple reason that if you accept Darwin's naturalism, you logically must reject the dogma of Orthodox Judaism. Naturalism is the antithesis of fundamentalism.

The problem for the Orthodox—and for all religious fundamentalists—is that it is becoming increasingly difficult to dispute the truth of evolution, because modern molecular biologists are proving Darwin right. Using new DNA technology they can now determine a branching tree for all plant life, with all plant species going back to a single plant algae. Taking this one step further, scientists are working on a single tree of life for *all* life, plant and animal (including human) alike, tracing it back to one source. The fact is, molecular biology has reached the point at which most scientists no longer consider evolution a theory. They consider it a historical fact.

This hasn't stopped conservative Christian groups across the country from mounting a broad attack on the teaching of evolution in the public schools. In 2004 the school board in Dover, Pennsylvania, ruled that biology teachers must read a statement to their students, telling them that "Darwin's theory of evolution is a theory . . . not a fact," and that "intelligent design is an explanation of the origin of life that differs from Darwin's view." A year later the citizens of Dover voted to oust this school board and replace it with a new board whose first action was to rescind the previous board's decision and to toss intelligent design out of the science classes. In reaction, Pat Robertson had this to say on the Christian Broadcasting Network's 700 Club:

> I'd like to say to the good citizens of Dover: if there is a disaster in your area, don't turn to God. You just rejected him from your city. . . . God is tolerant and loving, but we can't keep sticking our finger in his eye forever. If they have future problems in Dover, I recommend they call on Charles Darwin. Maybe he can help them.[6]

At roughly the same time that the Dover school board decision was being thrown out, the Kansas Board of Education, by six votes to four, went the other way, approving new public school science standards that cast doubt on the theory of evolution. This vote was a victory for the supporters of intelligent design.

Some "modern" Orthodox have also latched onto the theory of intelligent design as a way to reconcile creation with the world being billions, not thousands, of years old. They assert that they do not accept Darwinian evolution, but they also reject creationism. Of course, this stance requires them to finesse as metaphorical the Torah's description of the creation of the world and man. All well and good, but the fact remains that with the exception of its proponents—many of whom have close ties to Christian fundamentalist organizations[7]— the scientific community is united in the opinion that intelligent design theory has no absolutely no basis in hard science.

"Devilishly clever" is how Dr. Jerry Coyne, a professor of ecology at the University of Chicago, describes how the theory of intelligent design is constructed. "It has an appeal to intellectuals who don't know anything about evolutionary biology, first of all because the proponents have PhDs and second of all because it's not written in the sort of populist, folksy, anti-intellectual style. It's written in the argot of academia." Dr. Leonard Krishtalka, a biologist and director of the University of Kansas Natural History Museum and Biodiversity Research Center, puts it more colorfully: "Intelligent design is nothing more than creationism dressed in a cheap tuxedo."[8]

Andrew Newberg's experiments, in contrast, follow the scientific method and lead to some thought-provoking conclusions. Newberg and d'Aquili started out with a basic hypothesis: "Spiritual experience, at its very root, is intimately interwoven with human biology. That biology, in some way, compels the spiritual urge."[9] Using the latest neuroimaging techniques, they studied the neural patterns first of Tibetan Buddhists "during the peak moments of meditation" and then of Franciscan nuns "during [their] most intensely religious moments," and found—in both cases—that the parts of the brain involved in focusing attention become engaged, but while this is happening, the areas of the brain that orient people in space become increasingly inactive. It is this second phenomenon, taking place in what neurobiologists call the "orientation association area" of the brain, that offers us the more powerful clue about what is happening when we are lost in meditation or prayer.[10]

Remember the Franciscan nun, who, during the most intense moment of her prayer, felt a palpable sense of God's presence and an absorption of her self into his being? This is how she described her feelings at that moment:

> I felt communion, peace, openness to experience. . . . [There was] an awareness and responsiveness to God's presence around me and a feeling of centering, quieting, nothingness, [as well as] moments of the presence of God. [God was] permeating my being.[11]

Now listen to how one of Dr. Newberg's colleagues at the University of Pennsylvania describes what he felt at the moment of peak transcendence when practicing Tibetan Buddhist meditation:

> There was a feeling of energy centered within me . . . going out to infinite space and returning. . . . There was a relaxing of the dualistic mind and an intense feeling of love. I felt a profound letting go of the boundaries around me and a connection with some kind of energy and state of being that had a quality of clarity, transparency and joy. I felt a deep and profound sense of connection to everything, recognizing that there never was a true separation at all.[12]

In both cases—the Tibetan Buddhists and the Franciscan nuns— Newberg and d'Aquili observed exactly the same neural changes: When they were in deep meditation or in deep prayer, the regions of their brains that orient people in space tended to become inactive. The result was that they experienced exactly the same kind of feeling, a feeling Newberg describes as losing the distinction between self and non-self.

It's a pity no Orthodox Jews were included in Newberg's study, as it would have been illuminating to observe the workings of their brains, too, when they were deep in prayer. It is likely he would have encountered exactly the same neural phenomenon; as the Orthodox Jews, wrapped in their prayer shawls, swaying back and forth, and chanting their prayers, become more deeply immersed in intense emotional feelings, the orientation areas of their brains would become increasingly less active and they would feel at one with God.

You will recall Mordecai Kaplan's emphasis on ritual as a means by which Jews can identify with their Jewish civilization. Without knowing it, Kaplan was tapping into the biological receptivity to spirituality and religion that Wilson theorized about and Newberg's studies have tended to confirm.

There is no denying that religious ceremonies are moving emotional experiences for the participants. This is the power of ritual, whether it be the celebration of the Virgin of Guadalupe in Mexico, the colorful ceremonies of an African tribe, Christmas Eve mass, or some of the haunting liturgy that is part of the services for the Jewish High Holy Days.* Newberg and d'Aquili offer the following observations about the biology of belief, the first of which should sound familiar (emphasis mine):

> Anthropologists have long understood that the rituals of early human societies performed an important survival function by fostering, among a given clan or tribe, a sense of specialness and common destiny. Through the powers of ritual, clan members are constantly reminded that they were the people favored by the particular deity they worshipped, and that they were, in some sense, *chosen*. . . .
>
> Until recent years, anthropologists largely agreed that the urge to perform rituals was purely a cultural drive. Societies performed

---

* One's emotional experience from a religious ceremony doesn't even have to be religious. On the afternoon of 9/11, I was driving in my car, my attention glued to the radio. The station began to broadcast a boys' choir in a cathedral somewhere in America singing "Amazing Grace." This is a Christian hymn to which I don't relate, but the sound of those innocent young voices singing the beautiful, lilting melody in a memorial to those slain brought tears to my eyes, and I had to pull over.

rituals, they believed, because humans had learned over time that ritual behaviors offered powerful social benefits. . . . [R]ituals do provide powerful social benefits, but our growing understanding of neurological function leads us to believe that the ritual urge may be rooted in something deeper than the cultural needs of a given society. It suggests, instead, that humans are driven to act out their myths by the basic biological operations of the brain.[13]

In 2001 *Newsweek* published an excellent cover story by Sharon Begley on Newberg's work called "Religion and the Brain," which explained with remarkable clarity and in laymen's terms the neurobiological phenomenon of ritual in the context of Newberg's studies:

[Rituals]—drumming, dancing, incantations—all rivet attention on a single, intense source of sensory stimulation. They also provoke powerful responses. That combination—focused attention that excludes other sensory stimuli, plus heightened emotion—is key. Together, they seem to send the brain's arousal system into hyperdrive, much as intense fear does. When this happens, one of the brain structures for maintaining equilibrium—the hippocampus—puts on the brakes. It inhibits the flow of signals between neurons, like a traffic cop preventing any more cars from entering the on-ramp to a tied-up highway.

The result is that certain regions of the brain are deprived of neuronal input. One such deprived region seems to be the orientation area, the same spot that goes quiet during meditation [and prayer]. And in those states, without sensory input the orientation area cannot do its job of maintaining a sense of where the self leaves off and the world begins. That's why ritual and liturgy can bring on what Newberg calls a "softening of the boundaries of the self"—and the sense of oneness and spiritual unity. Slow chanting, elegiac liturgical melodies and whispered ritualistic prayer all seem to work their magic the same way: they turn on the hippocampus directly and block neural traffic to some brain regions. The result again is "blurring the edges of the brain's sense of self, opening the door to the unitary states that are the primary goal of religious ritual," says Newberg.[14]

E. O. Wilson's thesis and Andrew Newberg's conclusion—that, regardless of the specific religion, the human brain has evolved to treat spirituality exactly the same way—is not uncontested. In an article entitled "Hardwired for God?" Christian de Quincy, professor of consciousness studies at John F. Kennedy University and managing editor of *IONS Noetic Sciences Review*, questions the hypothesis that God is merely an experience generated in the brain's neural pathways and suggests that, instead, it may be that "the brain has evolved to detect a genuinely divine presence greater than the brain."[15] Others frame the question in simpler terms: If Wilson and Newberg are right that the human brain is wired for spirituality, then it was God who did the wiring. Perhaps, but there is no legitimate, empirical evidence to support either of these hypotheses, any more than there is for the hypothesis that yes, human beings did write the Torah but they were divinely inspired. To accept any of these hypotheses as true requires an act of faith.

Moreover, Wilson's thesis does not purport to be the whole story explaining man's religious experience. As we have seen, there are important sociological, psychological, and philosophical components. What Wilson does is add the biological component. But what does this really mean? When we say that evolution has configured human beings in a way that renders them receptive to religion, what exactly are we saying about the human mind?

To answer this question, think of the human brain's responsiveness to spirituality in terms of the interaction of the hardware, the operating system, and the software applications of a computer—a device that to a certain extent simulates the human brain. Some, including Wilson, have talked about our religious receptivity in terms of hardware, but I don't think that is the best approach. If our responses to religion were really hardwired, everyone would have some sort of religious experience, in much the same way that everyone responds fearfully to perceived danger. But religious experience is not a feature of everyone's life. There are, after all, atheists and agnostics. Nor are religious experiences inevitable, impervious to the influence of culture, or completely beyond our control.

A better analogy, I think, is the operating system, the underlying software without which a computer would be largely inert. Though more malleable than hardware, it is the operating system that determines to a large degree what a computer is capable of doing. The operating system constrains the behavior of a computer over time, but code can be rewritten. This means that although the operating system software is stable, code can be altered so that the computer's basic functionality changes. In a similar way, the brain's operating system makes the basic responsiveness to religion possible. But it does not *require* the expression of that basic responsiveness (it allows for atheism), nor does it dictate the *form* a given expression should take (it allows for the diversity of religious traditions).

Whether our basic capacity for religious experience is used, as well as *how* that basic capacity is used, are matters determined by culture and history. A commitment to a particular religious tradition can be thought of as a software application. Our general receptivity to religion (the operating system) makes it possible to "install" that application, but our distinctive environments determine whether an application is installed and, if it is installed, how it will be configured. Bringing all this together:

- In the same way that the hardware innards of a computer—the circuit boards, microprocessors, and memory chips—make computing possible, so does the basic hardware of the brain make high-level cognitive functioning possible. Certain human responses are genuinely hardwired (such as fear responses to danger signals), and certain capabilities are precluded entirely.

- The operating system of the brain—itself a product of eons of evolution—enables specific kinds of capabilities, such as a receptivity to spirituality and religion. The brain's operating system is selected in complex ways in response to evolutionary pressures, so it can be modified to accommodate the surrounding environment. But it also remains robust and relatively stable over time.

• Commitments to particular religious traditions are, in effect, applications.* These applications are molded by the cultural and social pressures of their time and place.

Emile Durkheim's thinking fits perfectly into this analogy. His landmark insight that a people precedes its religion makes it clear that specific religious beliefs and practices—the applications—are the product of human culture, not manna from heaven above. Mordecai Kaplan would agree. Durkheim's (and Kaplan's) sociology integrates seamlessly with Wilson's contemporary neuroscience. Indeed, one directly supports the other, with the result that, taken together, both explanations are strengthened.

Durkheim makes the historical and normative claim that religious practices developed in large part out of the need for social cohesion and that they will survive only if they prove useful in the here and now. But he encourages us to be extremely skeptical toward dogmatic religion: "What science disputes in religion is not its right to exist but the right to be dogmatic about the nature of things, the kind of special competence it claim[s] for its knowledge of man and the world."[16] For Durkheim, the function—the extremely important function—of religion is to bind us to one another, forging the social ties critical to a community's survival and flourishing. Spirituality survived the scientific revolution precisely because it gave us something science could not, namely, solidarity.

Mordecai Kaplan built on Durkheim's ideas by focusing not on religion's historical tendency to promote social stability, but on the role religion might play in renewing the Jewish people. Because "the worth of a civilization depends not only upon the values and ideals it professes, but upon its ability to energize them,"[17] Kaplan believed that Judaism could survive only if it became a morally superior religious tradition and ethical force. He hoped to revitalize Judaism by

---

* In the world of high technology, the holy grail for all software application companies is what is known in high-tech jargon as a "killer app" (killer application). Unfortunately, as we have seen all too often, extreme commitment to fundamentalist religious dogma can become a killer app, literally.

shoring up its positive aspects and revealing what he took to be its moral myopia, arguing that religious traditions ought to be in the service of humanity, and not the other way around. The true object of religion should be the welfare of the people, not God and what we speculate to be God's will.

E. O. Wilson is concerned with the sociobiological origins of religious tradition and practice. His Darwinian theory, which the studies by Newberg and d'Aquili tend to confirm, holds that the human brain has evolved to be receptive to spirituality, to believe in transcendental beings or forces.

Contemporary neuroscience explains the biological origins of religious experience, but not its social precursors. It is Durkheim's work that illuminates those social origins, because he identifies the most basic purposes of religious activity. While Wilson asks, what makes religion neurologically possible? Durkheim and Kaplan ask, what is the purpose of religious activity? When we integrate the answers to these two questions, as I have attempted to do here, the important conclusion we come to is this:

> Sociobiological evolution has embedded in humanity a propensity toward religious behavior and spiritual sentiment. Laid on top of these biological predispositions are the multifaceted social pressures that lead different peoples to create different religions that will bind them together into communities that can survive and flourish.

In the mind of the religious fundamentalist this synthesis is, unfortunately, taken to an extreme where he loses all sense of proportion. Which is why every fundamentalist, regardless of his religion, knows that it is he, and he alone, who is in sole, certain, and complete possession of The Truth.

It is why Ali and Ari, two little innocents born in the West Bank city of Hebron on the same day with exactly the same basic neurobiological hardwiring, with exactly the same neurobiological operating system that evolved to make them receptive to spirituality, grow up with different installed sociological "applications"—that is to say, with the different doctrines, beliefs, and practices their respective religious communities imbued in their minds, the dogma that will shape their lives.

This is why Ari grows up to be an Orthodox Jewish settler, who believes with all his heart that the dogma of Orthodoxy is true and, therefore, represents the only true path to God. Ari knows that *all* the "Land of Israel" is his people's (the chosen people's) eternal inheritance, God's timeless bequest to the Jewish "nation" in the covenant. How does he know this? The Torah says so—and so do the Orthodox rabbis, repeatedly. He grows up hating Arabs and venerating people like the murderous Baruch Goldstein.

And this is why Ali grows up to be a fundamentalist Muslim, who believes with all *his* heart that it is the dogma of *Islam* that is true and, therefore, represents the only true path to God. Ali knows that Western civilization is wicked, degenerate, corrupt, and determined to repress Islamic truth and, indeed, the whole Muslim world. How does he know this? The mullahs say so, repeatedly. He grows up hating the Jews, whom he considers interlopers not only in the West Bank and Gaza, but also in Israel proper, and celebrating the murderous suicide bombers, who think nothing of killing innocent little children riding on a school bus.

And they both started out in life exactly the same, as innocent babes in arms.

But think for a moment what would have happened if, through some mix-up, Ari and Ali were switched at birth and went home from the Hebron hospital with the wrong families. Ari would become Ali, and Ali, Ari—and as they grow up each would have the "wrong" religious application installed. The real Ali would grow up as the Orthodox Jewish settler who hates Arabs, and the real Ari would grow up as the fundamentalist Muslim who hates Jews and wants to destroy Israel.

The irony would be funny were it not all so terribly sad. Religious fundamentalism is never funny.

A FINAL WORD

As we have seen, the evidence weighs heavily, very heavily, against the truth of Orthodox Judaism. If we apply the same principles of rational belief that we rely on in our everyday life, it is difficult—I would say impossible—to reach any conclusion other than that the dogma of Orthodox Judaism is not true. It is false.

I will go further. Far from being divine immutable law, the doctrines of Orthodox Judaism—like fundamentalist dogma everywhere—are an anachronistic absurdity in this day and age, and they spawn a pious ignorance that subverts independent thought. Independent thought is anathema to all fundamentalists. Instead, they ask you to check your brains at the door of life.

I find a great deal of truth in Mordecai Kaplan's concept of religion in general and of Judaism in particular. In much the same way that Abraham Lincoln envisioned America as a nation *of the people, by the people, and for the people,* Kaplan held that the Jewish religion came from and should serve the Jewish people, not the other way around as the Orthodox would have us believe. Kaplan also held that Judaism is a civilization that values the well-being and moral excellence of its people, rather than what some self-styled sages interpret to be the word and the will of God.

In the final analysis, isn't this what is really important? Not what you believe about God, the cosmos, and the like, but the moral standards by which you choose to live your life. Thomas Jefferson summed it all up very well when he wrote that "it does me no injury for my neighbor to say there are twenty gods or no God. It neither picks my pocket nor breaks my leg."[1]

For me, the choice between the personal freedom embodied in Western democratic values and the bondage of a fundamentalist religious law based on fallacious dogma is a no-brainer. I choose freedom. I hope you will, too.

* * * * *

NOTES

PREFACE

1. Before the Common Era; often referred to as BC, Before Christ.

2. The last execution for blasphemy in Britain was carried out on January 8, 1697, when a young University of Edinburgh student named Thomas Aikenhead was hanged for railing against the doctrines of Christianity, which he allegedly claimed were "a rapsodie of faigned and ill-invented nonsense," consisting of "poetical fictions and extravagant chimeras." He is reputed to have called the Old Testament "Ezra's Fables" (Unitarian Universalist Historical Society, http://www.25.uua.org/uuhs/duub/articles/thomasaikenhead.html). In the ensuing sixty years, Edinburgh evolved from "a dour near-theocracy to a cosmopolitan center," so that when "an ecclesiastical society attempted to excommunicate the freethinking Scottish philosopher David Hume . . . perhaps the most thoroughgoing skeptic in the history of philosophy . . . the motion failed by a vote of fifty to seventeen. Hume's chief tormentor, a splenetic clergyman named George Anderson, died a few months later and . . . 'an ecclesiastical era drew to a close'" (David Denby, "Northern Lights," review of James Buchanan, *Crowded with Genius* [New York: HarperCollins, 2003], *New Yorker*, October 11, 2004).

3. To a lesser degree, Old Testament scriptures are also an important underpinning of Islam. Eid al-Adha, for example, is an important religious festival that made the news at the end of 2006 when Sunni Muslims in Iraq were chagrined that Saddam Hussein was executed at the beginning of the celebration. Eid al-Adha calls for all Muslims to sacrifice a sheep, in strict accordance with Islamic law (which includes facing the sheep toward Mecca when its throat is slit), to "celebrate the story of Abraham's willingness to sacrifice his son to God [and to commemorate] God's reprieve, which allowed Abraham to kill a ram instead of his son" (Mary Jacoby, "Ritual Sacrifice? Not on My Street, Some Belgians Say," *Wall Street Journal*, January 4, 2007).

The influential radical sheikh Yusef Qaradawi, who is regularly featured on Al Jazeera, said that, as Muslims, "we believe in the Jewish and Christian scriptures. Our Islamic faith is not complete without them" (Dinesh D'Souza, *The Enemy at Home* [New York: Doubleday, 2007], 179).

4. Roland de Vaux, *The Early History of Israel* (Philadelphia: Westminster, 1978).

5. *Wall Street Journal,* January 17, 2005.

6. Leonard Pitts, "GOP's Disdain for Separating Church and State Bubbles Over," *Miami Herald,* September 3, 2006.

The economist and political observer Paul Krugman agrees with Pitts's assessment and sees Republican hostility to modern science as sending the message that "today's Republican Party [is] increasingly dominated by people who believe truth should be determined by revelation, not research" (Krugman, "An Academic Question," *New York Times,* April 5, 2005).

7. Lexington, "Belief and the Ballot Box," *Economist,* June 5, 2004.

8. Thomas L. Friedman, "War of the Worlds," *New York Times,* February 24, 2006.

9. Sam Harris makes the broader point that "criticizing one's faith is taboo in every corner of our culture, ... [but] our religious beliefs can no longer be sheltered from the tides of genuine inquiry and genuine criticism" (*The End of Faith* [New York: Norton, 2005], 13, 225).

10. In 2005 *Business Week* published a special report by William C. Symonds called "Earthly Empires—How Evangelical Churches Are Borrowing from the Business Playbook" (May 23, 2005). In the report, Symonds focused on what he called "a new generation of evangelical entrepreneurs [who are] transforming their branch of Protestantism into one of the fastest-growing and most influential religious groups in America. ... Says pollster George Gallup, who has studied religious trends for decades: 'The evangelicals are the most vibrant branch of Christianity.'" Conversely, Symonds writes, "the so-called mainline Protestants who dominated in the twentieth century have become the religious equivalent of General Motors."

In 2005 the *New York Times Magazine* ran a cover story on the trend toward evangelical megachurches, focusing on one in Surprise, Arizona, called Radiant Church, whose membership went from 350 in 1999 to 5,000 in 2005. That's a large membership, but there are some much larger. Lakewood Church in Houston, for example, has over 30,000 members. Radiant is an affiliate of the Assemblies of God, a Pentecostal movement (it was noted that John Ashcroft was a member) whose adherents treat the Bible as fact and believe in miracles, faith healing, and speaking in tongues. To all outward appearances Radiant is a laid-back church, but its founding pastor told the *Times* writer that his church must continue to add even more members because "churches that have stopped growing have stopped hearing the screams of people being sent to hell" (Jonathan Malken, *New York Times Magazine,* March 27, 2005).

11. Christopher Hitchens, *God Is Not Great* (New York: Twelve, 2007), 150.

12. Nicholas Kristof, "Liberal Bible-Thumping," *New York Times,* May 15, 2005.

Lest you think that Kristof—who says he "often writes about religion because faith has a vast impact on society"—is being melodramatic with this characterization, it might be well to recall that in 2006 President Bush said that he senses a

"Third Awakening" of religious devotion in the United States (Peter Baker, "Bush Tells Group He Sees a 'Third Awakening,'" *Washington Post*, September 12, 2006).

13. Pitts, "GOP's Disdain."

14. In the Op-Ed section of the *New York Times*, the editorialist Brent Staples commented: "I am descended from generations of preachers and evangelists, dating back to my great-grandfather.... My grandmother was an evangelist who married a Baptist minister.... My mother taught me to respect religion, but to be wary of people who use piety as a license to run other people's lives" (April 27, 2003).

INTRODUCTION

1. The Torah (from the Hebrew, meaning *teaching* or *instruction*), also called the "Five Books of Moses" or "the written Torah," comprises the first five books of the Hebrew Bible (the Old Testament). Christians often refer to the Torah as the Pentateuch, from the Greek and meaning *five cases.* Orthodox doctrine holds that, in addition to the written Torah, God gave the Jewish people, through Moses, an "oral Torah," comprising all the books of the Prophets, the Midrash, the Agadah, and the Talmud. For our purposes, the Torah will mean the first five books of the Old Testament. The book of Joshua is the sixth book, immediately following Deuteronomy. Biblical scholars generally agree that the person who wrote Deuteronomy also wrote the next six books as a continuation of the purported history of the ancient Jewish people. As a result, he is often referred to as the Deuteronomistic Historian.

2. James D. Bennet, "Crossing Jordan; The Exit That Isn't on Bush's Roadmap," *New York Times,* May 18, 2003.

3. *Ha'aretz* (Tel Aviv, English edition), January 6, 2005.

4. There are those who argue that the U.S. government is carrying the separation of church and state too far, claiming that the country was founded on Christian principles that remain an integral part of the nation. They would do well to consult Article 11 of the treaty with Tripoli, which was *unanimously approved* by the Congress and signed by President John Adams in 1797: "As the Government of the United States of America is not, in any sense, founded on the Christian religion . . . ."

5. I heard this myself on CBS radio, and the quoted words do not convey the depth of this man's anger.

6. The straw man is a common trick of rhetoric. It works like this. You set up a weak position that is not in fact held by your opponent and then make a big show of demolishing this straw man. Your audience will almost surely be convinced by your argument and agree with your conclusion—and almost equally surely will not recognize that your opponent, too, would agree wholeheartedly. This is a way to convince an audience that your arguments and conclusions are reasonable while those of your opponents are not.

CHAPTER ONE

1. Emanuel Feldman, *On Judaism* (New York: Shaar Press, 1994), 95.

2. For example, the Reform rabbi Harvey Fields points out that "Rabbi Yochanan claims that God's voice was divided into seven voices, and the seven voices were further divided into seventy languages spoken by all the peoples of the world at that time. Other rabbis of Yochanan's time disagree. They claim that God spoke with one voice. Rabbi Isaac taught that 'the message of all the prophets who were to arise in later generations . . . was given to Moses with the Torah.' Rabbi Simeon ben Lakish agrees. Extending this idea that all the books of the Hebrew Bible were given to Moses at Mount Sinai, some of the ancient rabbis claim that God gave two Torahs to Moses . . . [the] 'Written Torah,' comprising the Five Books of Moses: Genesis, Exodus, Leviticus, Numbers, and Deuteronomy . . . [and the] 'Oral Torah,' made up of all the books of the Prophets, the Midrash, Agadah, the Talmud, and all decisions and explanations of Jewish law by rabbinic scholars through the ages" ("What Happened at Sinai?" in *A Torah Commentary for Our Times* [New York: UAHC Press, 1991], 2:47).

All this debate be as it may, there is no doubt that the Orthodox today do believe that the oral Torah was transmitted simultaneously with the written Torah, as interpretations and supplements to the written text. They believe that, in some mysterious way, the teachings of the Mishnaic and Talmudic rabbis were not innovations. Instead, they were uncovering the layers of meaning that were already inherent in the original revelation from God.

3. Moses Maimonides (1135–1204) was the leading intellectual figure of medieval Judaism. His *Thirteen Articles of Faith* is still today a theological bulwark for Orthodox Jewish belief. A towering intellect, Maimonides was a jurist and physician of note, as well as a leading philosopher and theologian.

4. The Orthodox extrapolate the census figure in the book of Numbers of 603,500 men twenty years and older to two million people to account for women and children and for the priestly tribe of Levites, who, on the instructions of God, were not to be counted.

5. Both Rabbi Emanuel Feldman and Rabbi Ezriel Tauber make this point explicitly. Feldman argues that, in addition to faith, "there is basis in reason [to believe the story of the revelation]. Note that the Torah tells us that there were some two to three million witnesses to this claim. . . . The very Torah which Moses brings to the people states that the Revelation was witnessed by all the people. Certainly if this claim were false, any one of them—all of them—would have risen up to call Moses a liar!" (Feldman, *On Judaism*, 94, 95). Tauber says: "Other religions are founded on belief; ours is founded on knowledge. . . . The Torah says that when G-d wanted to reveal His will to mankind, He left no room for doubt. He personally revealed Himself to *millions* of people at the foot of Mount Sinai! Moses didn't make the sale; the Torah itself tells us he had a speech impediment. The millions of people at Mount Sinai did not 'believe' the vision

Moses had; they heard it from G-d themselves" (Tauber, *Choose Life* [New York: Shalheves, 1991], 41).

6. *The Torah: A Modern Commentary,* Revised Edition, W. Gunther Plaut, ed. (New York: URJ Press, 2005), 912. It is this text, which is generally referred to as the Plaut Torah, that I have used throughout for quotations from the Torah.

7. In the Plaut Torah (see note 6, above), Professor Hallo provides a brief essay entitled "Genesis [or Exodus, Leviticus, Numbers, Deuteronomy] and Ancient Near Eastern Literature" immediately preceding each of the five books. These essays, which are abundantly footnoted with source references, place the Torah squarely in the context of the contemporary Near East.

8. "The twelve tribes are grouped in four divisions, made up of three tribes each. . . . Each division is identified by a standard (*degel*), which is precisely the term that denoted the socio-military unit of mercenaries, including Jews, that served in the frontier colony of Elephantine in Egypt under the Persian Empire [in the fifth century BCE]. And in both the Elephantine papyri and in Numbers, the priestly families were not enrolled in any of these divisions. What Numbers describes, then, is essentially a military organization familiar from postexilic times" (ibid., 891).

9. "Such archival texts typically display identical features, including not only minute detail and endless repetition but also the same relative position of summaries and totals, specification of the standards of measure used, uniformity of types and quantities of commodities involved, and a very minimal narrative setting" (ibid., 892).

10. Dovid Gottlieb, *Living Up . . . to the Truth,* rev. 2nd ed. (Jerusalem: privately printed, 1994), 33.

11. Rabbi Halevi presented his argument in the year 1140 in *The Kuzari,* a defense of Judaism against the dominant Christian and Islamic religions and Greek philosophies of the time.

12. Logicians define *armchair psychology,* a term we all tend to throw around loosely, as psychological "laws" discovered by introspectively imagining the way people will or will not behave.

CHAPTER TWO

1. Ze'ev Herzog, "Deconstructing the Walls of Jericho," *Ha'aretz* (Tel Aviv, English edition), October 29, 1999. Herzog goes on to assert that "it will come as an unpleasant shock to many that the God of Israel, Jehovah, had a female consort and that the early Israelite religion adopted monotheism only in the waning period of the monarchy and not at Mount Sinai."

2. *Red herring,* the term for deliberate misdirection, has a colorful origin. Poachers would position themselves between hunting dogs and their prey and drag a smoked herring across the trail. This would send the dogs off in the wrong direction, giving the poachers an opportunity to bag the prey themselves.

3. Amy Dockser Marcus, *The View from Nebo* (New York: Little, Brown, 2000), 76.

4. Israel Finkelstein and Neil Asher Silberman, *The Bible Unearthed: Archaeology's New Vision of Ancient Israel and the Origin of Its Sacred Texts* (New York: Free Press, 2001).

5. Ibid., 60.

6. Ibid.

7. Ibid., 61.

8. Ibid., 76–83.

9. Ibid., 77.

10. Ibid., 79.

11. Marcus, *View from Nebo*, 78, 79.

12. Finkelstein and Silberman (*Bible Unearthed*, 107) attach the following footnote to this statement: "Although there is no way to know if ethnic identities had been fully formed at this time, we identify those distinctive highland villages as 'Israelite' since many of them were continuously occupied well into the period of the monarchies—an era from which we have abundant sources, both biblical and extra-biblical, testifying that their inhabitants consciously identified themselves as Israelites."

13. Ibid., 118.

14. Ibid., 63.

15. Ibid., 186–88.

16. The Midrash is a collection of special commentaries on the Torah.

17. Dovid Gottlieb, *Living Up . . . to the Truth*, rev. 2nd ed. (Jerusalem: privately published, 1994), 30.

18. Finkelstein and Silberman, *Bible Unearthed*, 63.

19. William Foxwell Albright, *Archeology of Palestine*, rev. ed. (New York: Penguin Books, 1960); originally published as *The Archeology of Palestine and the Bible* (New York: Fleming H. Revell) in 1932. Gottlieb references Albright in his paper, and given the similarity of this quote to other things Gottlieb says, it would appear that this outdated book was the main source of Gottlieb's archeological claims.

20. Philip Davies, *In Search of "Ancient Israel,"* 2nd ed. (New York: Sheffield Academic Press, 1995).

21. Philip Davies, "What Separates a Minimalist from a Maximalist? Not Much," *Biblical Archeology Review* 26, no. 2 (March–April 2000).

22. Finkelstein and Silberman, *Bible Unearthed*, 64.

23. James K. Hoffmeier, *Israel in Egypt* (New York: Oxford University Press, 1996), 10.

24. Biblical archeologists and historians use the term *maximalist* to describe someone who accepts most of what an ancient text says as true, whereas the term *minimalist* is used to describe someone who is extremely skeptical and demands substantial corroborating evidence before accepting the veracity of any ancient text. Fundamentalist Christians and Orthodox Jews are maximalists. Academic biblical scholars tend to be minimalists.

25. Hoffmeier, *Israel in Egypt,* viii.

26. Ibid., 31.

CHAPTER THREE

1. I am assuming all events to be independent. To calculate the probability, we sum the probability of exactly three of the twenty-six predictions being correct, exactly four, exactly five, and so on. The probability of exactly n predictions being correct is computed by the formula $26!/(26-n)!n! \times .1^n \times .9^{(26-n)}$

2. Dovid Gottlieb, *Living Up . . . to the Truth,* rev. 2nd ed. (Jerusalem: privately printed, 1994), 27.

3. Paul Johnson, *A History of the Jews* (New York: Harper and Row, 1987), part 2.

4. Ibid., 132.

5. Ibid.

6. Deuteronomy 28:59–60.

7. Leviticus 26:3–8.

8. Deuteronomy 28:1–7.

9. Finkelstein, Israel, and Neil Asher Silberman, *The Bible Unearthed: Archaeology's New Vision of Ancient Israel and the Origin of Its Sacred Texts* (New York: Free Press, 2001), 276.

10. Ibid., 291, 292.

11. Richard Elliott Friedman, *Who Wrote the Bible?,* 2nd ed. (San Francisco: Harper, 1997), 136.

12. Brent Martel, "New Orleans Mayor Says God Mad at U.S.," Associated Press, January 16, 2006.

13. Scott M. Liell, "Shaking the Foundation of Faith," *New York Times,* November 18, 2005.

14. Deuteronomy 30:1–5.

15. "The Eternal said to Moses: You are soon to lie with your ancestors. This people will thereupon go astray after the alien gods in their midst, in the land which they are about to enter; they will forsake Me and break My covenant which I made with them. Then My anger will flare up against them, and I will abandon them and hide my countenance from them. They shall be ready prey; and many evils and troubles shall befall them. And they shall say on that day, 'Surely, it is because our God is not in our midst that these evils have befallen us.' Yet I will keep my countenance hidden on that day, because of all the evil they have done in turning to other gods" (Deuteronomy 31:16–18).

16. Richard Rubinstein, *After Auschwitz* (1966; repr. Princeton, N.J.: Princeton University Press, 1999), cited in Eugene B. Borowitz, *Choices in Modern Jewish Thought* (New York: Behrman House, 1983), 193.

17. Thomas Gilovich, *How We Know What Isn't So* (New York: Free Press, 1993). Readers who wish to pursue this subject can also see *Why People Believe*

Weird Things (New York: Freeman, 1997) by Michael Shermer, the founding editor of *Skeptic* magazine and the author of *How We Believe: Science, Skepticism and the Search for God* (New York: Holt, 2000); *Mathematical Carnival* by Martin Gardner, exp. ed. (1975; repr., Washington, D.C.: Mathematical Association of America, 1989); and an article by Patricia Cohen, "Poof! You're a Skeptic: The Amazing Randi's Vanishing Humbug," *New York Times*, February 21, 2001. The Amazing Randi is the stage name of the magician and professional skeptic James Randi, whom Shermer calls the pioneer of the skeptical movement, and who for many years has had a standing offer of a prize of $1 million for anyone who can prove supernatural or paranormal powers. As of yet, there have been no awards.

CHAPTER FOUR

1. Joel Greenberg, "For Israelis, New Tragedy Is a Challenge Sent by God," *New York Times*, March 3, 2001.

2. David D. Kirkpatrick, "Wrath and Mercy: The Return of the Warrior Jesus," *New York Times*, April 4, 2004.

3. www.cbsnews.com, November 3, 2006.

4. John F. Burns, "Israeli Rabbi Sets Off a Political Firestorm over the Holocaust," *New York Times*, August 7, 2000.

5. Jack Katzenell, Associated Press, August 7, 2000.

6. Jeremiah argued that resistance to the Babylonian onslaught was futile, because Nebuchadnezzar was God's agent, sent to punish the people of Judah for their wicked and sinful ways.

7. The notion of an afterlife in which justice would be done seems to have emerged in Judaism in the second century BCE, during the time of the Hasmoneans and the Seleucid persecutions. It is interesting, and not surprising, that Jewish notions of martyrdom seem to have arisen at the same time. (The story of Hannah and her seven sons is the classic example.) The Talmud and Midrash clearly operate with the assumption that there is a "world to come," but it is not always clear whether this refers to an afterlife or to the time of the messiah.

One of the things one notices when reading the Torah is that its blessings and curses are always temporal, restricted to this world. This is one of the principal ways Judaism differs from Catholicism. The Torah is not the *Divine Comedy*, nor is the Jew the medieval Catholic sparrow flying through the storm of life, accumulating good works for a just reward in the afterlife. But wherever it came from, the concept of an afterlife did not come from the Torah without an awful lot of artful jiggling.

Reincarnation is an accepted doctrine in traditional and mystical Orthodox circles, although it is not a given that every Orthodox Jew would embrace this idea in its entirety. The traditional Orthodox prayer book praises God "who revives the dead." This prayer was modified many years ago in the Reform prayer book, which now praises God "who gives life to all."

8. *The Torah: A Modern Commentary*, Revised Edition, W. Gunther Plaut, ed. (New York: URJ Press, 2005), 874, 875.

CHAPTER FIVE

1. Leviticus 11:2–7. These are the well-known dietary laws that permit the Jewish people to eat land animals only if they both chew the cud and have cloven hoofs.

2. *The Torah: A Modern Commentary*, Revised Edition, W. Gunther Plaut, ed. (New York: URJ Press, 2005), 712.

3. A subgroup of the Artiodactyla, ruminants, such as cows, sheep, and other hoofed animals, have multichambered stomachs and regurgitate their food and re-chew it—that is, chew a cud—as a normal part of the digestive process.

4. Rabbi Plaut agrees. In his commentaries he concludes: "The biblical writers were not scientific biologists" (Plaut, *Torah*, 712). The Orthodox respond, predictably, that the zoologists—and, presumably, the eminent Rabbi Plaut, too—do not understand what animals the original Hebrew text was indicating.

CHAPTER SIX

1. Ezriel Tauber, *Choose Life* (New York: Shalheves, 1991), 142–45.

2. Esther 9:14.

3. Bill Keller, "Is It Good for the Jews?," *New York Times*, March 8, 2003.

4. Underwood Dudley, *Numerology—or What Pythagoras Wrought* (Washington, D.C.: Mathematical Association of America, 1997).

Why Pythagoras? It has nothing to do with the famous theorem that bears his name, which, in all likelihood, he didn't prove. What Pythagoras *did* do, according to Dudley, was to "turn number mysticism loose on the world," and this, in turn, led to numerology (p. 5).

5. To understand numerology, you must first understand gematria, an obtuse word for the really very simple technique for turning letters into numbers. Most scholars believe that it was the ancient Greeks who first had the idea (*alpha* = 1, *beta* = 2, up to 10; then it goes 10, 20, and so on, up to 100; and then it goes 100, 200, up to 900). You can do the same thing in any language, including Hebrew (*aleph* = 1, *bet* = 2, and so on). Here's an example of how the biblical numerologists find sevens. In the first sentence of the Torah, the sum of the gematria values of the words "God" (86), "Heavens" (395), and "Earth" (296) is 777.

6. The gematria value of the word "Gettysburg" works out to be 144.

7. Dudley, *Numerology*, 110.

8. Lisa Belkin, "The Odds of That," *New York Times Magazine*, August 1, 2002, 34.

9. Anna Badkehn, "Orthodox See Mark of the Beast in New Russian Taxpayer IDs," *Boston Globe*, February 25, 2001.

10. Ibid.

11. For a complete discussion of the Law of Small Numbers and the Law of Round Numbers, see chapters 9 and 11, respectively, of Dudley's *Numerology*.

12. Belkin, "Odds," 34.

13. See chapter 3 for a reference to *How We Know What Isn't So* by Thomas Gilovich, a professor of psychology at Cornell University, who also demonstrates that what many people are convinced are discernable patterns are, in reality, nothing more than random events.

14. Dudley, *Numerology*, 117.

CHAPTER SEVEN

1. *The Torah: A Modern Commentary*, Revised Edition, W. Gunther Plaut, ed. (New York: URJ Press, 2005), xxxvii.

2. Recent books that present serious arguments for the atheist position are *The End of Faith* by Sam Harris (New York: Norton, 2005); *The God Delusion* by Richard Dawkins (New York: Houghton Mifflin, 2006); *God Is Not Great* by Christopher Hitchens (New York: Twelve, 2007); and *Breaking the Spell* by Daniel Dennett (New York: Penguin, 2006).

3. Richard Elliott Friedman, *Who Wrote the Bible?*, 2nd ed. (San Francisco: HarperSanFrancisco, 1997), 132.

4. Ibid., 9.

5. Thomas Paine, the English-born American whose thinking and eloquent writing inspired the American Revolution, disdained the fundamentalist religious beliefs of the time. His final work, *The Age of Reason*, was an assault on organized revealed religion. Paine was not an atheist. He was a self-described deist (as were probably several of the Founding Fathers, such as Franklin and Jefferson), one who eschews all organized religion in favor of a universal deity. In *The Age of Reason* Paine held that "the true Deist has but one Deity, and his religion consists in contemplating the power, wisdom and benignity of the Deity in his works, and in endeavoring to imitate him in everything moral, scientifical, and mechanical."

6. Michael A. Meyer, *Response to Modernity* (New York: Oxford University Press, 1988), 93.

7. To demonstrate his point, Friedman reproduces the story of the flood (Genesis 6:5 to 8:22), with the twist that the J story is printed in the normal typeface, whereas the P story (P is the third author) is printed in boldface capitals. Inviting us to read the story in its entirety, and then go back and read each story separately, Friedman concludes: "The two flood stories are separable and complete. Each has its own language, its own details, and even its own conception of God. And even that is not the whole picture. The J flood story's language, details, and conception of God are consistent with the language, details, and conception of God in other J stories. The P flood story is consistent with other P stories. And so

on. The investigators found each of the sources to be a consistent collection of stories, poems, and laws." (Friedman, *Who Wrote*, 60).

8. Why J and not Y? Because the biblical scholars who developed the Documentary Hypothesis were predominantly German, and "j-a" is pronounced "yah" in German.

9. Friedman, *Who Wrote*, 62–69, 75.

10. Ibid., 238, 239.

11. Shiloh, located roughly midway between Jerusalem, the capital of Judah, and Shechem, the capital of Israel, was the religious center of the land during Samuel's time. Samuel, the kingmaker for both Saul and David, was a Shiloh priest. But then things went badly for the priests of Shiloh. First, the Shiloh priest who was one of King David's two chief priests bet on the wrong horse in the fight for the succession to David's throne. Solomon (the winner) had him tossed out of Jerusalem, and the Shiloh priests lost all power in Judah. Jeroboam, the first king of Israel, had no use for the Shiloh priests either, because they condemned his prized golden calves. All priests were of the tribe of Levi, a tribe that, unlike the other tribes, had no land of its own. Finding themselves odd men out in both Judah (where the Aaronid priests were in control) and Israel, the Shiloh priests were, understandably, generally pretty bitter men.

12. The Aaronid priests were in authority at the central altar in Judah. Only those who claimed to be descended from Aaron could be priests. They excluded even those Levites who claimed to be descendents of Moses, and they looked down on the priests of Shiloh in Israel.

13. Friedman, *Who Wrote*, 53.

14. 2 Samuel 7:16.

15. Friedman, *Who Wrote*, 101, 102.

16. Ibid., 145.

17. Ibid., 238.

18. Amy Dockser Marcus, *The View from Nebo* (New York: Little, Brown, 2000), 240, 241.

19. Israel Finkelstein and Neil Asher Silberman, *The Bible Unearthed: Archaeology's New Vision of Ancient Israel and the Origin of Its Sacred Texts* (New York: Free Press, 2001), 153, 158, 159.

20. Ibid., 158, 159.

CHAPTER EIGHT

1. Emanuel Feldman, *On Judaism* (New York: Shaar Press, 1994), 39, 40.

2. The largest-selling books in the United States today (over 60 million copies) are the twelve volumes of apocalyptic novels in the Left Behind series, which is based on a literal reading of the book of Revelation. In the latest, *Glorious Appearing*, Jesus returns in the Second Coming and mercilessly (and grotesquely)

slaughters millions of nonbelievers. To some, the Left Behind novels are science-fiction fantasies, but it's a good bet that to many who buy them the stories that unfold are very real.

3. In 2004 the journalist Bill Moyers received the fourth annual Global Environment Citizen Award from the Center for Health and the Global Environment at Harvard Medical School. In accepting this award, Moyers delivered the following remarks: "Remember James Watt, President Reagan's first Secretary of the Interior? Watt told the U.S. Congress that protecting natural resources was unimportant in light of the imminent return of Jesus Christ. In public testimony he said, 'after the last tree is felled, Christ will come back.' Beltway elites snickered. The press corps didn't know what he was talking about. But James Watt was serious. So were his compatriots across the country. They are the people who believe the Bible is literally true—one third of the American electorate if a recent Gallup poll is accurate. [Moyers then described the Left Behind series and went on to say] I'm not making this up. I've read the literature. I've reported on [its readers,] following some of them from Texas to the West Bank. They are sincere, serious, and polite as they tell you they feel called to help bring the rapture on as a fulfillment of biblical prophecy. That's why they have declared solidarity with Israel and the Jewish settlements and backed up their support with money and volunteers" (posted on AfterNet, December 4, 2004).

The Reverend John Hagee offers an example of what Moyers was talking about. In October 2006, five thousand evangelicals gathered for a "Night to Honor Israel" at Hagee's megachurch in San Antonio, Texas. Earlier in the year Hagee "arrived in Washington with 3,500 evangelicals for the first annual conference of his newly founded organization, Christians United for Israel [where he pronounced that] support for Israel was 'God's foreign policy'" (David D. Kirkpatrick, "For Evangelicals, Supporting Israel Is God's Foreign Policy," *New York Times*, November 14, 2006).

The Orthodox rabbi Yechiel Eckstein disputes Moyers's view. In a cover story published July 24, 2005, in the *New York Times Magazine* and entitled "The Rabbi Who Loved Evangelicals (and Vice Versa)," Zev Chafets noted that "in the last eight years alone, an estimated four hundred thousand born-again donors have sent Eckstein about a quarter of a billion dollars for Jewish causes of his choosing," adding that "no Jew since Jesus has commanded this kind of following." In this article Rabbi Eckstein—the founder and head of the International Fellowship of Christians and Jews (abbreviated as the IFCJ)—was quoted as saying: "There are all sorts of crazy conspiracy theories out there about how evangelicals only support Israel to bring on Armageddon or because they want to convert Jews to Christianity. That's just not true." Maybe not. But the writer also quoted Sandy Rios, a former president of the conservative organization Concerned Women for America, in Washington, D.C., who had recently been hired as the IFCJ's vice president for programming, as saying: "The truth is, Christians do want to convert Jews ... we believe it's part of God's plan." Three days later, according to Chafets, Rios was fired.

4. I use the term *Jewish community* as a shorthand to refer to the total number of people in the world who consider themselves ethnically and/or religiously Jewish.

5. Dovid Gottlieb, *Living Up . . . to the Truth,* rev. 2nd ed. (Jerusalem: privately printed, 1994).

6. Because these events are clearly not independent, this cannot in principle be an actual calculation. Further, the actual number of events whose probability we would have to factor in is far greater than two hundred.

CHAPTER NINE

1. Dovid Gottlieb, *Living Up . . . to the Truth,* rev. 2nd ed. (Jerusalem: privately published, 1994), 13–15.

2. Amy Dockser Marcus, *The View from Nebo* (New York: Little, Brown, 2000), 20, 22.

3. *The Torah: A Modern Commentary,* Revised Edition, W. Gunther Plaut, ed. (New York: URJ Press, 2005), 1156.

4. Gottlieb, *Living Up,* 25.

5. Muhammad ibn-Musa al-Khwarizmi, who lived in ninth-century Baghdad, is considered by many to be the father of algebra. The word *algorithm* is a derivation of his name.

6. Here is a good example. The most authoritative academic translation of Genesis is by E. A. Speiser, who is universally regarded as one of the world's foremost academic scholars of the ancient Hebrew language. In the story of the Garden of Eden, God's discovery that Adam and Eve had eaten from the tree of knowledge is translated by Speiser as follows: "They heard the sound of God Yahweh as he was walking in the garden at the breezy time of day; and the man and his wife hid from God Yahweh among the trees of the garden" (*Anchor Bible,* 3rd ed. [New York: Doubleday, 1964]). The problem for the Orthodox with this passage is the fact that God's walking in the garden, if taken literally, conflicts with Maimonides' Third Article of Faith: the Aristotelian doctrine that God has no body.

To avoid this problem, the Orthodox rabbi Aryeh Kaplan gives this very loose translation in *The Living Torah* (New York: Moznaim, 1981): "They heard God's voice moving about in the garden with the wind of the day. The man and his wife hid themselves from God among the trees of the garden." Rabbi Kaplan adds the following note to the phrase "moving about:" "Literally, 'walking.'" The commentaries explain that it was the voice that was moving, not God. With his accommodating translation, Rabbi Kaplan is following the time-honored Orthodox tradition of adapting the text to explain away any apparent inconsistencies.

7. Max Weber, considered by many to be one of the founders of modern sociology, held that the basic social, political, and economic institutions in Western society today have their origin in Protestant religious values. Perhaps his most famous book is *The Protestant Ethic and the Spirit of Capitalism.*

8. Gottlieb, *Living Up,* 47. The Orthodox would likely argue that what Rabbi Gottlieb means is that because the Jewish people were chosen by God to bring his word to the world, of all the world's religions only Orthodox Judaism continues to contribute to the betterment of mankind. This argument works only if you buy into Orthodox dogma. If you reject this fundamentalist dogma as false, then Gottlieb's argument makes no sense at all.

9. As we saw earlier, the Zoroastrians also embraced monotheism over three thousand years ago, so the Jews were not unique in this regard, but the impact of Jewish monotheism was undoubtedly much greater.

CHAPTER TEN

1. Emanuel Feldman, *On Judaism* (New York: Shaar Press, 1994).

2. Ibid., 13.

3. Ibid., 14.

4. Ibid., 15.

5. Ibid., 16.

6. Ibid., 134.

7. Emanuel Feldman's book is not unique in its sharp-tongued denigration of Western civilization. Here is what Rabbi Ezriel Tauber has to say in his book *Choose Life* (New York: Shalheves, 1991)—which, likewise, follows the "growth" of a fictitious young man the rabbi has created, also named David, and also yearning for Jewish meaning in his life (again, I have italicized the tone words): "Take an honest look at the world. I think an objective person has to conclude that this last century has been the *most murderous and inhumane in world history.* . . . Upon close inspection, it is as if the more mankind has 'advanced,' the further away from a perfected world it has *drifted"* (p. 67). Tauber also uses the comparison to animals: "You can *eat exclusively to fill your stomach,* which is basically the same reason *animals* do, or you can turn your eating into a G-dly act by following the commandments the Creator gave you about eating" (p. 57).

8. Feldman, *On Judaism,* 18, 19.

9. Ibid., 122.

10. Ibid., 123.

11. Ibid., 19.

12. Ibid., 20.

13. Ibid., 23.

14. Ibid., 29.

15. Ibid., 20.

16. Ibid., 21.

17. Ibid., 25.

18. Ibid.

19. Ibid., 47.

20. Ibid., 93.

21. Ibid., 277, 278.

22. Ibid., 290.

23. Ibid., 17.

24. Ibid., 30.

25. Ibid., 135.

26. Ibid., 292.

27. Dovid Gottlieb, *Living Up . . . to the Truth*, rev. 2nd ed. (Jerusalem: privately printed, 1994), 6.

28. Ibid., 5.

29. Not quite all. Prejudice, and in some cases the law, thwarted the freedom and ambitions of many minorities until relatively recently. Over the past fifty years, however, American law has evolved to protect minorities and assure them a fair shot at the American dream, just like everyone else. More important, although some level of prejudice undoubtedly remains ingrained in the English and American peoples, there has been a sea change in their attitudes. The candidacy of Senator Barak Obama for President of the United States, unthinkable fifty years ago because of his race, is an eloquent testimonial to this change in attitudes.

30. Joel Greenberg, "Non-Orthodox Gain Support from Ruling in Israeli Court," *New York Times,* February 20, 2001.

31. Ibid.

32. Mary Curtius, "Ruling in Israel Stirring Emotions," *Los Angeles Times,* February 20, 2001.

33. Quoted in Richard Dawkins, *The God Delusion* (New York: Houghton Mifflin, 2006), 223.

34. Ibid., 247.

As for the revered (Dawkins calls it "disgraceful") story of Abraham and Isaac, he asks how "a modern moralist cannot help but wonder how a child could ever recover from such a psychological trauma." Richard Dawkins has a finely honed wit, which he sprinkles generously throughout his book. For example: Abraham's "murdering knife was already in his hand when an angel dramatically intervened with the news of a last-minute change of plan: God was only joking after all" (p. 242).

35. In 1989, in what became a cause célèbre throughout the world, Iran's spiritual leader Ayatollah Ruhollah Khomeini issued a decree condemning the Anglo-Indian novelist Salman Rushdie to death for blaspheming Islam in his satiric novel *The Satanic Verses.*

36. Michael A. Meyer, *Response to Modernity: A History of the Reform Movement in Judaism* (New York: Oxford University Press, 1988), 250.

37. Deborah Sontag, "Jerusalem Journal," *New York Times,* May 2, 2000.

38. Deborah Sontag, "Israeli Army Ousting Officer for Intolerance," *New York Times,* November 23, 1999. This is not an isolated incident. "Two weeks earlier . . . the president of the World Union for Progressive Judaism faced a similar assault

from a member of Parliament. He . . . had been invited to attend a Parliament committee meeting on conversion. A legislator from the [Orthodox] United Torah Party entered the committee room, [and, according to the rabbi] started screaming [that] he wouldn't sit with the Reformim because we've caused assimilation of millions of Jews, worse than the Nazis" (ibid.).

39. On August 20, 2002, the *New York Times* ran the following Associated Press release: "An Islamic high court in northern Nigeria rejected an appeal today from a single mother sentenced to be stoned to death for having had sex out of wedlock." Fortunately, unrelenting international pressure eventually led Nigeria's top civil court to set aside this judgment. On April 24, 2003, the *Wall Street Journal* reported: "An Iranian actress was sentenced to seventy-four lashes for kissing an actor on the cheek in public. The sentence was suspended barring a future offense."

40. Eugene Borowitz, *Choices in Modern Jewish Thought* (New York: Behrman House, 1983), 254.

41. Bill Broadway, " 'Suffer Not a Woman to Teach,' Baptist Group Reserving the Pulpit for Men," *Washington Post*, June 10, 2000.

42. Feldman, *On Judaism*, 97.

43. Deuteronomy 17:2–12 says:

2] If there is found among you . . . a man or a woman who has affronted the Eternal your God and transgressed the covenant—3] turning to the worship of other gods and bowing down to them, to the sun or the moon or any of the heavenly host . . . 4] and you have been informed or have learned of it, then you shall make a thorough inquiry. If it is true, the fact is established, that abhorrent thing was perpetrated in Israel, 5] you shall take the man or the woman who did that wicked thing out to the public place, and you shall stone them, man or woman, to death. 6] A person shall be put to death only on the testimony of two or more witnesses; no one must be put to death on the testimony of a single witness. 7] Let the hands of the witnesses be the first to put [the condemned] to death, and the hands of the rest of the people thereafter. Thus you will sweep out evil from your midst. 8] If a case is too baffling for you to decide, be it a controversy over homicide, civil law, or assault—matters of dispute in your courts—you shall promptly . . . 9] . . . appear before the levitical priests, or the magistrate in charge at the time, and present your problem. When they have announced to you the verdict in the case, 10] you shall carry out the verdict that is announced to you. . . . 11] You shall act in accordance with the instructions given you and the ruling handed down to you; you must not deviate from the verdict that they announce to you either to the right or to the left. 12] Should either party act presumptuously and disregard the priest charged with serving there the Eternal your God, or the magistrate, that man shall die. . . .

44. *The Torah: A Modern Commentary*, Revised Edition, W. Gunther Plaut, ed. (New York: URJ Press, 2005), 1292.

45. Borowitz, *Choices*, 254.

46. Paul Berman, "The Philosopher of Islamic Terror," *New York Times*

Magazine, March 23, 2003. This article was adapted from Berman, *Terror and Liberalism* (New York: Norton, 2003), which includes a fuller discussion of the thinking of Sayyid Qutb.

47. Feldman, *On Judaism,* 269.

48. Berman, "Philosopher of Islamic Terror."

49. Sameer N. Yacoub, "Terror Chief Declares 'War' on Democracy," Associated Press, January 23, 2005.

50. "Crazy Mahmoud," editorial, *Wall Street Journal,* May 10, 2006.

51. Berman, "Philosopher of Islamic Terror."

52. Stephen Holden, "Outrun Fate? Not for Iranian Women," review of film festival, *New York Times,* March 24, 2001.

53. Deborah Sontag, "Sharon Opens His Campaign," *New York Times,* January 11, 2001.

54. Noah Feldman, "Orthodox Paradox," *New York Times Magazine,* July 22, 2007.

Feldman, a law professor at Harvard, studied for twelve years at a yeshiva that considered itself "modern" Orthodox. His article explores the relationship between religious and cultural identity. After posing for a group photo at his tenth-year yeshiva reunion, Feldman and his Korean-American fiancée were intentionally Photoshopped right out of the picture. Not only that; every milestone that Feldman shared with the yeshiva's alumni director after that reunion—including his marriage and the birth of his son—never made it into his school's alumni newsletter. Feldman's article does not seem to reflect any bitterness on his part, but at times his words reveal a profound sadness at the way he has been treated by members of the Orthodox community.

Reaction to Feldman's article produced a full page of letters to the editor in the August 5, 2007, edition of the magazine. The first, by the executive vice president of the Orthodox Union, was predictable: "It was Feldman's choice to send as clear a signal as he could, through his marriage, that he was rejecting fundamental principles of the [Orthodox] community. His expression of surprise at the reaction of the community's institutions, including his alma mater, where he was taught these principles, strains credulity."

The last letter came at the question from a different perspective. A reader named M. J. Rosenberg wrote that "Feldman's article addressed a phenomenon that used to trouble me. No longer. Once I realized that the kind of small-mindedness he describes is not endemic to Judaism per se but to all forms of religious fundamentalism, I felt better. Fundamentalist Jews have more in common with fundamentalist Christians and Muslims than with the vast majority of Jews, Christians and Muslims who are not fundamentalists."

55. Ibid.

56. Deborah Sontag, "Powerful Israeli Rabbi Steps Up Attacks over Parochial Schools," *New York Times,* March 20, 2000.

57. Joel Greenberg, "Israel Destroys Shrine for Mosque Gunman," *New York*

Times, December 29, 2000.

58. Ibid.

59. Matt Spetalnick, "Peres: Sharon Risks Assassination for Gaza Plan," Reuters, October 19, 2004.

60. Jeffrey Goldberg, "Protect Sharon from the Right," *New York Times,* August 5, 2004.

61. Quoted in Sally Denton, "A Utah Massacre and Mormon Memory," *New York Times,* May 24, 2003.

What I find most interesting in this article on the Mountain Meadows Mormon massacre is how—and why—the current leadership of the Mormon Church is reluctant to accept responsibility, even though "several historians, including some who are Mormon, believe that church leaders, though never prosecuted, ordered the massacre. . . . The current church president, Gordon B. Hinkley—himself a 'prophet' who says he receives divine revelations—. . . [has] continued to hedge on the issue of church responsibility. . . . To acknowledge complicity on the part of the church leaders runs the risk of calling into question [the prophet] Brigham Young's divinity and the Mormon belief that they are God's chosen people. 'If good Mormons committed the massacre,' wrote a Mormon writer, Levi Peterson, 'if prayerful leaders ordered it, if apostles and a prophet knew about it and later sacrificed John D. Lee [the Mormon zealot—and adopted son of Brigham Young—who led the militia that carried out the massacre and was later blamed for it and executed], then the sainthood of even the modern church leaders seems tainted.'" In *Under the Banner of Heaven* (New York: Doubleday, 2003), Jon Krakauer offers a chilling account of the Mountain Meadow massacre and its aftermath.

62. Judith Miller, "Killing for the Glory of God, in a Land Far from Home," *New York Times,* January 16, 2001.

63. Gustav Niebuhr, "Baptists' Ardor for Evangelism Angers Some Jews and Hindus," *New York Times,* December 4, 1999.

64. Paul Hill was executed in 2003.

65. Dan Barry, "Tracing Anti-Abortion Network to a Slaying Suspect in France," *New York Times,* March 31, 2001.

66. Gustav Niebuhr, "Episcopal Dissidents Find African Inspiration," *New York Times,* March 6, 2001.

67. Gustav Niebuhr, "Recruiting Pitch: Monastic Life, for 3 Days," *New York Times,* January 13, 2001.

68. Matthew Barakat, "Va. Parishes Split from Episcopal Church," Associated Press, December 17, 2006.

69. Tom O'Neill, "Untouchable," *National Geographic,* June 2003, 30.

70. Michael Janofsky, "Young Brides Stir Outcry on Utah Polygamy," *New York Times,* February 28, 2003.

Krakauer (*Under the Banner*) details the fate of teenage girls (often as young as fourteen and sometimes younger) in the Mormon fundamentalist community. He also discusses the so-called Kingston Clan, which counts some fifteen hundred members "led by patriarch Paul Kingston, a lawyer who is married to at least twenty-five women and has sired some two hundred offspring" (p. 18). Krakauer cites another case in which a girl "reported to the police that immediately after her sixteenth birthday, her father, a businessman named John Kingston, had pulled her out of high school and forced her to become the fifteenth wife of his brother, David Kingston. . . . Twice the girl tried to run away from David, but she was caught each time. After the second escape . . . John Kingston then drove her to a remote ranch near the Utah-Idaho border that the Kingstons used as a 'reeducation camp' for wayward wives and disobedient children. He took the girl into a barn, pulled his belt off, and used it to whip her savagely. . . . [After the beating] the girl fled from the ranch and limped five miles along a dirt road [and] called the police. Both John and David Kingston were arrested and subsequently convicted. . . . John was found guilty of child abuse and locked up in the county jail for twenty-eight weeks; David was sentenced to ten years in prison for incest and unlawful sexual conduct" (ibid.). Unfortunately, the Kingstons are not alone in the Mormon fundamentalist community in their treatment of women in general and very young teenage girls in particular. All these men are 100 percent convinced that this is what God wants, that they are doing God's will.

71. David Firestone, "Child Abuse at a Church Creates Stir in Atlanta," *New York Times,* March 30, 2001.

72. Kathy Gannon, "Taliban Calls Ancient Relics' Destruction a Tribute to Islam," Associated Press, March 6, 2001.

73. The absolute certainty of the religious fundamentalist is also to be found among secular groups. While they may not base their beliefs on the word of God, they are as thoroughly convinced of the righteousness of their causes, justifying actions that offend and even harm those who do not share their convictions. In 2000 a group called People for the Ethical Treatment of Animals (PETA) launched an ad campaign aimed at young people to discourage them from drinking milk because dairy cows were being mistreated, and (I'm not kidding) advising them to drink beer instead. Beer is good for you, the ads said, because it contains no fat, cholesterol, or hormones. They grudgingly pulled the ads after receiving sharp criticism from many different groups who promote youth health and safety, but added as a parting shot that all the controversy had created an even greater awareness for their cause. (Karen Herzog, "Got Beer? PETA Wants College Students to Break the Milk Habit," *Milwaukee Journal Sentinel,* March 12, 2000). Fanaticism takes many forms.

74. Deborah Sontag, "In a Divided Israel, Thousands Rally for the Ex-Shas Party Leader as He Goes to Jail," *New York Times,* September 4, 2000.

75. Clifford J. Levy, "Both Clintons Met Supporters of 4 Hasidim," *New York Times,* January 24, 2001.

76. In April 2007 a former aide to U.S. Representative Don Young (R. Alaska) "pleaded guilty to taking bribes from Abramoff in exchange for tips on pending congressional action" (*Wall Street Journal,* April 25, 2007).

77. Michael Janofsky, "The Abramoff Case; The Money Trail; Many Millions in Kickbacks from Tribes," *New York Times*, January 4, 2006.

78. Philip Shenon, "Lobbyist in Congress Furor Is Sentenced in Florida Case," *New York Times*, March 30, 2006.

79. Feldman, *On Judaism*, 252.

80. Felicity Barringer, "Paper Seen as Villain in Abuse Accusation against Rabbi," *New York Times*, July 10, 2000.

81. Brandon Nailey and Robin Evans, "Sex-Abuse Study Faults Bishops," *San Jose Mercury News*, February 28, 2004.

In his provocative book *God Is Not Great* (New York: Twelve, 2007), Christopher Hitchens calls attention to the Vatican's "contemptible passivity and inaction" vis-à-vis Nazi Germany. Echoing Robert Bennett's observation that knowingly allowing evil to continue is cooperation with evil, Hitchens points out that "to decide to do nothing is itself a policy and a decision, [reflecting] the church's alignment in terms of a realpolitik that sought, not the defeat of Nazism, but an accommodation with it" (p. 238).

82. Toward the end of December 2000 "the Orthodox Union released a report [by a commission under the president of Hillel] documenting extensive abuse by the rabbi and allowing him to remain on the job despite the steady flow of complaints about his behavior over the years" (Andrew Jacobs, "Orthodox Group Details Accusations that New Jersey Rabbi Abused Teenagers," *New York Times*, December 27, 2000).

83. Ellen Goodman, "Debts—Moral and Financial—Are Coming Due in Boston," *Boston Globe*, December 8, 2002.

CHAPTER ELEVEN

1. The three principal branches of Judaism today are the Orthodox, the Conservative, and the Reform. Orthodoxy is Jewish fundamentalism. Reform is liberal Judaism. Conservative is somewhere in the middle, probably closer to Orthodoxy than to Reform.

2. Michael Massing, "New Torah for Modern Minds," *New York Times*, March 9, 2002.

3. Ibid.

4. For example, according to the eminent Yale scholar of the ancient Near East William Hallo, the "Deuteronomic Code," perhaps the most crucial portion of the book of Deuteronomy, is also the portion most explicitly indebted to older models.

5. Timothy Egan, "Tale Bigger than Life," *New York Times*, January 4, 2003.

6. Ibid.

7. "Bigfoot Risks Extinction, Says Canadian MP," Agence France-Presse, May 2, 2007.

8. Corey Kilgannon, "Miracle? Drama? Prank? Fish Talks, Town Buzzes," *New York Times*, March 5, 2003.

9. Emanuel Feldman, *On Judaism* (New York: Shaar Press, 1994), 53, 54.

10. Ibid., 143, 144.

11. Ezriel Tauber, *Choose Life* (New York: Shalheves, 1991), 149.

12. Ibid., 167.

13. Ibid., 168, 169.

14. Ibid., 186.

15. Ibid., 141, 142.

16. Rabbi Tauber echoes here what the eighteenth-century Talmudic sage Elijah ben Solomon—known as the Gaon of Vilna (The Learned One of Vilnius, Lithuania), or simply the Vilna Gaon—said in chapter 5 of his *Sifra Ditzniuta*: "The rule is that all that was, is and will be unto the end of time is included in the Torah . . . and not merely in a general sense, but including the details of every species and of each person individually, and the most minute details of everything that happened to him from the day of his birth, until his death; likewise of every kind of animal and beast and living thing that exists, and of herbage, and of all that grows or is inert." The Vilna Gaon is often cited by the Orthodox, who claim to see all sorts of hidden codes, patterns, and predictions in the Torah's text, which, they assert, could only have been put there by God.

17. Tauber, *Choose Life*, 141.

18. Joshua Hermalin, foreword to *Living Up . . . to the Truth* by Dovid Gottlieb, rev. 2nd ed. (Jerusalem: privately printed, 1994), 3.

CHAPTER TWELVE

1. Dovid Gottlieb, *Living Up . . . to the Truth*, rev. 2nd ed. (Jerusalem: privately printed, 1994), 28.

2. Amy Dockser Marcus, *The View from Nebo* (New York: Little, Brown, 2000), 134.

3. Gottlieb, *Living Up*, 28.

4. Israel Finkelstein and Neil Asher Silberman, *The Bible Unearthed: Archaeology's New Vision of Ancient Israel and the Origin of Its Sacred Texts* (New York: Free Press, 2001), 260.

5. George Melloan, "America's Problem Is Jihadists, Not the Whole of Islam," *Wall Street Journal*, November 26, 2002.

6. Adolf Eichmann, "My Memoirs," *Die Welt*, August 13, 1999.

7. *Economist*, Survey of the Twentieth Century, "Freedom's Journey," September 11, 1999.

CHAPTER THIRTEEN

1. "The Americanization of Reform Judaism," Jewish Virtual Library, a division of the American-Israeli Cooperative Enterprise;

http://www.jewishvirtuallibrary.org/jsource/Judaism/usreform.html.

2. Michael A. Meyer, *Response to Modernity: A History of the Reform Movement in Judaism* (New York: Oxford University Press, 1988), 229.

Meyer notes (ibid., 447) that "the complete texts of the petition, called a 'memorial,' and the constitution are in Barnett A. Elzas, *The Reformed Society of Israelites* (New York, 1916), 31–53; and L. C. Moise, *Biography of Isaac Harby* (Macon, Ga., 1931), 52–72."

3. Ibid., 231.

4. Thomas Jefferson, letter to Dr. Benjamin Rush, September 23, 1800. This quotation is inscribed in the rotunda of the State Chamber of the Jefferson Memorial in Washington, D.C.

5. Meyer, *Response*, 226–27.

6. The core meaning of the Hebrew root (the three Hebrew letters *koof, dalet,* and *shin*) is "to be set apart, separate," which appears to be the Torah's essential definition of holiness—that which is set apart from the ordinary. Thus, the *Kiddush* recited on the Sabbath declares that the seventh day is holy, that is, it is different and set apart from the other days. Leviticus 19 commands all Jews to live in a holy manner and sets forth a variety of laws that define a holy life. Some of these laws are commendable by any standard. They include such things as honoring the old, sharing one's food with the poor, treating one's employees fairly, not bearing a grudge, loving the stranger, and—as a precursor to Jesus's Golden Rule—loving one's neighbor as oneself. The Orthodox interpret the commandment to live a holy life as a separation from secular culture. Thus they avoid television, movies, and social settings where their children will encounter values they consider antithetical to theirs. Paradoxically, liberal Jews understand the commandment to live in a holy manner as actually *requiring* them to be fully engaged with the world. They reason that you can't really love the stranger if you refuse to have any contact with him.

7. Emanuel Feldman, *On Judaism* (New York: Shaar Press, 1994), 258.

8. David Aaron, "The First Loose Plank—On the Rejection of Reason in the Pittsburgh Principles of 1999," *CCAR Journal: A Reform Jewish Quarterly* (Fall 2001), 92.

The texts of the Pittsburgh Platform of 1885, the Columbus Platform of 1937, and the San Francisco Centenary Perspective can be found in Meyer, *Response to Modernity,* 387–94. They can also be found on the web site of the Central Conference of American Rabbis: www.ccarnet.org, along with the text of the Pittsburgh Principles of 1999.

9. Ibid., 98.

10. See note 8, above.

11. Aaron, "First Loose Plank," 95.

12. Bernard J. Bamberger, "The Torah and the Jewish People," in *The Torah: A Modern Commentary,* Revised Edition, W. Gunther Plaut, ed. (New York: URJ Press, 2005), xxxv.

13. Eugene Borowitz, *Choices in Modern Jewish Thought* (New York: Behrman House, 1983), 244.

14. Ibid., 245.

15. Emanuel Feldman, *On Judaism* (New York: Shaar Press, 1994), 75.

16. Ezriel Tauber, *Choose Life* (New York: Shalheves, 1991), 77.

17. George Will, "The Limits of Inclusiveness," *Newsweek*, November 10, 2003.

18. Meyer, *Response to Modernity*, 226, 227.

19. Borowitz, *Choices*, 52.

20. See note 8, above.

21. Aaron is responding here to a Commentary attached to the Pittsburgh Principles of 1999 in which it was held that "the culture in which we live no longer presumes that immortality is unscientific, irrational or unbelievable. Reform Jews are now liberated from the constraints of a religion based solely on rationalism, or a limited understanding of science" (ibid.).

22. Aaron refers to a Commentary attached to the 1999 Principles in which it is observed that "Jewish tradition holds that at Mount Sinai God gave the Jewish people a covenant reaffirming the promise to Abraham (Genesis 15) of an eternal people and an eternal claim to the Land of Israel" (ibid.).

23. Aaron, "First Loose Plank," 99, 101, 102, 104.

24. Ibid., 109.

CHAPTER FOURTEEN

1. Ira Eisenstein and Eugene Kohn, *Mordecai M. Kaplan: An Evaluation* (Philadelphia: Jewish Reconstruction Foundation, 1952), 289.

2. Mordecai Kaplan, *Judaism as a Civilization* (Philadelphia: Jewish Publication Society, 1994).

3. Durkheim offers a straightforward definition of religion: "A religion is a unified system of beliefs and practices relative to sacred things, that is to say, things set apart and forbidden—beliefs and practices which unite into one single moral community called a Church, all those who adhere to them" (Emile Durkheim, *The Elementary Forms of Religious Life*, translated and edited by Carol Cosman [New York: Oxford University Press, 2001], 40).

4. Durkheim's concept of a totem is much broader and much more complex than totem poles, those carved and painted vertical logs made by the Indians of the Northwest coast of the United States and Canada with which most of us are familiar. A totem pole is one type of totem, but not all totems are poles. When Durkheim talks of a *totem*, what he means is a symbol that a social group, usually a tribe, has selected as its main unifying emblem.

5. Durkheim, *Elementary Forms*, 76.

6. Like Kaplan, Durkheim was influenced by a number of important secular thinkers of his day, most notably Henri Bergson, the eminent philosopher. But with Durkheim, unlike Kaplan, the influence of these secular thinkers precipitated a personal (and painful) break with his family's religious tradition. For a discussion

of the effect of Durkheim's Jewish heritage on his sociological work, a good source is Deborah Dash Moore's article "David Emile Durkheim and the Jewish Response to Modernity," *Modern Judaism* 6, no. 3 (October 1986): 287–300.

7. Durkheim, *Elementary Forms,* 327.

8. Eugene Borowitz, *Choices in Modern Jewish Thought* (New York: Behrman House, 1983), 99, 100.

9. Mordecai Kaplan, *The Meaning of God in Modern Jewish Religion* (Detroit: Wayne State University Press, 1994).

10. Mordecai Kaplan, *The Future of the American Jew* (Philadelphia: Reconstructionist Press, 1981), 55.

11. Borowitz, *Choices,* 99–105, 116.

12. Kaplan, *Judaism as a Civilization,* 182. The *Shema Yisrael,* a brief prayer consisting of only six Hebrew words (translating to "Hear, O Israel. The Lord is our God. The Lord is One."), is the most important single prayer for all Jews, Orthodox and liberal alike. Jews call it "the watchword of our faith."

CHAPTER FIFTEEN

1. Sharon Begley, "Religion and the Brain," *Newsweek,* May 7, 2001.

2. Megan K. Stack, "Elvis' Eternal Encore," *Los Angeles Times,* August 16, 2002.

3. Edward O. Wilson, *Consilience: The Unity of Knowledge* (New York: Alfred A. Knopf, 1998), 210.

4. Andrew Newberg and Eugene d'Aquili, *Why God Won't Go Away: Brain Science and the Biology of Belief* (New York: Ballantine Books, 2001).

5. Andrew Newberg et al., "The Measurement of Regional Cerebral Blood Flow during the Complex Task of Meditation: A Preliminary SPECT Study," *Psychiatry Research,* Neuroimaging Section, 106 (2001).

6. "Pat Robertson Warns Pa. Town of Disaster," Associated Press, November 10, 2005.

7. A succinct discussion of the intelligent design theory is provided by James Glanz in an article published in the April 8, 2001, edition of the *New York Times:* "Darwin vs. Design: Evolutionists' New Battle." Glanz points out that Dr. Michael J. Behe, a professor of biological sciences at Lehigh University in Pennsylvania and the author of *Darwin's Black Box: The Biochemical Challenge to Evolution* (New York: Simon and Schuster, 1996), Dr. William Dempsky, who has a doctorate in mathematics from the University of Chicago and is on the faculty at Baylor University (which receives a small part of its funding from the Texas Baptist Convention), and Philip E. Johnson, a professor emeritus of the Law School at the University of California at Berkeley, "are regarded as the intellectual fathers of the design theory movement. Mr. Johnson's book, *Darwin on Trial* (Downers Grove, Il.: InterVarsity Press, 1991) has become its manifesto. Dr. Behe and Dr. Dempsky are fellows of the Discovery Institute, the Seattle research institute that promotes intelligent design in its Center for the Renewal of Science and Culture. The cen-

ter's $1.1 million annual budget is supplied largely by Christian foundations and [the center] broadly endorses intelligent design theory. Mr. Johnson is an advisor to the Institute."

8. Ibid.

9. Newberg et al., "Measurement of Cerebral Blood Flow."

10. Functional imaging studies usually involve PET (Positron Emission Tomography) and SPECT (Single Photon Emission Computed Tomography) scans, each of which uses different radiotracers to capture images of metabolically active regions of the brain. A radiotracer injected into the bloodstream of a subject emits signals that can be collected and processed by machines that are very sensitive to different kinds of gamma radiation. Special scanners process the gamma radiation, allowing relatively accurate images of the metabolic activity in the brain to be reproduced. It is these images that allow scientists to infer links between cognitive functions (for example, meditation and prayer) and increased—or decreased—levels of neural activity in certain areas of the brain.

For a functional imaging study to be valid, five assumptions must be valid:

The Discreet Processing Assumption. This is the idea that different regions of the brain are dedicated to the performance of specific cognitive tasks. This assumption has been confirmed by PET, SPECT, and EEG studies.

The Metabolism Assumption. This is the idea that neural activity is correlated with changes in local blood flow and metabolic activity. Two studies have confirmed the legitimacy of this assumption.[*]

The Measurement Assumption. This is the idea that radioisotopes can be used to indirectly measure changes in rCBF (regional cerebral blood flow). As long as radioisotopes are carefully chosen in accordance with the cognitive task at hand, there is no problem with this assumption.

The Physics Assumption. This is the claim that the physical properties, especially the decay rates, of radioisotopes are understood well enough to allow PET scanners to translate emitted gamma rays into meaningful images. There is nothing to suggest that this assumption is shaky.

The Data Transformation Assumption. This is the idea that the computer-facilitated transformation of gamma rays into meaningful images is not problematic. There is no need to doubt the legitimacy of this assumption.

Since all five assumptions have been demonstrated to be valid, it is safe to conclude that the functional imaging studies of the brain are using sound methodology.

11. Begley, "Religion and the Brain."

12. Ibid.

---

[*] M. Juieptner and C. Weiller, "Does Measurement of Regional Cerebral Blood Flow Reflect Synaptic Activity?: Implications for PET and fMTR," *Neuroimage* 2 (1995): 148–56; and P. J. Magistretti and L. Pellerin, "Cellular Mechanisms of Brain Energy Metabolism and Their Relevance to Functional Brain Imaging," *Philosophical Transactions of the Royal Society of London* B, no. 354 (1999): 1155–63.

13. Newberg and d'Aquili, *Why God Won't*, 92, 102.

14. Begley, "Religion and the Brain."

15. Christian de Quincy, "Hardwired for God?" *Cerebrum* 3, no. 3 (Summer 2001); adapted in de Quincy, "Data and the Divine," *IONS Noetic Sciences Review*, September–November, 2003.

16. Emile Durkheim, *The Elementary Forms of Religious Life*, translated and edited by Carol Cosman (New York: Oxford University Press, 2001), 325.

17. Mordecai Kaplan, *Judaism as a Civilization* (Philadelphia: Jewish Publication Society, 1994), 460.

A FINAL WORD

1. Thomas Jefferson, *Notes on Virginia*, 1782.

ACKNOWLEDGMENTS

Thanking those who make a book possible always has to be a pleasant task for any author. So it is for me. At the top of the list, unquestionably, is my wife, who, in every way possible, fully supported this endeavor.

Jacob Neusner, the brilliant scholar and theologian, first suggested I write this book and then unceremoniously proceeded to take a machete to the first draft of the manuscript. Jack's insightful critique led me to rewrite the book and, this time, to stay focused on what really matters. The eminent analytical philosopher John Etchemendy taught me how to look at complex questions of logic from new angles. I am indebted to John for his penetrating insights and innovative thinking. Janet Marder, with broad knowledge and a keen intellect, provided reasoned criticism that helped me see the wider picture more clearly. Geoff Emberling pointed me in the right direction to find what modern archeologists have uncovered about the real history of the ancient Near East. Best-selling author Dinesh D'Souza made several important recommendations to ensure that the book would be meaningful to the broadest possible reading audience. And George McCown gave me both valuable input and encouragement from the very beginning.

All authors should be lucky enough to have a research associate as good as John Eden. A highly intelligent young man who thinks out of the box, well read in philosophy, politics, and theology, articulate, tenacious, resourceful, hardworking, with a good sense of humor—that's a hard combination to beat. John made an important contribution to the book in a myriad of ways.

To transform a manuscript into a book takes a lot of talented people. My agent, Felicia Eth, is as good as they come. I signed on with Felicia because of her statement that she takes relatively few projects, but those she does take on she cares about. And she proved as good as her word, continuing to work closely with the publisher, making valuable contributions on a variety of fronts.

The arresting image on the dust jacket cover was created and painted by the talented and imaginative Dolores Avendaño, a world-class illustrator. The publisher asked Dolores to come up with something that would immediately convey the idea of a mind in bondage. You can't get any more creative than the concept Dolores produced and executed so well.

George Young has many years of publishing success under his belt producing and marketing books, and he is as adept and innovative as ever. Proofreader Karen Stough has an eagle eye that caught some potentially embarrassing lapses on my part. Book designer Brent Beck, who combines artistic talent with an unswerving attention to detail, did the layout of both the dust jacket and the text of the book, so that it would be attractive, legible, and a pleasure to read.

To all these good people, my sincerest thanks and appreciation.

Publisher's note: We provide quotations from a number of earlier works consistently with the doctrine of fair use. We are grateful to the following for explicit permission to use quotations from their works.

Excerpts from "Orthodox See Mark of the Beast in New Russian Taxpayer IDs" by Anna Badkehn, from the *Boston Globe*, February 25, 2001. Copyright © by Anna Badkehn 2001.

Excerpts from *Choices in Modern Jewish Thought* by Eugene B. Borowitz. Copyright © Behrman House, Inc. Reprinted with permission. www.behrmanhouse.com.

Excerpts from "The Odds of That" by Lisa Belkin, from the *New York Times Magazine*, August 1, 2002. Copyright © 2002 by Lisa Belkin. Reprinted with permission.

Excerpts from "The Philosopher of Islamic Terror" by Paul Berman, from the *New York Times Magazine*, March 23, 2003. Copyright © by Paul Berman 2003. Reprinted with permission.

Excerpts from "The First Loose Plank—On the Rejection of Reason in the Pittsburgh Principles of 1999" by David H. Aaron in the *CCAR Journal—A Reform Jewish Quarterly* are under the copyright protection of the Central Conference of American Rabbis and reprinted for use by permission of the CCAR.

Excerpts from "The Rabbi Who Loved Evangelicals (and Vice Versa)" by Zev Chafets, from the *New York Times Magazine*, July 24, 2005. Copyright © by Zev Chafets 2005. Reprinted with permission of Sterling Lord Literistic, Inc.

Excerpts from *The God Delusion* by Richard Dawkins. Copyright © 2006 by Richard Dawkins. Reprinted by permission of Houghton Mifflin Company. All rights reserved.

Excerpts from "A Utah Massacre and Mormon Memory" by Sally Denton, from the *New York Times*, May 24, 2003. Copyright © by Sally Denton 2003. Reprinted with permission.

Excerpts from "Freedom's Journey," Survey of the Twentieth Century, September 11, 1999. Copyright © by *The Economist*, 1999. Reprinted with permission of the Copyright Clearance Center.

Excerpts from "The Measurement of Regional Cerebral Blood Flow during the Complex Task of Meditation: A Preliminary SPECT Study" by Andrew Newberg et al., from *Psychiatry Research*, Neuroimaging Section, 106, 2001. Copyright © by Elsevier. Reprinted with permission.

Excerpts from *The Bible Unearthed: Archeology's New Vision of Ancient Israel and the Origin of Its Sacred Texts* by Israel Finkelstein and Neil Asher Silberman. Copyright © 2001 by Israel

Finkelstein and Neil Asher Silberman. All rights reserved. Reprinted with the permission of The Free Press, a division of Simon & Schuster Adult Publishing Group.

Excerpts from *Who Wrote the Bible?* by Richard Elliott Friedman. Copyright © 1987 by Richard Elliott Friedman. Reprinted with the permission of Simon & Schuster Adult Publishing Group.

Excerpts from "Israel Destroys Shrine for Mosque Gunman" by Joel Greenberg, from the *New York Times,* December 29, 2000. Copyright © by Joel Greenberg 2000. Reprinted with permission. Excerpts from "For Israelis, New Tragedy Is a Challenge Sent by God" by Joel Greenberg, from the *New York Times,* March 3, 2001. Copyright by © Joel Greenberg 2001. Reprinted with permission.

Excerpts from *Israel in Egypt: The Evidence for the Authenticity of the Exodus Tradition* by James K. Hoffmeier. Copyright © 1996 by James K. Hoffmeier. Reprinted with permission of the Oxford University Press.

Excerpts from *A History of the Jews* by Paul Johnson. Copyright © 1987 by Paul Johnson. Reprinted by permission of HarperCollins Publishers.

Excerpts from "Shaking the Foundation of Faith" by Scott M. Liell, from the *New York Times,* November 18, 2005. Copyright © by Scott M. Liell. Reprinted with permission.

Excerpts from *The View from Nebo* by Amy Dockser Marcus. Copyright © 2000 by Amy Dockser Marcus. By permission of Little, Brown & Company.

Excerpts from *Numerology: or What Pythagoras Wrought* by Underwood Dudley. Copyright © 1997 by The Mathematical Society of America (Incorporated). Reprinted with permission.

Excerpts from *Response to Modernity: A History of the Reform Movement in Judaism* by Michael A. Meyer, Oxford University Press. Copyright © 1988 by Michael A. Meyer. Reprinted with permission.

Excerpts from "GOP's Disdain for Separating Church and State Bubbles Over" by Leonard Pitts, September 3, 2006. Copyright © by the *Miami Herald.* Reprinted with permission of the Copyright Clearance Center.

Excerpts from "Untouchable" by Tom O'Neill, from *National Geographic,* June 2003. Copyright © by *National Geographic.* Reprinted with permission.

Excerpts from "Religion and the Brain" by Sharon Begley, from Newsweek, May 7, 2001. Copyright © 2001 by *Newsweek,* Inc. All rights reserved. Use by permission and protected by the Copyright Laws of the United States. The printing, copying, redistribution, or retransmission of the material without express written permission is prohibited. Reprinted with permission of Pars International.

The following excerpts copyright © The New York Times Co. and reprinted with permission:

• From "Paper Seen as Villain in Abuse Accusation against Rabbi" by Felicity Barringer, July 10, 2000. Copyright © 2000

• From "Crossing Jordan: The Exit That Isn't on Bush's Roadmap" by James D. Bennet, May 18, 2003. Copyright © 2003

• From "Israeli Rabbi Sets Off a Political Firestorm over the Holocaust" by John F. Burns, August 7, 2000. Copyright © 2000

• From "Child Abuse at a Church Creates Stir in Atlanta" by David Firestone, March 30, 2001. Copyright © 2001

• From "War of the Worlds" by Thomas L. Friedman, February 24, 2006. Copyright © 2006

• From "Darwin vs. Design: Evolutionists' New Battle" by James Glanz, April 8, 2001. Copyright © 2001

• From "Protect Sharon from the Right" by Jeffrey Goldberg, August 5, 2004. Copyright © 2004

• From "Outrun Faith? Not for Iranian Women" by Stephen Holden, Review of Film Festival, March 24, 2001. Copyright © 2001

- From "Young Brides Stir New Outcry on Utah Polygamy" by Michael Janofsky, February 28, 2003. Copyright © 2003
- From "The Abramoff Case: Money Trail: Many Millions in Kickbacks from Tribes" by Michael Janofsky, January 4, 2006. Copyright © 2006
- From "Is It Good for the Jews?" by Bill Keller, March 8, 2003. Copyright © 2003
- From "Miracle? Drama? Prank? Fish Talks, Town Buzzes" by Cory Kilgannon, March 5, 2003. Copyright © 2003
- From "Wrath and Mercy: The Return of the Warrior Jesus" by David D. Kirkpatrick, April 4, 2004. Copyright © 2004
- From "For Evangelicals, Supporting Israel Is God's Foreign Policy" by David D. Kirkpatrick, November 14, 2006. Copyright © 2006
- From "Liberal Bible-Thumping" by Nicholas D. Kristof, May 15, 2005. Copyright © 2005
- From "Both Clintons Met Supporters of 4 Hasidim" by Clifford J. Levy, January 24, 2001. Copyright © 2001
- From "New Torah for Modern Minds" by Michael Massing, March 9, 2002. Copyright © 2002
- From "Killing for the Glory of God, in a Land Far from Home" by Judith Miller, January 16, 2001. Copyright © 2001
- From "Baptists' Ardor for Evangelism Angers Some Jews and Hindus" by Gustav Niebuhr, December 4, 1999. Copyright © 1999
- From "Recruiting Pitch: Monastic Life for 3 Days" by Gustav Niebuhr, January 13, 2001. Copyright © 2001
- From "Episcopal Dissidents Find African Inspiration" by Gustav Niebuhr, March 6, 2001. Copyright © 2001
- From "Lobbyist in Congress Furor Is Sentenced in Florida Case" by Philip Shenon, March 30, 2006. Copyright © 2006
- From "Powerful Israeli Rabbi Steps Up Attacks Over Parochial Schools" by Deborah S. Sontag, March 20, 1999. Copyright © 1999
- From "Israeli Army Ousting Officer for Intolerance" by Deborah S. Sontag, November 23, 1999. Copyright © 1999
- From "Jerusalem Journal: More Than One Way To Remember" by Deborah S. Sontag, May 2, 2000. Copyright © 2000
- From "Sharon Opens His Campaign: U.S. Diplomat Puts Off Visit" by Deborah S. Sontag, January 11, 2001. Copyright © 2001
- From "To Worship Freely, Americans Need a Little Elbow Room" by Brent Staples, Editorial Observer, April 27, 2003. Copyright © 2003

Excerpts from *The Elementary Forms of Religious Life* by Emile Durkheim, translated and edited by Carol Cosman. Copyright © 2001 by Oxford University Press. Reprinted with permission.

Excerpts from *The Torah: A Modern Commentary*, Revised Edition, Edited by W. Gunther Plaut. Copyright © 2005 by the URJ Press. Reprinted with permission of URJ Press, 633 3rd Avenue, New York, NY, 10017, www.urjpress.com. All rights reserved.

Excerpts from "America's Problem Is Jihadists, Not the Whole of Islam," by George Melloan, November 26, 2002. Copyright © by the *Wall Street Journal*, 2002. Reprinted with permission of the Copyright Clearance Center.

Excerpts from "'Suffer Not a Woman to Teach,' Baptist Group Reserving the Pulpit for Men," by Bill Broadway, June 10, 2000. Copyright © by *The Washington Post 2000*. Reprinted with permission.

INDEX

Notes: To distinguish them from page references, numbers denoting chapter and verse in the Bible have been set in italics. Where note numbers are duplicated on the same page, relevant chapter numbers have been supplied.